THE FUTURE OF EDUCATIONAL PSYCHOLOGY

Sponsored by the
Division of Educational Psychology
of the
American Psychological Association

THE FUTURE OF EDUCATIONAL PSYCHOLOGY

Edited by
Merlin C. Wittrock
University of California, Los Angeles
Frank Farley
University of Wisconsin

1989

LAWRENCE ERLBAUM ASSOCIATES, PUBLISHERS
Hillsdale, New Jersey   Hove and London

Lawrence Erlbaum Associates, Inc., Publishers
365 Broadway
Hillsdale, New Jersey 07642

Library of Congress Cataloging in Publication Data
The future of educational psychology : the challenges and
opportunities / edited by Merlin C. Wittrock, Frank Farley.
    p.   cm.
Includes bibliographies and indexes.
ISBN 0-8058-0001-8
1. Educational psychology.   I. Wittrock, M. C. (Merlin C.), 1931–
II. Farley, Frank.
LB1051.F97   1989   88-16316
370.15--dc19   CIP
Printed in the United States of America
10 9 8 7 6 5 4 3 2 1

Contents

v

Preface

This book addresses people interested in the future of educational psychology. The field of educational psychology has a proud history of major contributions to research and theory in education and psychology. Because of recent developments in theory, research, and technology, educational psychology again has impressive opportunities to advance knowledge and practice in both these fields.

The recent emergence of research in cognition decidedly enhanced the role of educational psychology in the study of both education and psychology. Thinking skills, student and teacher thought processes, motivation, attention, comprehension, learning strategies, and metacognitive processes, all topics of central importance in educational psychology, now also interest a wide variety of educational researchers and psychologists.

As a result, the opportunities for educational psychology to contribute theory and research to education and psychology are unprecedented. The purpose of this volume is to see that these opportunities are realized. We want to focus the attention of people upon these sizable opportunities. Our objective is to facilitate the important contributions which can and will occur if educational psychologists define their field and their roles appropriately to take advantage of the opportunities that they now have.

We want to thank the many people who enabled this aspiration of ours to become a volume. The APA Division of Educational Psychology Committee on the Future of Educational psychology, consisting of Barbara McCombs, Chair, and Margaret Clifford, William Asher, Frank Farley, Sigmund Tobias, and Merlin Wittrock, contributed the definition of the field that appears in the final chapter. The Executive Committee of the Division of Educational Psychology supported our plans for the book, although we take full responsibility for any of its possible shortcomings. The chapter authors enthusiastically responded to our invitations to prepare manuscripts on the directions and the future of educational psychology. Christine Carrillo, Sarah Kincaid, and Cathy Smith processed much of the text of the volume. The LEA staff, including Larry Erlbaum, Sondra Guideman, and Carol Lachman, competently edited and revised all of the manuscripts of the volume. To all these people, and to many others who worked on this book, go our gratitude, appreciation, and thanks.

We hope that this book will contribute to the growth and development of the field of educational psychology, and to the future of educational psychologists. They, like their predecessors, again have impressive opportunities to contribute to the research and theory that will influence the future of the study of education and psychology.

Merlin C. Wittrock
Frank Farley

We dedicate this volume to the memory of *Sonja Verena Farley* for her longtime help and commitment to educational psychology.

We donate the royalties of this volume to the APA Division of Educational Psychology and its members.

Merlin C. Wittrock

Frank Farley

CHALLENGES AND OPPORTUNITIES

In this opening Section, we begin with an examination of the historical record of educational psychology by the historian of the Division of Educational Psychology of the American Psychological Association, Robert E. Grinder. Grinder notes that in the earliest teacher training institutions in America, the "normal schools," educational psychology was the guiding science, the "master science" for the education of prospective teachers. Grinder traces what he sees as a steady decline in the discipline (". . . fate has dealt unkindly . . .") from those halycon days, and proffers a number of reasons for the decline. But, not being an optimist defined as a well-informed pessimist, Grinder takes the highroad of genuine optimism, concluding his historical analysis by deriving from it recommendations and proposals for re-establishing educational psychology as a "master science" in education.

Farley's chapter also reviews some history, and looks at the current substantive content of the discipline. He argues that there are very positive and very negative developments in contemporary educational psychology. The most positive feature is the theory and research ferment generated by the integrating concepts of cognitive psychology and cognitive science (see also Di-Vesta's, and Wittrock's, chapters in Section II of the present volume). The most negative feature is the seeming disintergration of "organized educational psychology," referring mainly to the decline in size and impact of the main professional home of educational psychologists—APA's Division of Educational Psychology. He offers some diagnosis of the problems, and reports a survey of Division members concerning these issues. He points out that this seeming disintegration may have ended, and that, given a resolve to do so, the discipline of educational psychology can have a "shining future" in an increasingly learning-centered, mind-centered, and psychological-society. He projects a set of developments for the future, and encourages the flowering of educational psychology into all areas of a meaningful, learning life.

Wittrock, in chapter 3, discusses opportunities for educational psychologists that are provided by recent developments in cognitive theory and in educational technology. Recent research and theory in cognition have produced instructional strategies useful for solving or ameliorating some important educational problems. These strategies include (1) training attention among learning disabled and hyperactive children, (2) teaching comprehension skills to children and adults, (3) retraining attributions for learning among "learned-helpless" students, and (4) teaching metacognitive skills to learners in elementary and secondary schools.

The concurrent advances in educational technology have opened new possibilities for teaching strategies such as those world-wide in literacy programs in and out of schools. The advances in educational technology also offer possibilities for improving job training in industries throughout the world. This combination of cognitive theory and educational technology will result, he feels, in extensive opportunities for educational psychologists to contribute to the improvement of teaching.

1 Educational Psychology: *The* Master Science[1]

Robert E. Grinder
Arizona State University

Political movements in the 17th and 18th centuries—stirred by decline of feudalism, growth of industrialism, and extension of commerce—produced egalitarian governments in Western Europe. Leading statesmen called for general education as a means of ensuring enlightened public opinion and responsible citizenship. The clamor led, initially, to the establishment of public or "vernacular" schools for children, and, in the 19th century, to secular or "normal" schools for training prospective teachers. New conceptions of child development, learning, and instruction arose, and accordingly, educational psychology "became the guiding science [the 'master science'] of the school, and the imparting to prospective teachers proper ideas as to psychological procedure, . . . became the great work of the normal school" (Cubberley, 1920, p. 755).

No one referred 100 years ago to the guiding science as educational psychology, but it was indeed a master science. The pioneer educational psychologists integrated two distinct domains of discourse: (1) development and learning, from the realm of psychology; and (2) social reformation and policy, from the realms of politics, economics, religion, and philosophy. To explain the psychological domain they explored the hidden recesses of human nature; to devise educational policy, they scrutinized the complexities of culture. They faced the same questions that perennially vex educational psychologists: How do individuals develop and learn? How are processes of change in individuals to be explained? What is the purpose of education—toward what moral and social ends, that is, does instruction prepare the young? Educational psychology was understandable then

---

[1]An abbreviated version of this paper was presented at the annual meeting of the American Psychological Association, Washington, D. C., 1986.

3

as a unified discipline; both domains were taken into account simultaneously, and perspectives from each were melded intentionally into a coherent whole.

Unfortunately, no one alive today knows educational psychology either as a master science or a coherent discipline. Proclamations of a long succession of presidents of the Division of Educational Psychology [15] of the American Psychological Association testify to its lack of cohesion (Brownell, 1948; Clifford, 1983; Conrad, 1961; Gates, 1949). For example, one of them stated recently that educational psychology is "a field that is now difficult if not yet impossible to define—as a scientific discipline or as a professional community." "Well then so what," he asked, "if educational psychology is something like an onion—a collection of layers whose unity can be easily peeled away to reveal no core—still, all the peels remain onion and they do indeed go well with many other things" (Snow, 1981, p.1). From guiding science to seasoning in only a century! A metaphor describes the distinguished discipline of educational psychology as having become a pungency for the word salads of educators.

Fate has dealt unkindly with the discipline of educational psychology. Over the centuries, while other sciences evolved from naturalistic, empirical perspectives, the ideological content of educational psychology was shaped by metaphysical, philosophical, and later, pedagogical imperatives. During the past century, however, events indicate that when educational psychology emerged eventually as a relatively independent discipline, its 19th-century founders abandoned the modus operandi that "got them there" in favor of professional responses that have brought the discipline to the brink of disintegration.

My intent in this paper, therefore, is to indicate (1) some of the reasons why the discipline of educational psychology lost its mantle as a master science. My commentary is divided into two chronological periods. First, I trace briefly the development of ideology pertinent to educational psychology from the contributions of Plato to those of E. L. Thorndike. I contend that the pioneers who framed the discipline at the turn of the 20th century embraced viewpoints and approaches that diverted them from insights being drawn, at the time, from studies of cognitive phenomena. I believe, too, that these insights should be regarded as the primary heritage of contemporary educational psychology. Second, I describe three distinct consequences—withdrawal, fractionation, and cries of irrelevance—that arose from the narrow, restrictive perspective toward both substance and methodology that many members of the profession adopted during this century. I assert that the resulting divisiveness contributed considerably to the current malaise within the discipline.

Is reform possible? Is the discipline of educational psychology actually on the verge of extinction? In conclusion, I suggest, in agreement with several contemporary educational psychologists, how educational psychology can be reestablished as a master science and, thus, can be assured a future as promising as anticipated by its pioneers.

THE DEVELOPMENT OF IDEOLOGY IN EDUCATIONAL PSYCHOLOGY

Origins

Early Greek philosophers sought to ascertain the "first principle" by which to explain the origin of the physical world. Their probing turned eventually to queries about the source of knowledge. Plato, for example, examined the roles of heredity (nature) and experience (nurture). He reckoned all knowledge is innate at birth and is perfectible by experiential learning during growth. Plato reasoned, too, that knowledge derived through psychic activity, being of the essence, was stable and dependable, whereas that obtained from sense impressions, being variable and unreliable, was unstable and undependable. Plato thus deserves recognition as an early educational psychologist; he was among the first to make the nature-nurture distinction, and he recognized the significance of both reasoning and affect in acquiring knowledge.

Plato's distinguished pupil, Aristotle, is celebrated primarily for his work in philosophy and the natural sciences. Aristotle warrants equal acclaim for his contributions to educational psychology. He extended Plato's views about the nature of learning, and for more than two millennia, his outlook provided the psychological basis for all schooling. Aristotle was first to observe that "association" among ideas facilitated understanding and recall. Comprehension, he said, was aided by contiguity, succession, similarity, and contrast (Brubacher, 1966). Aristotle expanded also Plato's mind–body dualism into five "faculties" or "potentialities"—physical, appetite, sensory, locomotive, and rational. He believed the rational faculty to be stimulated primarily by sense impressions; however, its functioning could be affected by any one of the faculties. It stored knowledge, dealt with abstractions, ordered concepts into systems, and solved problems intuitively. Everyone possessed equal potential to realize his or her rational faculty, since it entered the body at birth from a primordial reservoir and returned to the reservoir after death.

Aristotle is credited with giving birth to "faculty psychology." Although he viewed the five faculties as functionally unified in their service to the soul, medieval scholars elected to reify each of them as a separate entity. They argued incessantly over the probable number of faculties, but they agreed generally on the rational and sensory. The medieval scholars also gave rise to the "doctrine of formal discipline," a psychological process of schooling which emphasized memory as the chief agent in knowledge acquisition. For example, from medieval times until well into the 19th century, children were regarded as miniature adults who were required to memorize and recite whatever was expected of them. Schooling made provision for developing innate potentialities but not for individual differences in reasoning capabilities or interests. Since intellectual processes were presumed to be similar in all pupils, disinclination toward memo- rization tasks was regarded as willful; hence, instructional policy relied mainly on corporal punishment to maintain discipline and ensure orientation to subject matter.

Renaissance Educational Psychology

John Locke (1632–1704), an English physician-philosopher, championed the doctrine of formal discipline, but for reasons opposite to those of medieval scholars. Locke swept aside Plato's theory of innate ideas, dismissed Aristotle's assumption of five faculties, and rejected the belief that knowledge is acquired solely through refining fundamental potentialities. Locke's examination of how people learn convinced him that knowledge is derived primarily from external experiences. The mind is like a blank wax tablet (tabula rasa), he said, and successions of simple impressions give rise eventually to complex ideas through association and reflection.

Locke saw in his theory of knowledge acquisition a new method for testing the validity of knowledge per se. Medieval scholars had assessed validity on the basis of coherence among metaphysical precepts, and thus, in their search for truth, they ignored experience and relied instead on disputation and rules of reason. Locke also recognized the importance of systematic reasoning, but he insisted that knowledge should be regarded as acceptable and valid only if a basis in experience could be found for it. The discipline of educational psychology is thus indebted to Locke for establishing "empiricism" as a criterion for testing the validity of knowledge, and thereby, for providing a conceptual framework for the later development of experimental methodology in the natural and social sciences.

Locke saw in the doctrine of formal discipline an instructional method for developing higher reasoning powers. He recognized that associationism and empiricism were incompatible with the principles of faculty psychology, but the emphasis on discipline in the latter appealed to him. He proposed disciplining the body by diet and exercise, the character by subordinating desire, and the mind by drill and exercise, especially in mathematics. Whereas Locke's pedagogy has not survived, his theory that mental life can be decomposed into simple associations subsequently flourished in the 20th century. It formed the core of mechanistic interpretations of learning, and in turn, produced for a time a dynamic dimension of educational psychology.

The emergence of educational psychology was affected, too, by the develop- mental perspectives of John Comenius (1592–1670) and Jean Jacques Rousseau (1712–1778). Comenius, a Moravian clergyman, recognized age differences in children's ability to learn. And he preceded Locke in observing that children learn more effectively when they are involved with experiences that they can assimilate. Rousseau, who was born 8 years after Locke's death, expanded

Comenius' ideas about human development and Locke's ideas about learning into a new theory of educational reform that was destined to dominate 19th-century pedagogy. Rousseau argued that children are not naturally depraved, as held by the theologians of his day. He presented his view in *Emile,* which was published in 1762, a time when society was rejecting authoritarianism in favor of egalitarianism. In brief, Rousseau popularized Locke's emphasis on health and physical exercise, knowledge acquisition through experience, and reason and investigation as replacement for arbitrary authority. He had found in the works of Comenius and Locke a prescription for educating children according to their natural inclinations, impulses, and feelings.

Among the prominent teachers who attempted to put Rousseau's ideas into practice, Johann Heinrich Pestalozzi (1746–1827) developed the strongest following. Pestalozzi taught among the poor, and, lacking resources for books for materials, he was challenged to draw upon children's natural interests and activities. Pestalozzi believed that pedagogy, as Rousseau had urged, could regenerate society. As a consequence of his carefully developed methods and observations, he exerted enormous influence upon pedagogical practices throughout Western Europe. Pestalozzi may be embraced as the first applied educational psychologist in that he "tried to organize and psychologize the educational process" by harmonizing it with the natural development of the child (Cubberly, 1920, p. 542).

Nineteenth Century Educational Psychology

Until mid-19th century, for as long as anyone could remember, metaphysicians, theologians, and philosophers had dictated the content and practice of instruction. They presumed that adequate knowledge of the subject matter to be taught provided sufficient background for teaching. Who was to contradict them? The pedagogy described in Plato's *Republic,* the writings of the Scholastics and the Jesuits, Locke's *Some Thoughts concerning Education,* and Rousseau's *Emile,* conveyed only personal judgments. Times, however, were changing.

Charles Darwin presented *The Origin of Species* to the world in 1859 after personally collecting observations of plants and animals distributed throughout the world and exhaustively analyzing the patterns of variation that he saw. He thereby determined that a uniform principle of evolution accounts for species mutability. In any given population of plants and animals, he said, the environment "naturally selects" which of the random variants will be hereditarily favored. Darwin lent enormous credence to the belief that humankind is a product of natural forces. Specifically, he inspired philosophers and others to conceive the mind to be a function of the brain and nervous system and to surmise that ways of reasoning and behaving have less to do with supernatural powers than with changes in nervous energy. By the 1860s, growing interest in empiricism and successes in applying methods of science to natural and physical phenomena stimulated interest in dealing similarly with mental phenomena. In 1860, for example, Herbert Spencer, intellectual *sui generis* of his time, issued this timely call for the scientific study of educational processes:

> Men read books on this topic and attend lectures on that; decide that their children shall be instructed in these branches of knowledge and shall not be instructed in those; and all under the guidance of mere custom, or liking or prejudice; without ever considering the enormous importance of determining in some rational way what things are really most worth learning. (Spencer, 1860/1912, pp. 7–8)

Spencer, along with others, helped transform sentiments about pedagogy into systematic theory and method, but the substantive impetus for change stemmed primarily from the monumental scholarship of Johann Friedrich Herbart (1776–1841). Earlier in the century, Herbart had distinguished instructional processes from subject matter, and he had sought to identify the more effective of them on the basis of his understanding of psychology. He is the acknowledged " 'father' of scientific pedagogy" (Flugel & West, 1970, p. 19).

Herbart had visited Pestalozzi's school, and he had written approvingly of his methods. His observations led him to formulate a dynamic new concept of mental activity, which is based on his interpretations of metaphysics, mathematics, and experience. First, he started from the metaphysical assumption that the psyche or "soul" possesses one original tendency—to preserve itself. It begins as a colorless void, without qualities, but as it attempts to assimilate experiences, ideas collide with one another, giving rise to a sense of consciousness. The ideas and sensations that enter the mind remain there to influence later learning, and those that maintain themselves in consciousness exert the most influence on the psyche. These ideas, Herbart said, following Locke's views on associationism, constitute an "apperceptive mass." Second, he believed that as ideas become psychic forces, they can be assessed quantitatively; thereby, Herbart linked pedagogical theory to empiricism. Third, and perhaps most importantly for subsequent developments in educational psychology, Herbart directed the attention of educators to the importance of beginning the learning process at a point commensurate with children's readiness to address meaningfully the content of subject matter.

According to Herbart, interest develops when already strong and vivid ideas are hospitable toward new ones, since pleasant feelings arise from the association of old and new ideas. Noteworthy past associations thus motivate apperception of current ones. Herbartianism, in predicting that learning follows from building up sequences of ideas important to the individual, gave teachers a semblance of a theory of motivation.

Herbartian psychology provoked American educators to found in 1895 the National Herbart Society for the Scientific Study of Education [renamed in 1902 the National Society for the Scientific Study of Education]. In papers, debates, and discussions, participants considered the philosophical and psychological implications of apperception, interests, experience, and measurement. However, as they struggled to develop integrative theories linking learning and instruction, metaphysical and philosophical speculation yielded eventually to more systematic, psychological analyses (Leary, 1924). As Cubberly (1920) put it, "to the Herbartians we are indebted . . . for a new and truer educational psychology" (p. 763).

Herbartian psychology led also to the founding in 1879 of Wilhelm Wundt's (1832–1920) laboratory in Leipzig for the experimental study of psychology. The new laboratory marks both the moment when psychology became an independent, creditable science and when scientific methods and procedures were institutionalized specifically for the study of psychological phenomena. Never before had research of this kind been conducted on such a scale!

Wundt extended Herbart's theory of apperception into a theory of consciousness, whereby he sought to explain associations among mental processes. He elicited data via introspection, and he described them in relation to measurable stimuli and reactions. Nonetheless, Wundt eschewed the study of reasoning. In his view, introspection was applicable only as an intensive, short-range, carefully prepared observational strategy, and when used in the study of complex mental processes it led to unreliable, "mock experiments" (Heidbreder, 1933).

The realization that aspects of mental activity could be measured and treated experimentally attracted a cohort of brilliant, eager students to Leipzig. Many of them—G. Stanley Hall, James McKeen Cattell, Hugo Munsterberg, Frank Angell, and Charles Judd—were subsequently appointed in the 1880s and 1890s to establish experimental psychological laboratories in the United States. They became educational psychologists, and in the eyes of Wundt, heretics all! A new, urban, industrial society was rising in America, and social circumstances drew them away from Wundt's strict precepts to pedagogical problems. Schooling now was expected to foster citizenship and encourage social mobility as well as teach basic subjects. How were the schools to adapt? The tempo of the times coincided with tensions arising among Herbartians to become more scientific (Joncich, 1968). And Wundt's students were admirably prepared. They responded swiftly to the call that they apply their psychological training in helping solve pressing social concerns.

One of Wundt's students who came to America, an Englishman, Edward Bradford Titchener (1867–1927), however, proved to be a staunch disciple. Titchener was appointed director in 1892 of the psychology laboratory at Cornell University, and he, too, regarded the study of the generalized mind to be the only legitimate purpose of psychological investigation. Titchener distinguished the subject-matter of physics from that of psychology by viewing the former as independent of the individual and the latter as dependent on the experiencing person. Questions of psychological meaning pertained only to those which asked how persons interpreted consciously the context of their experiences (Titchener, 1896).

Titchener, nonetheless, strayed somewhat from Wundtian orthodoxy (Blumental, 1985). More than had Wundt, he emphasized the significance of sense experiences to such higher mental processes as concept formation, he argued that introspection is valid for interpreting a great variety of sensations and feelings, and importantly, he insisted that the major task of psychology is to show how complex reasoning can be accounted for via combinations of basic elements (Titchener, 1896).

But for all his careful systematization, Titchener could not stem the counterforces in American psychology that were at work defining an applied educational psychology. New psychological viewpoints, more responsive to the social concerns of the day, were on the horizon. William James (1842–1910) was unwilling to take for granted, as did Titchener, that psychology was already a science. He regarded it as a mental philosophy based on associationism, and he was unsympathetic toward Titchener's attempts to analyze states of consciousness into elements (Heidbreder, 1933). Many of the psychologists who had studied with Wundt joined forces with James in seeking instead to understand ways in which the mind functions, adjusts, and adapts to its environment.

John Dewey (1859–1952) launched a devastating attack upon Titchenerian psychology in a paper he presented in 1896 at the annual meeting of the Herbart Society. Dewey focused on mental processes, not merely as static elements, but as purposeful activities (Dewey, 1896). In brief, he argued that a stimulus and the response it elicits constitute a reflex arc, an arc should be the minimal unit of analysis, and its function should be the basis for understanding it. Dewey also drew upon functional ideology to correct an error he saw in Herbart's interpretation of the role of interest in the theory of apperception. As he interpreted Herbart, interest arising from the association of ideas produces only a passive reflex. Dewey argued that interest is self-propulsive, inherently motivational, and functional. Individuals address aspects of their environment, not because these features possess the quality of being interesting, but because they are viewed instrumentally as ways of realizing a purpose.

Dewey thus initiated a new system of psychology, which came to be known as functionalism. At the turn of the century, functionalism encouraged developments in mental testing, investigations of individual differences, and studies of adaptive behavior. And as it opened new vistas, it evolved to become the first organized stand in American psychology against domination by Titchenerian psychology. Titchener adopted the phrase "structural psychology" in order to contrast his viewpoint with functionalism. He retorted by distinguishing cryptically between the two, saying that the data of the former signify "Is" whereas those of the latter signify "Is for." Titchener regarded functionalism as a lapse into common sense as opposed to scientific theorizing, an evasion of the strict demands of experimental psychology, and an unwelcome intrusion of teleology. To him, it represented a confusion of science with both technology and philosophy (Heidbreder, 1933). But Dewey's depiction of mental processes as instruments for more effective living complemented Darwinism and the adaptive orientation it presupposes. It gave pedagogues the impetus to draw upon psychology for breaking new ground in educational psychology.

The hostile atmosphere that once separated structuralists and functionalists has long since evaporated. The structuralists recognized problems of activity and adaptation; the functionalists agreed that consciousness was interesting and important (Murphy & Kovach, 1972). The real source of the schism was probably Titchener's relentless passion for formal correctness (Heidbreder, 1933). His Wundtian compatriots in America shared Titchener's reverence for scientific exactness but not his extremism. In his zeal to be scientific, he stifled curiosity about the purposefulness of mental activity. Educational psychologists were poised to address a variety of practical problems, which could not be investigated within the narrow research framework of late-19th century structuralism.

Edward L. Thorndike (1874–1949) emerged as the man of the hour (Grinder, 1981). A brilliant young psychologist on the professional horizon, he had earned a master's degree from Harvard in 1897 and a doctorate, based partly on his thesis. *Animal Intelligence,* from Columbia in 1898. After teaching briefly in Cleveland, he accepted an invitation to return to Columbia as an instructor. He had eschewed opportunities to study in Leipzig, and now, he was prepared to bulwark a revitalized version of Locke's associationism against Titchenerian ideology. Like Titchener, Thorndike disdained intuitive, common sense psychology. He embraced functionalism; however, he preferred to be identified as a "connectionist," because he sought to explain learning in terms of stimulus-response connections (Roback, 1964). In formulating "laws" of learning, namely "The Law of Effect," to account for the strengthening or weakening of connections as a result of experience, Thorndike gave the fledgling science of educational psychology an entirely new perspective. He drew upon Herbart's basic assumptions about the soul, apperception, and measurement (a) to recast the soul as original nature and native traits; (b) to couch apperception in terms of stimulus-response bonds; and (c) to view the quantitative elements as the measurement of abilities, individual differences, and rates of learning (Leary, 1924).

Following publication of Thorndike's (1913–1914) masterful three volume series, *Educational Psychology,* conceptual advance in educational psychology rested on a plateau for nearly a half-century. Thorndike so thoroughly melted and fused the views of Locke, Herbart, and others with his own into an original proclamation of the learning process that reverential educators treated it thereafter as dogma. He was not solely responsible, however, for the triumph of associationism. John B. Watson sensationalized behaviorism, and he reduced higher mental processes to subvocal, mechanical associations. Watsonian behaviorism pained Thorndike, because he could not accept its rejection of heredity and instincts as influences upon individual differences; nonetheless, it swept across the landscape, too, to exert a strong, but superficial impact between 1920 and 1950 upon American psychology (Hilgard, 1980).

Talk of different learning theories slowed. Discussions of learning in the leading textbooks in educational psychology written between those of Thorndike and the immediate post-WW II years testify to the overwhelming impact upon pedagogy of his S-R position and the lesser influence of behaviorism (Ellis, 1951; Pillsbury, 1926; Skinner, 1936; Starch, 1919; Stroud, 1935). Textbook authors genuflected to The Law of Effect, and they laid waste to Wundt and Titchener by wholly ignoring their contributions to understanding such structural elements of the mind as attention, perception, memory, language processing, concept formation, and logic of problem-solving. Washburne (1936), for example, in an exhaustive review of systems in educational psychology could come up with a mere four: connectionist, behaviorist, Gestalt, and genetic or developmental.

Eventually, during the mid-1950s, cognitive views of learning gained ascendancy over stimulus-response positions (Hilgard, 1980, 1987). By mid-20th century, few would have disputed the assertion that adjustment or adaptation constitutes the basis of both behavioral *and* cognitive activity. Functionalism had been absorbed into the major themes of psychology, and it no longer was a distinct frame of reference. With purposefulness taken for granted, questions pertaining to the role of mental phenomena in learning and development were resurrected. The changes in outlook emanated from theory and research not in educational psychology but in academic psychology (Hilgard, 1980; Kessel & Bevan, 1985). For example, Tolman (1932) emphasized the significance to learning of intervening variables and cognitive structures. Gestalt psychologists showed that animals can solve problems in ways that reveal intellectual activity; social learning theorists then found that imitation can occur in the absence of the gradual shaping of behavior. As psychologists began to consider how individuals acquire, retain, recall, and transform information, investigations of higher mental processes achieved unprecedented levels of sophistication (Hilgard, 1980).

Wundt and Titchener would be indeed pleased! The mind is once again at the forefront of theory and research in contemporary psychology. Current thrusts in educational psychology are in keeping with the times (Mayer, 1983; Treffinger, Davis, & Ripple, 1977). But during the conceptual maelstrom the discipline had been reactive rather than proactive. Educational psychology was bounded initially by functionalism and a mechanistic interpretation of learning. For a time it was the master science; then it allowed itself to fall out of step. Educational psychology owes its heritage to Wundt and Titchener more than it has acknowledged. The insights of early cognitive psychologists, and the great body of literature that they inspired, still are largely ignored by contemporary educational psychologists. Our 19th-century predecessors have much to teach us about both the substance and breadth of our discipline. But we plunge forward blindly. We allow data to pile up higher and higher. Are we unwittingly repeating earlier discoveries, reconceptualizing earlier theories, and creating pathways to research that long ago proved to be blind alleys? Perhaps, if we continue to cultivate a tradition that ignores the past, our present will increasingly have less and less meaning, and our current contributions will be no more significant to 21st-century educational psychologists than those of the 19th century are now to us.

EDUCATIONAL PSYCHOLOGY IN THE TWENTIETH CENTURY

E. L. Thorndike was among the first in the 20th century to surface among the titans who sought to establish educational psychology as a compelling science. When Thorndike contributed the lead essay in the first issue of the *Journal of Educational Psychology* [the preface stated that the journal would apply the "methods of exact science" to educational problems], he declared that the purpose of educational psychology was to clarify educational aims by defining them in measurable terms and in showing statistically the probability of their attainment. Just as those in the physical sciences had defined the volt, calorie, erg, and ampere as measures of change, so, he said, educational psychologists would define units of human nature and behavior, which in turn, would enable them to study problems whose solution depended on some amount of measurable change in boys and girls (Thorndike, 1910).

Thorndike's professional aim to establish educational psychology as a reputable science was sustained immeasurably by his abiding faith in the efficacy of science. As a young man, he had read Karl Pearson's, *The Grammar of Science,* and he accepted its assertion that science, properly deployed, is competent to solve all problems (Joncich, 1968). In 1912, as Thorndike was putting the finishing touches to the third of his three volumes in educational psychology, unprecedented scientific achievements were becoming commonplace. Technological progress during the 19th century paled by comparison. Flying machines were beginning to appear in the sky, horseless carriages were proliferating, electrification was sweeping across the nation, phonographs were enlivening households everywhere, and on April 14, 1912, the fateful night of the sinking of the Titanic, hundreds of lives were saved through the incomparable accomplishments of wireless telegraphy. The citizens of 1912 were probably awed more by the events of their day than we would be today should humans be sent to Mars!

Thorndike and a cohort of similarly persuaded psychologists believed that science had revealed to them the fundamental parameters of learning. They reasoned, therefore, that they should, on the one hand, retreat to their research activities to refine their theoretical assumptions, and on the other, promote educational psychology as an applied engineering discipline. For example, Starch (1919) insisted that educational issues should determine the problems and scope of educational psychology. Worcester (1927) said that educational psychology should first examine factual teaching problems, and then, look to general psychology for application of principles. Charters (1945) observed that engineers apply knowledge gained in mathematics, physics, chemistry, and geology to build roads, dams, and skyscrapers; similarly, educational psychologists must start with practical educational problems and solve them by making use of knowledge from basic scientific disciplines, including psychology. And Brownell (1948) suggested similarly that educational psychologists should start with the problems of instruction and "go from there to knowledge of the learning process to select what is most useful."

The faith that many educational psychologists professed in science, and, in turn, their laboratory investigations, never wavered while they proclaimed that solutions to pesky problems in education were on the horizon. But it isolated them from messy, ongoing educational issues. Unfortunately, it also affected the emerging structure of educational psychology in three significant ways:

Withdrawal. In 1948, a report of an APA Division of Educational Psychology [15] committee on the contributions of educational psychology to education noted that for several years educational psychologists had disavowed responsibility for the value or direction of education (Rivlin, 1948). In brief, the report identified educational psychologists as interested only in the laws of learning, as unable to understand or be understood by those who were conducting the actual business of education, and to be in the process of breaking down their areas of research even more minutely. An APA committee on relations between psychology and education chaired by Donald Snygg in 1954 pointed out that more and more of the influential theorists in educational psychology were withdrawing from the general problems of education and human relations into the more limited fields of experimental psychology (cited in Grinder, 1967).

Fractionation. When Washburne (1936) identified four viewpoints in educational psychology [connectionist, behaviorist, Gestalt, and genetic], he noted that proponents of each believed that their particular viewpoint was entirely different from the others. Washburne observed, too, that since each of them contributed to the same end—"improved problem solving ability"—all were equally right. Each viewpoint, he said, simply concentrated on different aspects of the same phenomena, and consequently, "none of them is wrong except when he claims the others are wrong" (p. 731).

Later, Woodruff (1950), after surveying the breadth of activity in educational psychology, questioned whether there was any common ground on which to converse. "We have no fundamental field which is our own to a greater extent than it belongs to anyone else." The APA "divisions of Evaluation and Measurement, Childhood and Adolescence, Personality and Social, School Psychologists, and Maturity and Old Age," he said, "have as much claim as we on such functions as learning, adjusting, individual differences, tests and measurement, statistics, and growth and development" (p. 5).

Irrelevance.   The retreat-to-the-laboratory mindset of many educational psychologists, an apparent expression of their disinterest in practical educational problems, has led to a great deal of dissension among the ranks. Schroeder (1913) started the ball rolling when he declared: ''I hope the time is near when the academic psychologist will be willing to renounce for once the claims of pure science and give practical assistance to those in urgent need of it'' (p. 470). Ellis (1951) stated that ''professional educators have doubted that our teaching is better today as a result of the developments in educational psychology during the past forty years'' (p. 5). Brownell (1948) commented that it would be difficult to prove that principles in educational psychology had improved classroom teaching over a thirty year period. And the Rivlin Committee (1948) report held that too many educational psychologists assumed responsibility only for making learning more effective, regardless of its value.

THE REFORM OF EDUCATIONAL PSYCHOLOGY

The promise held forth at the turn of the century for the new discipline of educational psychology had turned by mid-century into despair. Internal factiousness had fractured unity of purpose and aloofness had alienated practicing educators. Terman (1950) lamented that perhaps the time had come to stop viewing educational psychology as a discipline. A small contingent of educational psychologists, however, has argued in recent years that the discipline can be rescued by elevating discussions of theory and research among members to a common plane of discourse. The effort began with the Rivlin Committee (1948) report to the APA Division of Educational Psychology, which stated:

> What we need may be not just Educational Psychology or Psychology in Education, but a systematic application of unified and integrated facts and concepts from all the social sciences, including psychology. . . . Teachers need educational psychologists . . . who can explore more thoroughly than do other psychologists those psychological questions that arise from education. Teachers need educational psychologists who are familiar with many areas of psychology and with related studies in human relations even though their own research is confined to one area. (pp. 13–15)

Arthur Gates (1949), a member of Rivlin Committee, and incoming President of the Division, expressed the quintessence of the new solution in a personal letter to the membership: ''The educational psychologist should pioneer, open up new vistas, bring to bear upon the work of the educator new techniques, sources of information, and forms of orientation. This, it seems to me, should be one of the major purposes of the Division of Educational Psychology of the APA.'' Later, Ausubel (1969) made a comparable plea in a vigorous defense of educational psychology as a discipline, while Wittrock (1967) proclaimed that "educational psychology goes beyond the archaic conceptualization that it is 'the application of psychological principles to education.' It is time for us to practice a liberal conceptualization of educational psychology as the scientific study of human behavior in educational settings" (p. 4). The tendentiousness of these leaders was followed by the Treffinger et al. (1977) volume and the Scandura et al. (1981) report, both of which represent closely the spirit of the Rivlin Committee manifesto.

Unfortunately, the calls for reform—which would bring educational psychology into alignment with the practices that enabled it a century ago to attain the status of master science—have gone unheeded. Consider, for example, the following statement in the Scandura et al. (1981) report: "we feel at this time that the paradigm shift from S-R to information processing should be encouraged . . ." (pp. 385–386). Why? No rationale is given. Is it because information processing leads to more efficient learning? Of what kind? Does it lead to more cost-effective procedures in classrooms? Will it lead to a more informed citizenry? And, importantly, why did not Thorndike think of it? During the feverish days of the National Herbart Society, such a proposal would have been debated endlessly for its implications both to psychology and to society.

The reformists might have been taken seriously had they traced the heritage of the discipline from its exciting, nineteenth-century beginnings and had they endeavored to restore it to its original form and function. To regain pre-eminence, educational psychology must be re-asserted as a discipline dedicated primarily to analysis and synthesis of concepts and issues, and two decisive steps must be taken. First, the dwindling members of the cohort must represent educational psychology to the world of pedagogy as *the* integrative discipline. Second, to inspire academicians, scholars, and researchers to re-create a dynamic discipline—one that will stimulate participation because of the comprehensive perspectives it offers—inclusion of pertinent commentary on historical, theoretical, and social issues must become required criteria for presentations at the annual meeting and in the publications of the Division of Educational Psychology. The future of the discipline of educational psychology depends on it.

REFERENCES

Ausubel, D. P. (1969). Is there a discipline of educational psychology *Psychology in the Schools, 4,* 232–244.

Blumenthal, A. L. (1985). Shaping a tradition: Experimentalism begins. In C. E. Buxton (Ed.), *Points of view in the modern history of psychology* (pp. 51–83). New York: Academic Press.

Brownell, W. A. (1948). Learning theory and educational practice. *Journal of Educational Research, 41,* 481–497.

Brubacher, J. S. (1966). *A history of the problems of education* (2nd. ed.). New York: McGraw-Hill.

Charters, W. W. (1945). Is there a field of educational engineering? *Educational Research Bulletin,* Ohio State University, *24,* 29–37.

Clifford, M. M. (1983, June). President's message. *Newsletter for Educational Psychologists, 6,* p. 1.

Conrad, H. S. (1961, September). *Research in educational psychology: Directions and misdirections.* Presidential address, at the meeting of Division 15, APA, New York.

Cubberly, E. P. (1920). *The history of education.* Cambridge, MA: Houghton Mifflin.

Dewey, J. (1986). The reflex arc concept in psychology. *Psychological Review, 3,* 357–370.

Ellis, R. S. (1951). *Educational psychology: A problem approach.* New York: Van Nostrand.

Flugel, J. C., & West, D. J. (1970). *A hundred years of psychology* (3rd ed.). New York: International Universities Press.

Gates, A. I. (1949, April). The functions of educational psychology. *Division 15 Newsletter,* American Psychological Association, pp. 3–6.

Grinder, R. E. (1967, March, May). The growth of educational psychology as reflected in the history of Division 15. *Educational Pychologist.* pp. 2, 15, 23; 27, 30–31, 35.

Grinder, R. E. (1981) The "new" science of education: Educational Psychology in search of a mission. In F. H. Farley & N. J. Gordon (Eds.), *Psychology and education* (pp. 354–366). Berkeley, CA: McCutchan.

Heidbreder, E. (1933). *Seven psychologies.* New York: Appleton-Century-Crofts.

Hilgard, E. R. (1980). Consciousness in contemporary psychology. In M. R. Rosenzweig & L. W. Porter (Eds.), *Annual review of psychology* (Vol. 31, pp. 2–26). Palo Alto: Annual Reviews.

Hilgard, E. R. (1987)). *Psychology in America: A historical survey.* New York: Harcourt Brace Jovanovich.

Joncich, G. (1968). *The same positivist: A biography of E. L. Thorndike.* Middleton, CT: Wesleyan University Press.

Kessel, F. S., & Bevan, W. (1985). Notes toward a history of cognitive psychology. In C. E. Buxton (Ed.), *Points of view in the modern history of psychology* (pp. 259–294). New York: Academic Press.

Leary, D. P. (1924). Development of educational psychology. In I. L. Kandel (Ed.), *Twenty-five years of American education* (pp. 91–114). New York: Macmillan.

Mayer, R. E. (1983). *Thinking, problem solving, cognition.* New York: W. H. Freeman.

Murphy, G., & Kovach, J. (1972). *Historical introduction to modern Psychology* (3rd ed.). New York: Harcourt Brace Jovanovich.

Pillsbury, W. B. (1926). *Education as the psychologist sees it.* New York: Macmillan.

Rivlin, H. N. (1948, November). Report of the Committee on the "Function of the Division of Educational Psychology of the A.P.A." *Division 15 Newletter,* APA, pp. 3–16.

Roback, A. A. (1964). *A History of American psychology* (2nd ed.). New York: Collier Books.

Scandura, J. M., Frase, L. T., Gagne, R. M., Stolurow, K. A., Stolurow, L. M., & Groen, G. J. (1981). Current status and future directions of educational psychology as a discipline. In F. H. Farley & N. J. Gordon (Eds.), *Psychology and education* (pp. 367–388). Berkeley, CA: McCutchan.

Schroeder, H. H. (1913). A real problem for educational psychology. *Journal of Educational Psychology, 4,* 465–470.

Skinner, C. E. (1936). *Educational psychology.* Englewood Cliffs, NJ: Prentice-Hall.

Snow, R. E. (1981, November). President's message. *Newsletter for Educational Psychologists, 1,* p. 1.

Spencer, H. (1912). *Education: Intellectual, moral, and physical.* New York: Appleton. (original work published 1860).

Starch, D. (1919). *Educational psychology.* New York: Macmillan.

Stroud, J. B. (1935). *Educational psychology.* New York: Macmillan.

Terman, L. M. (1950, September). Letter to Lee J. Cronbach. *Division 15 Newsletter,* American Psychological Association, p. 7.

Thorndike, E. L. (1910). The contribution of psychology to education. *Journal of Educational Psychology, 1,* 5–12.

Titchener, E. B. (1896). *An outline of psychology.* New York: Macmillan.

Tolman, E. C. (1932). Purposive behavior in animals and men. New York: Appleton-Century.

Treffinger, D. J., Davis, J. K., & Ripple, R. E. (Eds.). (1977). *Handbook on teaching educational psychology.* New York: Academic Press.

Washburne, J. N. (1936). Viewpoints in educational psychology. In C. E. Skinner (Ed.), *Educational psychology* (pp. 705–732). Englewood Cliffs, NJ: Prentice-Hall.

Wittrock, M. (1967, March). Focus on educational psychology. *Educational Psychologist.* pp. 17, 20.

Woodruff, A. D. (1950, February). Functional structure needed. *Division 15 Newsletter,* American Psychological Association, p. 5.

Worcester, D. A. (1927). The wide diversities of practice in first-courses in educational psychology. *Journal of Educational Psychology, 18,* 11–17.

2 Challenges for the Future of Educational Psychology

Frank Farley
University of Wisconsin-Madison

Few current graduate students in educational psychology know much about the history of this field, and few of them can make solidly anchored projections of its future. However, the significant shortfall in historical knowledge is not a gaping hole in the curriculum vitae of the the graduate student only. It is also a wide-open space in the knowledge structures of much of the professoriate. There are few courses in North America on the nature and history of educational psychology. Indeed, if it wasn't for the periodic attention to history and definition given by the Division of Educational Psychology (Division 15) of the American Psychological Association, there would be little attention given at all. But fortunately for all of us, Division 15 has performed well in this area over the years, in articles published in its journal and its newsletter, culminating in the present volume.

I would like to summarize some of these historical efforts and discussions, before prognosticating about the future. Let me start with some stagesetting quotations:

Human history becomes more and more a race between education and catastrophe. (H. G. Wells, 1923)

. . . we shall continue to teach educational psychology to teachers with a mixture of pious optimism and subdued embarrassment. (J. B. Carroll, 1963)

The world of educational psychology . . . looks . . . like a swamp crosscut with intersecting channels, stagnant pools, and brackish backwaters. Clouds cover the moon, owls hoot in the distance, and a loon cries from across the lake. Out of the encircling mist a bark emerges carrying Jacques Barzun, who . . . offers a helping hand. ". . . on closer look," he counsels, "the actual choice for serious minds is never between an old unsatisfactory mode and a new exciting one. That is mere appearance. The choice is not *between*— it is *among* a multiplicity of tendencies, hopes, pretensions, routines, verbalisms, misrepresentations, fads, discoveries, and genuine new thought. (P. W. Jackson, 1981)

Educational psychology and all is well. (J. F. Feldhusen, 1976)

. . . the special task of the social scientist in each generation is to pin down the contemporary facts. (L. J. Cronbach, 1975)

It is . . . fruitless to look for a single, all-purpose 'scientific method': the growth and evolution of scientific ideas depends on no one method and will always call for a broad range of different enquiries. (S. Toulmin, 1961)

There are signs that concerns for basic psychology on the one hand and education on the other are coming together . . . Educational psychology is the *bridge* between these two disciplines. And though . . . it may be the fate of a bridge to be trampled on by those who approach it from either side, let it be known that educational psychology remains open for traffic. (F. Farley, 1973)

The history of educational psychology up to the recent past has, I believe, been well documented. The writings of Grinder (this volume and previous work), Watson (1961), and others has given us a good sense of where we've been. The pages of the *Educational Psychologist* have over the past decade kept historical discussion alive. The more important articles include Grinder's (1978) "What 200 Years Tells Us About Professional Priorities in Educational Psychology" and his 1981 chapter entitled "The "New Science" of Education: Educational Psychology in Search of a Mission." Another is William's (1978) "Analysis of the Journal of Educational Psychology": Toward a Definition of Educational Psychology."

In 1948 a special committee of Division 15 chaired by Donald Snygg attempted to define and outline the field. Thirty years later, in 1978, another Division 15 committee, chaired by Joseph Scandura, tried to do the same thing. The year 1984 found us with a new Division 15 committee, chaired by M. C. Wittrock, and charged with consideration of the definition of the field, its present status and likely future, and such matters as training and employment. It is this committee that led to the development of the present book. Clearly the frequency and intensity of concerns about the nature, and future, of our discipline are increasing.

Finally, one of the most recent historical analyses was written in 1985 by Ash and Love-Clark. They undertook an analysis of the content of 48 textbooks in educational psychology produced over the past 30 years. They were particularly interested in how much space was given to various topics over those 30 years. Two topics showed no charge in extent of coverage—*Teacher Effectiveness* and *Measurement*. A few topics showed massive declines in coverage, particularly *Mental Health* and *Emotional–Social Development*. A few topics showed massive increases in coverage—*Classroom Management and Interaction,* and the *Exceptional Child* and *Disadvantaged Child.* Other topics showing increases included *Motivation* and *Teacher Evaluation.*

Why do our concerns about the status of educational psychology seem, as indicated by the foregoing, to be on the increase? I believe there are a number of reasons for this.

We have never had it so good, and we have never had it so bad.

At the level of theory and research, educational psychology is probably in better shape now than it has ever been. Cognitive psychology has provided, perhaps for the first time in our discipline, a coherent unifying theory and viewpoint about human nature and mental life that is researchable and relevant to education. It has captured the imagination of a majority of researchers in educational psychology. Indeed, much of the important thinking and research in cognitive psychology has arisen from the domain of educational psychology. Thus, cognitive approaches to mathematics and science education, cognitive analyses of reading and reading instruction, memory training and learning strategies in educational contexts, cognitive analyses of intelligence and the teaching of thinking, have to a significant extent taken place within the field of educational psychology and have led to theoretical advances and significant changes in practice (see DiVesta, and Wittrock, this volume).

That's the good news. Or at least much of the good news. Thus, research and scholarship in educational psychology is vigorous and exciting, fueled by powerful theory. On the other hand, for the professional and human resources side of educational psychology, the news is not so good. The theoretical and research ferment has not led to notable increases in the number of students entering into graduate majors in educational psychology programs; nor has it increased the membership of Division 15, the principal professional home of educational psychologists. I think one problem here is that the rising cognitive tide floats *all ships,* that is, most areas of psychology are elevated by the cognitive tide, including educational psychology. Educational psychology is functioning at a more vigorous level of research and scholarship, but it remains in a small craft. Students who would study the training or teaching of thinking and intelligence in school settings may take their graduate work in a cognitive psychology program in a psychology department rather than in an educational psychology program. Also, members of APA with an interest in cognitive psychology and instruction may find APA's Division of Experimental Psychology (Division 3) or Division on the Teaching of Psychology (Division 2) satisfactory for their professional interests.

Let us look briefly at some disturbing developments in Division 15. Since 1977, membership in Division 15 has declined by almost 1400 members, an almost 40% decline over the decade. For comparison purposes, consider that many APA Divisions don't have a total current membership equal in size to Division 15's 10-year loss of 1400 persons. In 1977 Division 15 was one of the three largest Divisons in APA. A decade later it barely made the top 10. It should be pointed out, however, on a more positive note, that the decline in membership in Division 15 seems to have stopped, and a plateau, or slight increase, has been the rule for the past 2 or 3 years. But this is only part of the story. Over the same period of time, the number of program hours in the APA Annual Convention given to Division 15 dropped from approximately 60 hours to approximately 25 hours, a decline of greater than 55%. Obviously the range and coverage at these conferences of research and theory specifically in educational psychology has been dramatically curtailed. We have some of the most exciting research the field of educational psychology has seen for many decades, but we have an interestingly meagre platform upon which to present and discuss this work. The venue for discussion of this important work is shifting elsewhere, to special societies, e.g., the Psychonomics Society, to other Divisons of APA, or, more specifically, to education-centered organizations such as the American Educational Research Association (AERA). The formula by which APA assigns convention program hours to its various Divisions weights heavily the number of members in a particular Division and the number of that Division's members who register and attend the Annual Convention. If Division 15's membership goes down, or a declining percentage of its members attend conventions, its program hours are slashed. Thus, the decline in size of our Division is not a trivial issue. It impacts on the type of forum we can provide for the discussion of developments in our field.

I have no ready solution to this problem. Clearly AERA has been very attractive to educational psychologists with its low dues, ample program time, "special interest groups" organized around specific research themes or issues facilitating dialogue among researchers with common interests, and its interdisciplinary nature. AERA has had one dues increase in the past 15 years, and at one-third the annual dues of APA includes three journals as well as other benefits. APA, by contrast, has an automatic dues increase every 3 years, with current dues considered exorbitant by many members holding academic positions. For APA dues, one receives *Psychology Today,* the *APA Monitor,* and the *American Psychologist* as well as other benefits. The "street value" of these three publications is relatively small compared to the annual dues paid. A cost conscious educational psychologist might well decamp APA for AERA, and obviously many have done so.

I have outlined some possible reasons for the decline, or lack of growth, in Division 15 membership. One I haven't mentioned is the proliferation of new Divisions in APA. As of this writing there are 45 Divisions in APA. In most recent years one or two new Divisions have been established each year. Some of these new Divisions are in areas of substantive and/or professional interest that overlap aspects of Division 15, thus representing a degree of competition for educational psychologists' allegiance. They can be assumed to draw away some members from Division 15. APA is considering encouraging the development of

"Special Interest Groups" (SIGs) in the Association, which would represent relatively small groups of individuals with focused common interests. This trend might also lead to a reduction in commitment to Division 15.

In order to obtain the viewpoints of members of the Division of Educational Psychology on many of the issues raised above, in 1984 I undertook a mail survey of a random sample of Division members. The survey asked for an open-ended, essay-type, response. It read:

> A number of people have expressed strong concern recently about the future of our discipline. I, for one, am deeply concerned over the substantial decline in the size of membership in Division 15 over the past years. Some concern has been expressed over the job market for educational psychology graduates, over the nature of training for a changing discipline and changing job prospects. No longer do most doctoral graduates in educational psychology go on to become professors in educational psychology or psychology departments at universities. New interdisciplines are arising, such as cognitive science, that are having an impact upon educational psychology. What is the relation between educational psychology and school psychology? How shall educational psychology be defined for the years ahead; what is its likely future and what sort of future should we be working toward? All of the foregoing is by way of asking for your opinions and thoughts about the future of educational psychology. Where are we going? Where should we be going? Do things look good to you? If so, why? Do they look bad? If so, what can we do about it?

The response to the survey was substantial, with several hundred returns. The respondents represented a cross-section of the Divisional membership, including newer members, older members, and a number of former presidents. It was not unusual to receive 5 or 6 page single-spaced letters, and an assortment of relevant reprints, convention presentations, and so on. Respondents all expressed deep concern for the Division and the discipline. A number of themes and issues emerged from our analysis of the responses received, and I have grouped these as follows:

1. *Definition of the discipline*
   A. Education versus psychology as the primary basis of the discipline.
   B. An identity crisis exists, creating an image problem for educational psychology in the extended family of psychology.
   C. Educational psychology is becoming a melting pot of basic science and educational practice.
   D. There is a polarization of quantitative and qualitative scholars.
2. *Employment and job opportunities*
   A. The future for educational psychology lies in business and industry, and to some extent in the military services.
   B. We also need to look to adult education and adult learning.

    C. We need to expand more into computer technology, including computerized needs assessments, databases for research, computerized guidance systems and computer-based testing.

3. *Training and Education*
    A. Issue of a well-defined curriculum (e.g., core curriculum) versus a more open curriculum.
    B. Increased requirements for the Ph.D. in the work place.

4. *Research*
    A. Cognitive psychology is where the action is.
    B. Research should in this field always be an *interplay* between practical and theoretical issues.

5. *Current Gripes*
    A. Relevance to education of educational psychology journals.
    B. APA is too large and educational psychology is lost in the structure.

The foregoing analysis gives us, I believe, a *sense* of what items are of concern to educational psychologists at this time.

At this juncture I turn to the future of educational psychology and to some prognostications and proposals, in line with the title of this chapter and this book.

THE FUTURE OF EDUCATIONAL PSYCHOLOGY

Looking into the future is a dangerous business. You can never prove that your views are more correct than someone else's, without waiting around an inordinate length of time. Some people avoid consideration of the future altogether. They are in good company. Albert Einstein eschewed prognostication of any sort, allegedly saying "I never think of the future, it comes soon enough."

But the *future business* is big, and growing. However, the things we know with any certainty about the future are very few. A wag might say that all we know for sure is that it lies ahead.

Looking at the *broad context* of speculation and prediction about the decades ahead, what are some general expectations we should have for society at large?

I report briefly here on general expectations derived from two sources, from professional futurists, and from the field of science fiction writing.

Turning to the futurists, I quote from one of the leaders in this relatively new "discipline," the president of the World Future Society and editor of *Futurist* magazine, Edward Cornish (1980):

> Perhaps the most important insight that futurists can offer is that the future cannot be predicted! The future is not a world that lies before us quietly awaiting our arrival but rather a world that we ourselves are creating. The future, then, is not fixed. Many different 'futures' may develop out of the present moment in which we

live. For that reason, we should explore a number of possible future worlds, not just a single 'most likely' possibility. Again and again, experience has shown that something viewed as wildly improbable or even impossible turns out to be what actually occurs. We may lack the time to study carefully all the possibilities, but experience suggests that we ought to at least look at more than one. Even if no possibility turns out to be precisely on target, the experience of considering several alternatives keeps our minds open and ready for whatever contingencies may actually occur.

That quotation is mighty compatible to all of us in education committed to the importance of psychological and educational diversity!

Futurists have identified a laundry list of expectations and issues for which critical choices must be made. Let's look at their list:

1. Complexity and democracy
   The increasing complexity of modern life makes it more and more difficult for voters to understand policy issues and make wise choices. Many voters give up and stop voting at all.
2. The enormous scale of industrial society
3. Industries endangered by foreign imports
4. Issues of minority cultures
5. Nuclear power
6. Crime
7. Family breakdown
8. Growing armaments
9. International migration (e.g., Cuba, Vietnam, Cambodia)
10. Poverty in wealthy nations
11. Rich vs. poor nations (the haves vs. have nots)
12. Ownership of the oceans
13. Automobiles
14. The extension of human life
15. The value of human life
16. The cost of government regulations
17. New technology
18. Destruction of the environment
19. Extinction of many animals and plants
20. Artificial conception and birthing—also choosing the sex of one's children
21. Smoking, drugs
22. Who's responsible for human health?

23. Terrorism
24. Disorder in the financial world
25. Overpopulation
26. Credentialling—including such ideas as licenses for parents

Where science fiction writers are concerned, an examination of their work suggests that they generally agree on at least *two* overriding developments in the future. These are: (1) increasing world population, and (2) increased technology.

Let's get away from these very general background expectations for the future, and look more closely at some of the many possible specific expectations for educational psychology.

Despite some of the things I've said to this point, I foresee a shining future for educational psychology, and a yet closer relationship between psychology and education. The infusion of cognitive psychology into science and mathematics education, reading instruction, and techniques of assessment has been remarkable, and its end is certainly not in sight (cf. Gagné & Briggs, 1983).

Keeping a close marriage of psychology and education alive is very important to the health of both parties. Psychology is the most remarkable of modern scientific disciplines, setting itself the unique task of using the mind to experiment upon itself, while meeting conventional canons of science. Education, on the other hand, is an endeavor that provides the greatest possibility for the long-term improvement of the human condition. Thus, the experimenting spirit of psychology coupled with the potential of education to improve this troubled world represents a match made in heaven!

Let me elaborate further on why I see an ever-stronger union of psychology and education developing.

We are Creating the Psychological Society.   As one of the many examples of this, one can cite the increased public vocabulary, discourse, conceptions, and perspectives that are derived from psychology. A related example is the tremendous role for psychology in the coming Information Revolution and the Information Age. Most scholars of contemporary society and the growing legions of futurists and technology watchers agree that we are entering or are already in an Information Age, a condition wherein the primary coinage of society is information in its various representations, and the dominant technology is that designed to process information, that is, the computer. Ten or 15 years ago the psychological science called human information processing was an arcane subdiscipline of psychology, known to few outsiders. Now the concepts, methods, and findings of human information processing are front-stage center in a dramatic social and technological upheaval. We cannot at this time anticipate all the possible outcomes of the Information Revolution, but some of these should strike close to home for educational psychology.

The computer, and particularly, of course, the anticipated artificial intelligence or AI computer, is a quick-witted little metallic and silicone mind, and it is a natural, logical ally of the human mind. It amplifies, interacts, stimulates, and resonates to the human mind—being thusly unlike all earlier major technologies. Educational psychology needs to prepare for the exciting years ahead in this emerging computer-based Information Age. Learning, thinking, and comprehension and their high points as in the gifted child, and their lower points as in learning disabilities and special education, will increasingly be redefined and newly described using information terminology and will ultimately be mediated primarily by computer. New assessment methods will have to be developed and employed, many or most of which will be computer-based assessment. Computers in education will lead to new conceptions of ability and intelligence. Computer-learning and information-processing styles may be quite different from traditional learning styles. Intelligent behavior in a computer world may not be quite the same as in our traditional environments. Computer-learning failure and computer-learning disabilities may involve new twists we haven't anticipated. Affect, emotion, and motivation may have different outcomes and implications in computer learning than in traditional schooling. In all of this, educational psychologists, as the new cognitive scientists in educational settings, will have a shining role. We best soon get about the business of preparing for it.

Parenthetically, in terms of the ultimate jobs and careers of contemporary school children, we can predict with confidence that by far the majority will be working in the Information Sector of the labor force. Currently, approximately 50–55% of the U.S. labor force is in the Information Sector. Here are some interesting comparisons: In 1860 40% were in Agriculture, and 5% in what might be called Information occupations. By 1980, however, 3% were in Agriculture and 50% in Information occupations, and the growth of the Information Sector continues.

There will be many other new roles and employment opportunities for graduates in educational psychology.

I've speculated briefly about computers. The *media*, as in TV and radio (which is more popular than ever), offers many opportunities. In a 1983 article in *Professional Psychology*, Jane Zimmerman for example outlined some of the many opportunities in television.

An aging population opens up opportunities for adult educational psychology, life-long learning, and so on.

Consumer educators will increasingly be needed. There are roles for educational psychologists here.

Expanding the job opportunities in educational psychology is limited only by our imagination, and by our university training capabilities. A lesson in creating a demand can be learned from experimental psychology. The pioneering application of cognitive psychology to the law and particularly to courtroom processes and eyewitness testimony has begun to create a demand for researchers whose experimental knowledge of these processes is seen as useful. We can do the same. Education is not restricted to the schools, and will increasingly take place in other settings. We can be helpful in these new settings and developments in education. Newsome and Stillwell (1984) recently undertook a survey of job prospects in universities, business, and industry for four categories of psychologists: counseling psychologist, school psychologist, educational psychologist, and developmental psychologist. In hiring new doctoral graduates, the data showed a fairly low employment rate in universities, and a nearly zero rate in industry, *except for educational psychology graduates.* Thus a major bright spot in their survey was for educational psychologists working in industrial settings.

I could discuss further the expanding roles and job prospects for educational psychologists. And we haven't touched on the graduate training issues and designation issues that would arise! Other chapters in this book will be considering these topics.

Instead, I turn in closing, to theoretical and research directions I think we should take in the 1990s.

First, we must do better research than we're doing now, because there will probably be fewer individuals engaged in the research enterprise. I hope this selectivity will force an emphasis of quality over quantity. We should increasingly open-up our criteria of acceptable methodologies, allowing a wider scope of inquiry. This broadening of our criteria would be in accord with the beginning quotation from the philosopher of science Toulmin, and with many recent developments in the philosophy of science. I would also argue for statistical approaches, such as bootstrapping, as viable alternatives in a number-crunching computer age to traditional logical inference or optimization procedures.

But much more important than the argument over methodologies is the need radically to expand our *conceptions of human nature,* and therefore education. Cognitive psychology has expanded our horizons. But we are barely off the ground. I believe that in the next century *mind* will become a central concept of advanced cultures, as will self-awareness, consciousness and creativity. Let us strive to research, know, teach, and communicate what is essentially human and humane, such aspects of a meaningful life as curiosity, wonder, love, generosity, creativity, aesthetics, moral development, stages of consciousness, spiritual knowledge, and enjoyment of life.

Lee Cronbach has elaborated on his definition of the main task of the contemporary social scientist as "pinning down the contemporary facts," referred to earlier, adding that "To know man as he is is no mean aspiration." In league with Jackson (1981), I would further add that "To know humans as they *might be,* is no mean aspiration." Educational Psychology—the psychology of humans in the process of becoming educated—can contribute to the realization of this dream.

REFERENCES

Ash, M. J., & Love-Clark, P. (1985). An historical analysis of the content of educational psychology textbooks, 1954–1983. *Educational Psychologist, 20,* 47–55.

Carroll, J. B. (1963). The place of educational psychology in the study of education. In J. Walton & J. L. Kuethe (Eds.), *The discipline of education.* Madison: University of Wisconsin Press.

Cronbach, L. J. (1975). Beyond the two disciplines of scientific psychology. *American Psychologist, 30,* 116–127.

Cornish, E. (1980). Editorial. *The futurist, 14*(1).

Farley, F. H. (1973). Editorial. Whither *EP? Educational Psychologist, 10*(1).

Feldhusen, J. F. (1976). Educational psychology and all is well. *Educational Psychologist, 12,* 1–13.

Gagné, R. M., & Briggs, L. J. (1983). Instructional psychology. *Annual Review of Psychology.*

Grinder, R. E. (1978). What 200 years tells us about professional priorities in educational psychology. *Educational Psychologist, 12,* 284–289.

Grinder, R. E. (1981). The "new science" of education: Educational psychology in search of a mission. In F. H. Farley & N. J. Gordon (Eds.), *Psychology and education: The state of the union.* Berkeley, CA: McCutchan.

Jackson, P. W. (1981). The promise of educational psychology. In F. H. Farley & N. J. Gordon (Eds.), *Psychology and education: The state of the union.* Berkeley, CA: McCutchan.

Newsome, T., & Stilwell, W. E. (1984). Unpublished manuscript. Lexington: University of Kentucky.

Toulmin, S. (1961). *Foresight and understanding.* New York: Harper & Row (cited in Jackson, 1981).

Watson, R. I. (1961). A brief history of educational psychology. *Psychological Record, 11,* 209–242.

Wells, H. G. (1923). *The outline of history.* Cited in B. Evans (1978) (Ed.), *Dictionary of quotation.* New York: Avenel Books.

Williams, J. P. (1978). Analysis of the *Journal of Educational Psychology:* Toward a definition of educational psychology. *Educational Psychologist, 12,* 290–296.

Zimmerman, J. D. (1983). Psychologists multiple roles in television broadcasting. *Professional Psychology: Research and Practice, 14,* 256–269.

3 Opportunities in the Future of Educational Psychology

M. C. Wittrock
University of California, Los Angeles

OPPORTUNITIES IN EDUCATION AND TRAINING

The improvement of the education of millions of students in elementary schools, secondary schools, colleges, and universities around the world presents an enormous opportunity for educational psychology. Adult literacy is a world-wide objective of educators. Basic skills in reading, mathematics, and physical science are essential in modern, technologically advanced societies.

Job skills in industry, business, and the military services need to be acquired by large numbers of adults each year. Competence in medicine, dentistry, nursing, engineering and related professions needs to be maintained and advanced through training programs appropriate for busy practitioners.

Effective training programs are also needed to teach people around the world how to build, maintain, service, and operate the ever-changing machines and equipment that pervade our industries, offices, and homes. The need to learn about this technology and to keep up with its advances presents significant training opportunities.

If it is taught in an understandable and memorable way, research-based information about health, wellness, nutrition, and preventive and curative medicine can improve the quality and longevity of many people's lives. The amelioration through education and training of complex social problems, such as crime and drug-abuse, could add enormously to the quality of life and to the productivity of individuals around the world.

Knowledge about the social sciences and the humanities is an important and enriching part of our daily lives. Through education, this knowledge should be available to adults who were not fortunate enough to have the opportunity to acquire it in a school or college.

RECENT ADVANCES IN EDUCATIONAL PSYCHOLOGY

Recent developments in educational psychology provide useful ways to contribute to these important educational and training opportunities. The recent research in cognition gives educational psychologists a better understanding than they have ever had before of how students learn from teaching. This recent research also provides useful ideas about motivation—especially attribution processes—about attention, memory, anxiety reduction, knowledge acquisition, comprehension, learning strategies, and metacognition. The useful ideas in these areas include strategies for changing student attributions, for focusing attention, for monitoring comprehension, and for teaching students self-control of their thought processes during learning (Wittrock, 1984, 1985).

In addition to these advances in the understanding of teaching and in the strategies of learning from instruction, recent advances in the technology of instruction have been impressive. The hardware of teaching now includes microcomputers installed, or soon to be installed, in many American classrooms. However, the programs of instruction for use in these machines are only beginning to be effective and sophisticated. Their potential, including their graphics, opens new avenues for educational psychologists to design interesting and understandable instruction for students in elementary and secondary schools and colleges, in homes, and on the job. These potentials for augmenting training and education are awesome. People who understand how students learn from instruction are needed to write understandable instructional materials.

In measurement, assessment, and evaluation, the contributions of cognitive science and high technology are also impressive. Recent cognitive conceptions of intelligence emphasize students' learning strategies. The measurement of learners' strategies, as it has developed in the recent research on mathematics learning, produces useful diagnostic instruments for classifying learners' thought processes, and for designing instruction appropriate for different learners. In science learning, comparable progress has been made in identifying some of the models children have of scientific phenomena.

These recent advances introduce extensive opportunities for educational psychologists in teaching, curriculum development, instruction, teacher-training, inservice education, assessment, and evaluation occurring in schools and in other contexts, such as industry, business, and the military services. The possibilities for using these recent advances in psychological theory and research, along with the modern innovations in the technology of instruction, to address the problems of teaching children in schools and adults on the job or at home seem limited only by our creativity and imagination.

Ironically, in this time of unprecedented advances in knowledge and technology within educational psychology, there is not a proportionate growth in the number of educational psychologists, at least not those active in Division 15 of APA. The reasons for this disparity are not well understood. But they could include the expanding roles of other branches of psychology, such as experimental psychology, and the growing base of educational researchers who routinely receive some training in the methods and theory of educational psychology. Neither of these groups views themselves as educational psychologists. Yet each of them plays a role of the educational psychologist. Unlike 40 years ago, today it is acceptable for experimental psychologists to study reading comprehension, mathematics learning, science teaching, written composition, and thinking skills in the schools. Unlike 40 years ago, today educational researchers who study instruction and curriculum incorporate in their research many of the recent findings and models of cognitive psychology on motivation, attribution, comprehension, group processes, attention, and knowledge acquisition.

Because of the relatively nontechnical vocabulary of cognitive psychology, the middle ground between psychological theory and the practice of education has shrunk. The vocabulary of cognitive psychology includes, as central concepts, attention, motivation, comprehension, and knowledge acquisition, all terms commonly used by educational researchers as well as by theorists and researchers in psychology. That these two groups often have different meanings for these central concepts does not seem to retard communication. The common tongue unites them, facilitates the exchange of ideas, and appears to diminish the role of the mediator, the educational psychologist.

Is there a problem? Educational psychology has succeeded extraordinarily in the last 25 years. Its subject matter, methods, and theory have contributed to training of a new generation of educational researchers. Through cognitive psychology, whose recent ascent began in large part in educational psychology, the field has had a major impact upon psychological research and theory. The influence of field is widespread. Its central problems are being studied by an increasingly wide range of talented psychologists and educational researchers. The progress on these problems is impressive, and so is the promise of the future.

LEADERSHIP FROM EDUCATIONAL PSYCHOLOGY

It is the promise of the future that we must emphasize. The extraordinary energy invested into research on complicated problems in educational psychology represents an unprecedented opportunity. We need to see that this opportunity realizes equally unprecedented advances in what we know and do in educational psychology. To help bring about these advances, we need to understand what educational psychology is and can become. We need ideas and leadership from educational psychologists.

We need a definition of educational psychology that indicates the value of training and experience in the theories, findings, and methods of doing psychological research in applied educational settings, such as schools. It must show what one must know and be able to do to be an educational psychologist. It must indicate the dual responsibilities of educational psychology, to understand and improve education and teaching, on the one hand, and to contribute advances to knowledge and theory in psychology, on the other hand. It must show how training in other branches of psychology, or in other fields of education, is a useful, but not sufficient, preparation for a career in educational psychology as a researcher or teacher who conducts psychological research in educational settings. It should specify the academic preparation, as well as the experience, and training in applied settings that qualifies an educational psychologist to conduct psychological research in schools and other educational contexts. We need to insure that the people who are conducting psychological research and applying psychology in the schools are properly trained and experienced for their roles as educational psychologists.

We have an outstanding opportunity to contribute to psychology and to improve the education of people around the world. We must provide the leadership needed in the next 20 years to realize the benefits that can come from the recent and widespread resurgence of interest in educational psychology. We must provide the organization and coherence that enables the recent research interest to cumulate findings into useful psychological theory, and into knowledge-based advances in teaching.

These are the opportunities we have as educational psychologists. We must take advantage of them.

REFERENCES

Wittrock, M. C. (1984). The president's message: New opportunities for educational psychologists. *Newsletter for Educational Psychologists, 8*(1), 1–2.
Wittrock, M. C. (1985). The president's message: Enlarging the conception of educational psychology. *Newsletter for Educational Psychologists, 8*(2), 1–2.

II EMERGING DIRECTIONS OF THE SCIENCE AND THE TECHNOLOGY

Research, theory, and technology in educational psychology promise to continue to change substantially in the next decade. The direction of this change emanates in large part from the impact on the field of the last 20 years of cognitive science and its ways of perceiving teaching, learning, and human aptitudes. The three chapters in section II explore related facets of these changes that promise to continue to develop and to lead to conceptual and technological advances in descriptive and prescriptive knowledge in educational psychology.

In chapter 4, Francis DiVesta discusses some of the changes he foresees in cognitive models of the learners and of learning events. These changes portend educational applications that will follow from the research on problems in teaching and learning. The problems to study include gaps left by behaviorism, such as the effects upon learning of (1) learner aptitudes, (2) learners' processing of information, and (3) higher order thinking. The educational applications he emphasizes include (a) cognitive objectives, (b) prior learning and schema, (c) the learner's representation of knowledge, (4) social influences, including cooperative learning, (e) domain-specific thinking skills, (f) classroom management analyses in terms of learner processes, (g) attribution processes, (h) the measurement of cognitive processes and learning outcomes and (i) learner generation of knowledge.

Wittrock develops several of these topics. He focuses on research that studies (1) prior knowledge in learning, (2) attention and attribution in learning, and (3) effective cognitive training programs for teaching learners strategies to generate meaning from instruction and teaching. He explores three domains: learning disabilities, mathematics and physical science, and reading comprehension. Research in these areas shows substantial promise for improving understanding of learning and for enhancing school achievement.

Richard Clark explores the promise of a research-based technology and its implications for teaching methods, curricula, courses, teachers, and instructional devices. He sees instructional technology moving from a focus on teaching as a craft to teaching as an applied science based on prescriptive knowledge. The prescriptive knowledge base, in turn, will derive from declarative knowledge and procedural knowledge developed in the scientific study of educational psychology. In this interesting perspective he develops, the instructional strategies, not the hardware of instruction, will create the advances in effective teaching. The hardware is a way to implement a strategy of teaching. In his model, achievement is enhanced by the students' thought processes during learning, which are influenced by the instructional methods and strategies. From this focus, he foresees a synthesis of experimental and correlational studies of educational psychology that will produce a new methodology for prescriptive research on teaching and its measurement.

4 Applications of Cognitive Psychology to Education

Francis J. Di Vesta
The Pennsylvania State University

The present chapter addresses the theme that current cognitive theories have made significant contributions to a number of cognitive models of the learner, and of learning events, important to educational applications in general and to educational psychological research in particular. They set the stage for implying needed future research directions in educational psychology. Each of the major sections of this chapter may be viewed as underlying an issue on which research is being conducted (to a large extent by educational psychologists) but for which more definitive answers have yet to be obtained. Each section is based on a direction where extended conceptualizations and research directions are needed rather than to review areas of research (e.g., adjunct question research) where considerable literature is already available.

No one model presently accounts for all the complexities of learning and instruction. However, it is apparent that there are models that correspond to each of the processing phases in which a student participates during the learning process and that correspond to the influences (e.g., social influences in the classroom) that impinge on his or her performance. In the course of this discussion it has been necessary to omit many topics that are, indeed, relevant and important to understanding the learner and to education in general. Thus, topics such as memory, problem solving, individual differences, and the psychology of school subjects are not discussed because of space limitations rather than because of neglect.

Cognitive models can be and are being shaped to applications in instruction and for improving tools for thinking. With the development of current vast resources such as encyclopedic data bases, opportunities for representing knowledge graphically in three and four dimensions, introduction of 500 megabyte CD ROMs, computer networking, and new video technologies there is emerging immense potential for a new generation of cognitive educational engineering. Concern for applying cognitive theories to education comes from many quarters of psychology. In a recent publication, for example, Thorndyke (1984) has argued that " . . .(1) the enterprise of cognitive and aducational psychology should be the development of cognitive technologies for use in applied settings, and (2) schema theory currently promises more as a prescriptive theory than it delivers as a descriptive theory" (p. 188). Other similar positions are noted throughout this chapter from both experimental and educational psychologists.

In the presentation in this chapter there are statements of reviews about the current status, issues, and potential research thrusts. The areas discussed involve the necessity for a concern with ecological approaches; the need to orient instruction toward the objective of understanding; needed research on the role of prior knowledge in learning; issues related to assimilative, activation, and generative processes that are concerned with active rather than passive learners; implications of the learners' *state of knowledge* for guiding instructional events; and cognitive components of motivation. During the past 25 years there has been a growing interest in cognitive psychology to the almost complete exclusion of strict associationistic principles. In this transition the educational psychologist has played no small part. What more influential field can there be than one that is concerned with, or influences, in no small way, the education of people in virtually all civilizations?

A major change in the emergence of cognitivism has been in filling the gaps, neglected by behaviorism, related to (a) the effects of the characteristics of the learner on learning outcomes; (b) the role played in learning by a processing organism; (c) the requirements for effective higher order thinking; (d) what was processed by the learner during a learning or problem-solving event; (e) the consequences of given forms of processing; and (e) how outcomes of learning are to be measured.

To emphasize that these variables were being ignored consciously by psychologists of an earlier era, they had introduced the concept of the "black box" as a metaphor to imply that the "contents" and "processes" of the brain were inaccessible to experimental observations and thus investigations of behavior and behavioral changes could be made entirely in terms of external observable stimuli and observable behavior. Thus, the internal workings of the mind would remain a mystery inaccessible to scientific investigation. Neglecting to study the thinking process as we know it today was intentional and purposeful during a period (the first half of the century) in which the young science of educational psychology was attempting to avoid the difficulties posed by using anthropomorphic and often tautological, interpretations of behavioral phenomena.

Regardless of behavioristic dominance there has always been a cognitive psychology in the background, in which many dominant figures were educational psychologists. For example, from the beginning of scientific psychology there was E. B. Huey's work on the psychology and pedagogy of reading (Huey, 1908/1968), and Dewey's (1910) concern with problem solving. The works of

Duncker (1945), Koffka (1935), Max Wertheimer (1945), and other Gestalt psychologists were major contributors to our current understanding of problem solving as it applies to the classroom. However, many educational psychologists who might have been considered to be "behaviorists" often employed cognitive constructs. For example, Thorndike (1917; 1932) noted the importance of belongingness, understanding, and meaningfulness when he spoke of verbal learning.

The more recent influences in the development of cognitive psychology also came from quarters closely allied to education, if not from educational psychologists themselves. The most dominant were the influences of the developmental psychology of Piaget (1926; Flavell, 1963), computer research on artificial intelligence (Simon, 1965) and simulation of human problem solving (Newell & Simon, 1972), a volume on cognitive psychology by Neisser (1967) and psycholinguistics among whom were the first contributors—W. Wundt and E. B. Huey and the recent contributor—N. Chomsky (see Blumenthal, 1970).

The recent era of transition from behavioral to cognitive psychology was clearly marked during the decade of the '60s, (Di Vesta, 1974). It was also during this period that Ausubel's theoretical work on the influence of cognitive structures was introduced. His comment, in the foreword to his (Ausubel, 1968) textbook titled *Educational Psychology: A Cognitive View*, was, "If I had to reduce all of educational psychology to just one principle I would say this: The most important single factor influencing learning is what the learner already knows. Ascertain this and teach him accordingly." "What the learner already knows" stands out as a proclamation that schemata . . . their contents and structure . . . are influential factors in acquisition, memory, and transfer. The statement seems as relevant today as it did when it first appeared.

These contributions to cognitive psychology brought about a renewal of concern about the learner's role in instruction; a concern for new ways of thinking about education and the educational process. The era of schema theories; theories about (a) the learner's knowledge of the materials, tools and media of the subject matter (e.g., number systems or linguistic knowledge); (b) cognitive and learning skills employed by the learner; and, (c) cognitive development was opened. Cognitive science has been directly responsible for the introduction of innovative experimental methodology and theory building, for constructs to represent mental structures and processes in scientific terms, for understanding reading, writing, and acquisition in other school subject-matter areas, and for providing the foundations for the technology of cognitive engineering.

ECOLOGICAL VALIDITY

An important question, in the face of these new innovations and in the use of the results of psychological experiments, is the extent to which the empirical findings are functionally useful. The answer to this question has always been a concern to educational researchers and continually arises in discussion of the *relevance* of experimental laboratory research for education. Some of this chapter section is based on Wagner and Sternberg's (1986) discussion of this concern which they call *practical intelligence*. Within this framework, the distinction once made between basic (or "pure") research versus applied research now seems *academic*. Psychologists, in general, have closed ranks on this question; research is expected to yield information about human learning, learning in everyday, natural situations, and learning as it occurs in the formal educational process, as well as in the highly constrained laboratory setting. Some educators may feel that all educational research ought to be directly and immediately applicable to education, and immediately useable by instructors, students, and other educational personnel. However, a sound psychology of education does require the support of experimental evidence and theory building to identify variables, new and hypothesized, that significantly affect learning and instruction; but obtaining such scientific support is a slow process at best. Furthermore, it is unlikely that a single variable, found to have influential effects on behavior in the laboratory, will in itself, have profound effects outside the laboratory. The utility of experimentation occurs from the identification of new constructs for labeling variables along with identification of constraints that define the effects of variables both in isolation and in interaction with other variables.

In the course of research, whether experimental, descriptive, ethnographic, or historical, educational psychologists currently strive for ecological validity. Neisser (1982) has stated the problem well. He says, "we expect students to learn from the educational practices we employ, and we administer examinations to see whether they have learned that which had been taught. If we are to take seriously the point that education is what is left over after what you have learned has been forgotten" (p. 5) most of us, as instructors, would be dismayed at what traces are left of our teaching. Neisser goes on to say,

> How much, then, do students retain? This really is an important question. Higher education has become a central feature of Western culture, involving millions of people every year, and it depends heavily on the assumption that students remember something valuable from their educational experience. One might expect psychologists to leap at the opportunity to study a critical memory problem so close at hand but they never do. It is difficult to find even a single study, ancient or modern, of what is retained from academic instruction. Given our expertise and the way we earn our livings, this omission can only be described as scandalous. (p. 5)

Discussion with any lay person will bring out interesting problems related to the educational process as it occurs in natural settings. To be explained are common observations that people have about memories of specific events, events that were not taught directly but had an important bearing on other critical events in that person's life; the influence of contexts of learning situations created by various teachers; the kinds of things that were never taught but were learned anyway (e.g., fantastic memory strategies that some people develop incidentally and the ability of some people, such as "hackers," to master complex computer systems without outside help); ease of remembering during childhood compared to what is remembered after deliberately applying oneself to learn and remember in the adult (even early adult) years, and so on. An important question in all of these observations is why these kinds of events occur for one person and not for another and why some people learn more from *incidental learning* situations than do others of equal "intellectual" ability. A related question is, "How much and what is learned from incidental learning situations compared to academic learning situations?"

As a psychologist deeply immersed in experimental investigations and theories of memory, Norman (1980), too, has commented on the need for ecological validity from the viewpoint of the school. He says,

> It is strange that we expect students to learn yet seldom teach them anything about learning. We expect students to solve problems yet seldom teach them about problem solving. And, similarly, we sometimes require students to remember a considerable body of material yet seldom teach them the art of memory. It is time we made up for this lack, time that we developed the applied disciplines of learning and problem solving and memory. We need to develop the general principles of how to learn, how to remember, how to solve problems and then to develop applied courses, and then to establish the place of these methods in an academic curriculum. (p. 97).

We have come a long way during the past century toward examining our research from the standpoint of its ecological validity. But it was not always so. For example, Ebbinghaus' (1885/1913) outstanding research on memory led to the development of the nonsense syllable because he had noted the importance of individual differences and wanted to eliminate or control for their effects (Anderson, 1985b). Despite the ingenuity of the invention of the nonsense syllable, he also effectively led a few generations of psychologists to ignore the effects of background knowledge on memory. Since his was the first systematic program of experimental studies of memory, these comments are not intended as a derogation of Ebbinghaus' important leadership on memory research through his substantive and methodological contributions (Tulving, 1985b). Rather, the comments are directed only toward illustrating changes over the past century in our current view of memory research in comparison with the first experimental program.

Evidence that today's researcher is concerned with the many classes of variables that affect learning and memory in "real-life" situations (Jenkins, 1974a, 1974b) comes from many quarters. Wagner and Sternberg (1985), for example, demonstrate the importance of tacit knowledge acquired in the course of extensive experience in successful performance in real world pursuits. Neisser (1976a) had also made a similar point by noting that academic intelligence is a subset of "real world" intelligence, i.e., the kind of intelligence that is required for successful performance in vocational pursuits. Wagner and Sternberg (1985) remind their readers that others before them have also considered the measurement of competencies in the real world. These approaches include the motivational approach of McClelland and his colleagues (McClelland, 1953), the critical incident technique developed by Flanagan (1954), the simulation approach represented by the In-Basket Test developed by Frederiksen (Frederiksen, 1986; Frederiksen, Saunders, & Wand, 1957) and the assessment center approach, a combination of the previously described techniques (Thornton & Byham, 1982). The latest approach to examining intelligence in every day situations that has implications for education is the study of differences in the thinking skills of experts and novices. As described in a later section of this chapter, the difference in the two stages of development of learning ability is primarily in what novices and experts know, how what they know is organized, and the *depth* of support they are able to provide for explanations of what they know (e.g., Chase & Simon, 1973; Chi, Feltovich, & Glaser, 1981). Such knowledge, being tacit, is not typically taught directly (although it could be) but is learned through experience in practical or formal learning situations. Wagner and Sternberg (1985) include in their description of tacit knowledge three classes of variables: managing others; managing career reputations and goals; and managing self so as to maximize one's productivity.

The attainment of ecological validity and the extent to which evidence is ecologically valid is, indeed, a pressing issue. Although the issue has had a long history of concern and debate, without satisfactory resolution, it will probably be dealt with by psychologists and educators more directly in their research in the future years, whether such research is conducted in the research laboratory, in the field, or in the instructional setting. This point becomes evident in the subsequent sections of this chapter.

OBJECTIVES OF INSTRUCTION

Educational objectives have appeared in many forms, however adventitiously their shapes may have been produced. The work of G. Stanley Hall on child and adolescent development was eventually applied in the form of educational goals or developmental tasks. Problems attacked by philosophers and experimenters alike were directed at what educational goals should be and, in some cases, defined the nature of the goals such as problem solving (Dewey, 1910), transfer and verbal learning (Thorndike, 1932).

Recent landmarks in the formal definitions of different forms of educational objectives were the *Taxonomy of Educational Objectives* (Bloom, Engelhart, Furst, Hill, & Krathwohl, 1956) and the description of behavioral objectives within the behavioristic framework (Mager, 1962). These approaches emphasized the statement of objectives in terms that were testable by objective (e.g., multiple-choice or true-false) tests. Unfortunately, this philosophy, inadvertently perhaps, placed the notions of reliability and other statistical characteristics of the test ahead of *what* the test measured and *how* to instruct for a given objective. Particularly neglected has been the goal of how to achieve comprehension and understanding since to achieve highly reliable statistical characteristics often depends on the testing of minutiae. This practice has become habitual with most educators. (Most college testing services, for example, will produce a multitude of statistics to describe the characteristics of each ''teacher made'' test. These are given serious attention by the constructor of the tests, who knows how to improve the statistical characteristics of the tests on the basis of the data provided.) The lessons on how to improve the statistical characteristics of tests have been well-learned; the definition of how to test for understanding and comprehension are less well understood by test constructors, psychologists, and educators alike.

The necessity for going beyond current types of tests and measuring problem-solving strategies and styles and for measuring processing components involved in higher level thinking behavior has been noted by Frederiksen (1986). Tests do influence the hidden agenda of objectives and their content and processing requirements are interpreted accordingly by students. Clearly, standardized tests, and their accompanying norms, are highly influential in what is taught in the curriculum even though their primary emphasis is on facts. Educational curricula and practices in general might be considerably changed if the tests placed emphasis on higher thinking skills and emcompassed the kind of knowledges and strategies required in practical settings.

Educational psychologists are currently taking on the challenge of teaching for understanding from a number of quarters. Although it is difficult to define exactly, understanding, as an objective, has several observable manifestations in behavior, although it is not in itself a behavior. Without understanding knowledge may have little transferability. With understanding new learning will be retained better and will be retrieved better than if we merely teach ''to the test'' and students learn ''for the test.'' Understanding is finding meaning structures in situations that on the surface seem disorganized or unrelated (e.g., as in the widely dispersed events that eventually become integrated to form a concept). Texts read with understanding are comprehended and structured by the reader. Math principles that are understood are supported by more and deeper reasons than poorly understood principles. Students who learn concepts with understanding can *explain* the concept better than those who learn the concept in a superficial manner (e.g., by its label or by a dictionary definition). Deese (1969) has argued strongly that without the achievement of understanding by the learner instruction is less than an optimal effort. Learners should be able to acquire new knowledge with facility, to know its meaning, to retain it, and to use it in thinking . . . all of which outcomes are the result of learning with understanding (see also, Simon, 1980).

Research during the decades of behavioral domination placed this important objective on the back burner. Educational methods emphasized (and still do) the input-output relations between what teachers do and what students learn as a consequence of teacher activity. Little concern, if any, was given to what goes on in between that might foster understanding. Fortunately, this state of affairs is changing. The current burgeoning of research on reading comprehension and on learning and instructional strategies are examples of a systematic attack on means for helping students to achieve understanding.

PRIOR KNOWLEDGE AND SCHEMA THEORY: THE REPRESENTATION OF KNOWLEDGE

Understanding can be observed by manifestations in thinking and in the way memories are represented. Descriptions of such representations are to be found in the constructs of schemes and schemata cited, at least as early as in the philosophical works of Immanuel Kant (1781/1877), and later in the works of O. Selz on the nature of intellect (1927), Sir Frederic Bartlett on memory (1932), and the developmental epistemology of Jean Piaget (1926; also see Flavell, 1963).

A cognitive theory especially oriented toward education and using the notion of schemata (cognitive structure) was developed in the decade of the '50s by David Ausubel (see Ausubel, Novak & Hanesian, 1978, for a recent description). His theory was clearly constructed around principles with which we are still concerned today. By use of the contruct of cognitive structure Ausubel acknowledged the importance of memorial representations of experience and of their organization. The optimal organization was said to consist of hierarchically arranged concepts. These concepts and their arrangement (relations to one another) were the main components of the scaffolding that guided and provided anchors for the subsumption of new learning. As a result of organized representations of prior knowledge, new learning could become assimilated into the existing knowledge structures. Assimilation was not hypothesized to occur automatically; the text or other verbal input had to be potentially meaningful and the learner had to be motivated (a meaningful learning set) to derive the meaning in the text. A number of further deductions were made from these few principles such as the hypothesis that specific learning would be recalled more or less in terms of its particulars, but over a period of time the new learning would become an integral and dissociable part of the structures to which it had been linked. Nevertheless, the meaning of the original concept would become extended by incorporation of new learning but the specifics of original learning would be no longer recognizable . . . a process called obliterative subsumption. One can see the similarity between this view and current empirical evidence that shortly after learning the recall of meaning and gist takes precedence over verbatim recall (Sachs, 1967).

An important application of his theory was made by advocating the use of advance organizers. Recent research and reviews by Mayer (1979a, 1979b) has provided experimental evidence for the use of advance organizers in aiding assimilation of new learning. Other research by Helm and Novak (1983) has employed Ausubel's theory in a number of applications to science education particularly with respect to elementary school children's misconceptions about scientific principles.

Experiences, per se, are not stored in memory; they are represented in imaginal, propositional, or other form. They are organized according to their locations, their status within hierarchical organizations, their temporal arrangement in experience, and so on. In this form they comprise the schemata. Contributions to current versions of schema theory have emerged from a number of sources: in cognition in human learning (e.g., Bransford, 1979), in education and reading (e.g., Anderson, 1984; Anderson & Ortony, 1975) and in research on artificial intelligence as it relates to school-like situations (Collins, 1985; Schank & Abelson, 1977; Simon, 1965). Assumptions about the nature of the schemata, units of knowledge representation, are continually undergoing revision. Nevertheless, although a fuzzy concept, the *schema* construct has had important heuristic value for current research on human learning. In fact, it would be difficult to visualize a person without schemata representing prior experience. Questions that arise here are similar to those raised in Ausubel's theory: Are the schemata static, dynamic, or both? One of the assumptions appears to be that they are comprised of both qualities (see the next section on declarative and procedural knowledge). Another question is, "how are schemata organized?" Are they hierarchically organized or do they comprise a highly complicated integrated network of concepts and relations? The current evidence implies that both kinds of organizations exist in the schemata, probably hierarchies of superordinate and subordinate relations embedded in networks comprised of packets of both specific (declarative) knowledge and means (procedures) for using that knowledge (Norman, 1982).

Related to the schemata is the question of whether scripts (Schank & Abelson, 1977) are also embedded in the network of representations. Scripts are sometimes referred to as "giant schemata" comprised of regularly experienced orders of activities within similar events (such as attending a lecture, eating at a restaurant, or going to a physician's office). Recall may be organized around such relatively stabilized sequence of events or event-structures (Bower, Black & Turner, 1979). Representations of knowledge within the schemata are not always rigid, but have a range of attributes that are acceptable for general everyday situations (prototypes).

Scripts can be viewed as a series of expectations about events thereby allowing for predictions of typical behavior required in a given type of situation. It is unclear whether the assumed effects of scripts are different from those that might be predicted from schema theory without the notion of scripts. Within situational constraints scripts, nevertheless, appear to be reliable for given commonly and frequently experienced events within a culture.

In common with Ausubel's (Ausubel et al., 1978) view of cognitive structure, schema theory offers a multitude of opportunities for research on the functions schemata serve in (a) acquisition of new knowledge, (b) in representing general and domain-specific strategies for thinking, and (c) representing means of assessment and evaluation (Thorndyke, 1984, p. 183). With the emergence of emphases on prose learning, as opposed to verbal paired associate learning paradigms, schema theory has been oriented toward the effects of schemata on perspective-taking, motivational expectations, and interpretations of newly experienced situations. Relevant schemata enhance comprehension and memorability of passages read in text. They provide the foundations, framework and structures for understanding. They allow predictions for classifications of new experiences. They are crucial for *understanding*.

Schema theory has led to a number of imaginative studies. Among them are studies of the role of context in relating new information to existing schemata. For example, titles attached to ambiguous passages aid disambiguation of the meaning of those passages. Cultural differences (Cole & Means, 1981) and individual differences in schemata provide implicit contexts that differentially affect the reconstruction of event representations, learners' expectations about events and recall of events (Anderson, 1984; Steffensen, Joag-Dev, & Anderson, 1979). Generalized concepts in texts are instantiated in terms of the contexts within which they are embedded (Anderson & Ortony, 1975).

It is probably correct to say that schema theory is a part of the framework for most current innovations in educational research. It has certainly influenced many of the studies of classroom management, effective teaching, teaching of learning strategies, views of the effects of expectations on test taking, studies of experts and novices, and studies on school subjects. It is doubtful that an up-to-date textbook on teaching methods or supervision would be written without some reference to schema theory.

THE ACTIVATION OF KNOWLEDGE

The sheer encoding and storage of knowledge is insufficient for success in academic or real-world pursuits. The information must be activated, accessed, and retrieved on appropriate occasions. It must be patterned in accordance with situational demands as, for example, an electronics technician might pattern the circuitry systems in an amplifier. The representations and patterns must be capable of being used, and transferred, on demand and at a relatively automatic level for efficient application.

Although ordinarily considered somewhat separately from schema theory, activation theory (J. R. Anderson, 1983, 1984, 1985a) is a useful supplement to schema theory. Activation theory assumes the building of networks or systems of relations just as does schema theory but provides theoretical bases for understanding how knowledge representations enter into learning and thinking. Knowledge representations are of little value if they merely *exist* somewhere in storage. To be useful, knowledge has to be activated.

Within this theory, knowledge networks are comprised of propositions and production systems. Propositions comprise the system of declarative knowledge as the smallest units of meaning. They consist of arguments (concepts) and relations (verbs, adjectives, adverbs, etc.) between or among them. Production systems are based on procedural knowledge in a form such as "if-then" statements (see also, Lesgold, 1984).

Upon continual use, such as might occur in the diagnosis of a disease by a physician or in the use of a theorem for solving a geometry problem by an engineer, *declarative knowledge* becomes interrelated with procedures through *knowledge compilation*. Knowledge compilation involves *proceduralization,* a process that provides the learner with a series of perspectives about how the skill will appear or of how the knowledge will be used. It also involves *composition* whereby the use of procedures will be made more efficient by deleting irrelevant parts of the procedure or by combining multiple procedures into a single (or fewer) procedure(s). In the final, or *procedural* phase, the series of processes (if-then statements) are tuned by relating them to specific input patterns. Tuning occurs by strengthening (through repeated use), generalization (through increasing breadth of usage), and discrimination (through comparison and contrast of examples and nonexamples).

The importance of these constructs can be seen in the observation that students often seem to know the information required to solve problems but are unable to use the information appropriately (i.e., in a given situation or at the right time). The information has not been efficiently proceduralized. With sufficient practice, procedures become automatic (Schneider & Fisk, 1982; Shiffrin & Schneider, 1977) freeing cognitive space for thinking.

LaBerge and Samuels (1974) theorized that the performance of skilled readers required that word recognition and other basic processes had to become automated; fluency could not be accounted for by functioning only at the level of knowing what processes were involved. The assumptions in activation theory are useful for understanding such notions as interference in memorial processes, pattern recognition, priming through contexts, expectations in predicting, and the ability to generalize or to discriminate among concepts.

In addition to premises regarding the representation of information, activation theory considers that information must be active to be processed effectively. For example, ideas are more easily linked if they occur together in working memory. Further, the activation of one concept existing in the schema spreads to other concepts linked to it. Thus, priming by use of "advance organizers," contexts, or other means will activate a series of propositions related to the "primer." The importance of this premise can be seen in the illustration that a color primer for the concept of "cardinal" will spread to quite different associated concepts than if "member-of-the-clergy" or number primers are used (see also Cofer, 1957, 1973, for other examples). Underlying activation theory are not only assumptions about *how* knowledge is represented but also the *state* of that knowledge (see following sections) at a given time and the mechanisms by which activation occurs.

When applied to education, the theory does not leave the learner as a sheer collector of information. Through knowledge of the use of production systems the teacher would be strongly aware of the necessity for guiding the student to the point of using knowledge, how to use it effectively, and how much and what kinds of practice the learner should be given to reach efficient performance levels.

The theory appears to have implications for making information functional, a necessity if learning with understanding is to be an outcome of teaching. At least one textbook in educational psychology (E. Gagne, 1985) has been written based on activation theory. An incidental (and interesting) observation on E. Gagne's (1985) text is that although the text is based on J. Anderson's (1983, 1985a) theory, the position taken is consistent with, but independent of, the emphases in R. Gagne's (e.g., 1985) books on educational technology in which procedural knowledge in instruction is emphasized.

STATES OF KNOWLEDGE: EXPERTS AND NOVICES

To design curricula effectively, the instructional designer (teacher) must be aware of the learner's knowledge state. Learners with undeveloped schemata for a given subject-matter area must be taught differently and at different levels of conceptualization than learners with better developed concepts.

A major research thrust has been emerging during the past 20 years comparing how experts in an area differ from novices in their knowledge, conceptualizations, understanding, and problem solving. The current emphasis began about the time of de Groot's (1966) and Chase and Simon's (1973) studies that initiated investigations of the processing of chess positions by master chess players and duffers. Other studies ranged from investigations of the extent to which people knowledgeable in an area such as baseball differed in their understanding of a report of a game to problem solving in the social sciences (Voss, Greene, Post & Penner, 1984).

A study by Chase and Ericsson (1981) was particularly unique because it demonstrated that learners could be trained in short-term memory. They identified a learner who was knowledgeable about records for track-running times. By relating these memorial contents to random inputs of numbers the learner was able to extend his working memory to 80 digits. He employed strategies for finding patterns or chunks related to running times and through these techniques he was able to retrieve them at later times.

These studies were often cast within the framework of schema theory. However, it can be seen that Chase and Ericsson's (1981) and Chase and Simon's (1973) studies also identified higher-order processes that go beyond the basic characteristics typically associated with so-called short-term memory. They demonstrated *the importance of declarative knowledge in proceduralization* and the relation between the two. Thus, they showed that the working memory is dependent upon the nature of the patterns stored in long-term memory. These experiments provide a link for understanding the relation between the availablility of expert cognitive skills and the knowledge to which they are applied. The focus was on the state of the knowledge representations in the "mind" of the expert.

Neisser's (1982) recent orientation places emphasis on the knowledge patterns of experts as well. Expertise does not occur in a vacuum but rather, emerges through identifying environmental structures relating them to what is known, and modifying what is known. An aspect of the environment to be understood is the nature of the medium with which the expert works ("A conversation with Ulric Neisser," *Psychology Today,* May 1982). A mark of genius is the ability to extend the medium in new ways, as in sculpture or other art forms. The skilled person of course, has distinct information and excellent memorability for whatever his or her activity demands. Persons who are skilled in something others are not, do have prodigious memories for the amount of information they can recall in *their* areas of expertise, and prodigious knowledge about the characteristics of materials with which they work.

The study of the thinking patterns of experts and novices has underscored the importance of how experts arrive at understanding. Estimates are that between 5000 and 10,000 hours of training is required to achieve expertise. It is also estimated that a chess expert has between 10,000 and 50,000 meaningful patterns (Norman, 1980) at his or her disposal. Lesgold (1984) provides an excellent summary of the effect of knowledge on expertise (p. 34): Knowledgeable readers are better able to keep track of the flow of text as they read. Experts can retain more information in working memory especially for information related to the main theme of the text. As a result of patterning and chunking of information experts are better able to retain more complex information and events in the domain of their expertise than are novices. More knowledgeable persons are able to anticipate occurrences more accurately and as a result free cognitive space for high level processes.

With high levels of experience required for expertise, it is unlikely that novices should learn to perform tasks in exactly the same way that experts do. Nor should they be expected to know the same things at the same levels that experts do. With regard to acquisition of vocabulary, for example, Herman, Anderson, Pearson, and Nagy (1985) say,

Acquisition of word knowledge generally occurs in small increments. When learners initially encounter an unfamiliar word, they may grasp only some portion of its meaning. For example, while reading a passage on the development of river systems, a student who knows nothing about rills beforehand may know only that rills contain water. This partial knowledge of rills may be sufficient to respond to a multiple choice item when none of the distractors mention water, but it would be insufficient to respond to a multiple-choice item that required discrimination among definitions of three or four kinds of waterways. On the other hand, a second student may already know that rills are waterways and, by reading the same river systems text, figures out how rills fit into a water system. This second student added to his or her existing partial knowledge about rills. Thus, both students made incidental gains in word knowledge; but if researchers are unaware of the instrumental nature of vocabulary acquisition and fail to devise tests that are sensitive to partial gains in word knowledge they may conclude erroneously that not much, if any, incidental acquisition of vocabulary knowledge has occurred. . . .If researchers then proceed to test only for full adult understanding, the wrong conclusion might be reached, that is, that little incidental learning took place. (p. 3–4)

Different "states of knowledge" characterize the extreme (and in-between) phases of acquisition as well as suggesting descriptions of the course of learning. The idea of different states of knowledge may be the unifying link needed for a theory of how the student arrives at expertise with accompanying implications for instructional design (see Chipman, Segal, & Glaser, 1985; Segal, Chipman, & Glaser, 1985).

Following are three models that imply similar phases of learning from the state of arbitrary knowledge to functional, comprehended, and meaningful knowledge. The three models should be considered in conjunction with J. R. Anderson's activation theory, described earlier, that also characterizes three states of knowledge: declarative knowledge; knowledge compilation; and proceduralization (unitization).

A model proposed by Norman (Norman, 1978) and Rumelhart (1980) describes three stages in learning: accretion, reconstruction, and tuning. In the accretion stage information is assimilated into the schemata in relatively isolated fashion as discrete facts or propositions. With additional experience and exposure to learning situations in a given knowledge domain, ideas are linked to other ideas. Eventually the links form patterns through the reconstruction of the relations among ideas. The emerging patterns are characteristic of the emergence of "expertise." Superimposed on the continuing cycles of accretion and reconstruction is the tuning cycle during which is acquired the ability to use the information, whether ideas or patterns, under a variety of situations, with accuracy and more or less automatically. The latter is characteristic of an expert researcher who may support an hypothesis with highly reasoned deeply structured principles compared to the relatively superficial support given hypotheses by uninititated researchers.

Fitts's (Fitts, 1964; Fitts & Posner, 1967) model of motor skill learning is comprised of components similar to those in J. R. Anderson's (1984) and Norman's (1978, 1982) models. It, too, assumes three phases in the development of motor skills: cognitive, associative, and autonomous. During the cognitive phase the elements (declarative knowledge) of the skill are learned and represented memorially as verbal plans. In the associative stage the verbal plan is translated into a motoric representation. The skill is practiced until the sequence takes on program-like qualities, with routines and subroutines that will eventually be run off in smoothly performed and automatic sequences. Practice fixes the organization, sequence, and timing of the skill subcomponents. The third phase, that of achieving automaticity of the skill, refines (tunes) the skill, adds depth (the amount of explanatory support the leaner is capable of providing for a given decision), increases flexibility (the ability to perform the skill at different levels depending upon the circumstances), permits generalization with regard to recognizing patterns (experts functioning as diagnosticians perform trouble shooting tasks by examining specifics within general patterns), and allows discrimination (experts know which action-sequences go with which patterns).

A parallel model has recently been proposed by Tulving (1985a) for representing three systems of memory arranged in a monohierarchical arrangement: procedural, semantic, and episodic. The procedural system is at the bottom and it develops through active responding and adaptation to environmental demands. The semantic system, next in the hierarchy, provides internal symbolic memorial representations of meaningful events and ideas that do not have perceptual counterparts. There is a great deal of flexibility in thinking provided by this system since it means that schemata, world views, or models of the world, can be constructed and reconstructed through covert exploration and manipulation of internal models. Episodic memory is at the top of the hierarchy. In it are represented both personal and temporal representations of experience. Relating these three models of memory to Norman's model, Tulving suggests that acquisition in the tuning phase is based on procedural knowledge, acquisition in the reconstruction phase requires semantic use of the semantic memorial system, and acquisition in the accretion phase involves episodic memory.

The convergence of these independent models from various vantage points of perception, knowledge acquisition and activation, acquisition of cognitive and motor skills, and memorial processes are displayed in Table 4.1. They provide the promise of eventually building more refined substantial models for instruction and for investigations of learning in the classroom. The most promising of these, at present, is Norman's (1978) model, mainly because it provides differential implications and performance expectations for instructional methods, study skills, and evaluation at each of the states of knowledge and understanding.

In the accretion stage, learners may be exposed to a wide array of knowledge, terminology, explanations, events, and the like, all of which seem foreign and, indeed mysterious to them. Attempts will be made to link this material to existing knowledge structures, that is, instruction will be geared to adapting to the readiness of the student. The typical procedure at this point would, perhaps, emphasize the presentation of information, probably by the lecture method. Even when understanding is the objective, the discovery method is used or when demonstra-

TABLE 4.1
Convergence of Models Describing Phases of Learning
and States of Knowledge and Memory

Kind of Theory	Phase or State		
	Initial	Intermediate	Advanced
General	arbitrary	meaningful	functional
Schema Theory	accretion	reconstruction	tuning
Norman (1978)			
Activation Theory	declarative	knowledge	proceduralization
Anderson (1985a)	knowledge	compilation	or unitization
Memory	episodic	semantic me-	memory for pro-
Tulving (1985a)		morial sys-	cedural knowl-
		tem	edge
Perceptual motor	cognitive	asssociative	autonomous
Fitts (1964)			

tions are provided the initial period will require some presentation of information by an instructor, the seeking of information from resources, or the recall of discrete pieces of information. Because the knowledge structures are poorly developed and ideas are only partially related, recall tends to be fragmented rather than highly structured, reasoned, or organized. Study methods typically used are review and rehearsal of the material. Information in this state is not readily transferable or useable because of its isolated quality even though it may have been incorporated into a part of the schemata. Evaluation is made on the basis of simple recognition or cued recall tests. Since the qualities associated with the accretion stage are characteristic of most educational settings, it would appear that most formal education emphasizes the accretion phase, leaving the reorganization of learning and proceduralization to the learner.

Knowledge in the reconstruction phase may be structured initially in the form of prototypes such as the kinds of concepts that are used on an everyday basis (Rosch, 1975, 1977). These concepts are more like impressions that need no precise definition. Most people, for example, use the word "game" in communication without ever defining it. Indeed, arguments about its definition by lay persons and philosophers alike might take on the form of an endurance match. Such concepts can only be defined in terms of "family resemblances" since they are only applied within certain ranges of attributes. For example, it is clear that a sparrow is a bird, it is less clear that a chicken or ostrich is a bird, and many people mistake a bat for a bird and consider a penguin a nonbird because the attributes of bats and birds depart radically from the prototypes of mammals and birds, respectively. With increased training concepts become more refined and well-defined taking on the characteristic of constructs (e.g., technical terms). During the reconstruction phase, multidimensional attributes of concepts become interlinked with numerous relationships within the concept and with relationships to other concepts. The instructional methods that might be appropriate here are the "Socratic Dialogue," the inquiry method, the discovery method, or similar approach. The study method might also require some such technique as spatial mapping (Dansereau, 1985; Novak & Gowin, 1984; Weinstein & Mayer, 1985) by which the individual organizes and elaborates the material in ways that will identify the relation of the concept to other concepts (e.g., part of, characteristic of, subsumed under, example of, and so on) and that will also provide explanations of why certain relations exist.

The refining of concepts is the outcome of long cycles of accretion and reconstruction. The typical methods of evaluation in the reconstruction phase would be in the form of essay tests, comparison and contrasts, and somewhat limited applications. Because of its many links to other facets of the learner's world view understanding is being acquired and the material being learned can be transferred more effectively than in the accretion phase.

Transition to the tuning phase does not occur abruptly as though reconstruction stopped and tuning began suddenly. All states of given knowledge overlap with more emphasis to one, perhaps, than to the others depending on the amount of training the learner has endured. Knowledge that is highly tuned consists of a wealth of patterns that are easily accessed and deeply structured to the point of being available on an automatic basis and explainable by the learner. Ultimately a given concept or skill can be employed flexibly and automatically in novel settings together with other concepts and skills. As previously indicated this state may take many thousands of hours of training and experience (Schneider, 1986). The instructional method of practice, with informative feedback, in a variety of settings is required to help the learner to acquire breadth of understanding concepts within numerous contexts (a variety of conditions). Particularly useful would be the application of the material in decision-making or problem-solving situations. The study method in the tuning phase incorporates practice and application to achieve self-regulation of behavior and to achieve automaticity in retrieving information and relating it to new situations or to information already known. The method of evaluation would include such measures as (a) the extent to which the material could be easily and rapidly employed in trouble-shooting, problem-solving, and other decision-making situations; (b) testing the automaticity or latency of accessing or retrieving information or performing the skill; (c) performance of the activity or use of the knowledge under stress, and (d) evaluating the timing of the components in different sequences involved in the skill or procedure (e.g., in diagnosis of an ailment by a physician or a teacher's timing of the administration of arithmetic exercises to a 5th grade class).

Obviously, Norman's model does not provide for all instructional events. Nevertheless, it provides a skeletal model that does cover a variety of instructional events into which other events might be incorporated. At the least, it provides a guide for a number of concerns that must be considered in the development of a workable model of instruction for learning over the long haul.

THE GENERATIVE MODEL OF LEARNING AND INSTRUCTION

The human learner, from whatever theoretical viewpoint one takes, is recognized as an active agent in the learning process. He or she is no longer considered as a passive recipient of information. The constructivist's view of cognitive processes in education considers that the learner, as an active participant in the learning process, transforms the input at every turn. Memorial events are structured rather than passive copies of experiences. Learners do not merely absorb information presented by the teacher or other delivery system; they transform the information in terms of their expectations, of the relevance of the information from their perspective, and of what they are able to perceive as relevant, given their prior knowledge.

An important facet of the cognitive movement in education was the conscious recognition of the learner as an active participant in the learning process. This view had been implicit in nearly all theories from the turn of the century including Freud's defense mechanisms, the Gestalist's emphasis on configuration or "good figure," the Piagetian descriptions of operational and figural knowledge, and the Hull-Spence and neo-behavioristic models of mediated generalization and the distinction between nominal and effective stimuli. Early schema theories (e.g., Bartlett, 1932) recognized that the way experiences were represented and organized in long-term memory had important effects on attention, perception, learning, memory, and retrieval. Provisions were made within their models (Ausubel, 1968; Ausubel et al., 1978) for assimilation of new learning into the knowledge structure or schema.

Soon after current schema theories were introduced the functions of control mechanisms for the sensory register, working memory and long-term memory raised the question of what role was played by the learner in the control of these mechanisms (i.e., to what extent could they come under conscious control and to what extent could capacity of short-term memory be increased and how could retrieval be enhanced). The relevance of attention, encoding, and other processing mechanisms to understanding became incorporated into models of learning.

Very little attention was given in any of these theories to the way in which transformations were formed by the learner/performer. Nor was much attention given to the view that since learners are active participants in the learning process they should be able to learn better if they were given opportunity, with guidance, to construct meanings, inferences, explanations, and problem solutions. If this was the case, active construction of meanings should lead to increased understanding and increased memorability of the information learned.

In an early paper, Wittrock (1974a) addressed this problem in the form of a generative model of learning. The fundamental premise of the model was that learners tend to make sense out of their environment by generating perceptions and meanings for new experiences consistent with their knowledge representations (i.e., prior learning). What is learned, the durability of what is learned, and its transferability is a function of how and to what extent the information in the learning situation is related to already acquired knowledge. This model implies that learners construct meanings based on the interaction of perceptual experiences and stored meanings. These outcomes may occur automatically, since there is a tendency for people to pattern their experiences under any circumstance. The implications for instruction, on the other hand, are that the learner's achievement and understanding can *be controlled*. Such control can be achieved by requiring the learner to engage in productive activities aimed at guiding generative processes. The nature of the activities in which the learner engages determines what is learned. In essence, the model indicates that what the learner does, what processes are used, and what relations are (or are not) discovered depends on environmental (classroom) opportunities, what the learner knows, and the motivation of the learner to participate in those activities. What is learned is not necessarily that which is stated in the title of the course, what is described in the curriculum or syllabus, or the behavior described in a behavioral objective or the content of the course defined by texts, assignments, delivery system, and curricular materials. What *is* learned depends on processing requirements that are actually carried out by the learner.

A supportive position to the generative model was implicit in Neisser's (1976b) ecological approach to perception. The three fundamental elements in his model of the perceptual cycle are: the schemata of the present environment (representations of prior experience), *direct* exploration (including perceptual exploration, hypothesis formation, and physical forms of locomotion) that *samples* available information in the present environment (environmental opportunities). The information sampled *modifies* the schemata and the cycle is repeated (p. 112).

There are important differences between Norman's (described earlier in this chapter) and Neisser's approaches, which are beyond the scope of this chapter for discussion. However, both suggest a model that implicates the necessity for considering the learner's activity, for providing activities with designated outcomes, and for guiding activities in ways that will provide understanding.

Although the generative model is still in transitory development, Wittrock (1985a, 1985b, 1985c) has mustered a great deal of support, through his own research and that of others, for the general premise that engaging the learner in generative processes is, indeed, a desirable instructional event. The evidence stems from studies conducted by him in collaboration with his students and by other investigators who have used the model as the basis for their studies. The topics studied have included reading (Linden & Wittrock, 1981; Wittrock, Marks, & Doctorow, 1975), mathematics (Wittrock, 1974b), notetaking (Peper & Mayer, 1986), outlining (Dee-Lucas & Di Vesta, 1981), concept development (Di Vesta & Peverly, 1984) and science (Osborne & Wittrock (1983). In sum the outcome of these studies, conducted under a variety of environmental settings clearly supports the assumption that guided activity, on the part of the learner, is a desirable, if not necessary condition, for understanding.

The model holds promise for further development and refinement. For example, a taxonomy of the kinds of activities for given outcomes is needed. How to teach learners the strategies necessary for understanding and comprehension is an obvious need. . .in fact it is the subject of much study at the present time especially in the field of reading. How to make efficient strategies durable and flexible; how to make them self-regulated is a critical problem in the teaching of strategies.

Related problems also require consideration. It has been well established, for example, that elaboration and organization of text material have powerful effects on learning. But it is not mere elaboration—the making of an idea more complex, that facilitates learning and memory. Rather, it is precise and relevant elaboration that is important; elaboration that meaningfully relates new target information to old, that makes the new information understandable, that goads the learner to say, "Of course, now I see the reasons" (Bransford et al., 1982; Franks et al., 1982; Norman, 1982).

Similarly, not all forms of text organizations have equal effects on learning. This observation was made in an earlier era by educators who debated the value of psychological organization (organization that was motivating and appealing to the learner) vs. logical organization (organization that was appealing and acceptable to the expert in the field). Organization can have several effects: Organization of text can function as an advance organizer to affect the students expectations. Organization can affect the flow of ideas so that the material can be easily comprehended. And, organization can encourage generative learning, i.e., thinking skills, by requiring the learner to relate new information to what he or she already knows, by requiring him or her to relate information from different parts of connected discourse, by requiring the learner to determine whether literal comprehension or inferential comprehension is required, and by requiring the learner to monitor his comprehension.

The generative model also holds the promise of being integrated to account for many of the conditions of learning, their effects on learning, and their effects on outcomes. Nevertheless, research on classroom management (e.g., Berliner, 1983a, 1983b, 1983c) suggests that most teaching methods are still directed toward traditional achievement-centered goals (e.g., passing an entrance examination) rather than understanding preempting the goals of generative learning. Those methods often emphasize input-output relations based on the premise that what the teacher knows and does are the sole determiners of the students learning; a view commonly held not only by teachers, but by students at all educational levels and by their parents. Even today, the input-output premise ignores, neglects, or only gives lip-service to the role played by the learner in determining educational outcomes.

THE LEARNER'S ACTIVITIES: COGNITIVE SKILLS

Emerging on the scene of research on learning is the currently popular topic of what cognitive skills are, how they influence learning and memory, under what conditions, and how they can be trained . . .concerns that appear to be natural concomitants of the generative theory of learning.

For purposes of discussion, some distinctions can be made among the facets of cognitive skills research. The first of these is the study of *"cognition about cognition"* or "knowing about knowing." This area of research, called metacognitive research assumes that people gain an awareness of some skills and strategies that can be used to facilitate or shortcut their thought processes (Brown, Bransford, Ferrara, & Campione, 1983). The second area is research focused on the identification and functional characteristics of cognitive skills (e.g., Sternberg, 1984). Cognitive skills or learning strategies are activities such as identifying scripts within narratives, the use of mnemonic aids for memorizing facts, or the use of recursive rules in multiplication, "that help the learner achieve some learning goal."

Some contributions to the *identification* of cognitive skills have been made from the study of metacognitions, from research on artificial intelligence, and from developmental psychology. In the area of writing, for example, Scardamalia (1984) distinguishes between the "knowledge-telling" writing processes of the novice and the "knowledge-transforming" writing processes of the expert author. The novice treats writing as an associative device assuming that he or she has all the available information and that the task is simply "to put down on paper all that one knows." The expert uses that information too, but realizes that writing requires keeping the reader in mind and that organization, elaboration, and editing must be coordinated to make communication with the reader possible.

An important area of cognitive skills research is the *training* of such skills. This is the "proof of the pudding," i.e., if an identified cognitive skill can be trained in some portion of the population, according to a sound theoretical approach, and with reliable, enduring, and flexible (or, at least, identifiable) outcomes then the skill, as a construct, has a degree of "psychological reality."

The assumptions regarding general techniques for external (teacher) manipulations of instruction appropriate for all students are also brought into question by the research on metacognitions. This research indicates that no two students have the same thoughts on how to study the same material despite whatever prescriptions for study might be made.

Nevertheless, the study of metacognitions has helped to identify some commonly used strategies that can be trained to facilitate learning. For example, Sternberg (1984) has described some deficits (potentially capable of being remediated through training) in younger and poorer reader's metacognitions including: understanding the purposes of reading; modifying reading strategies for different purposes; identifying important information in a passage; recognizing how new information relates to what is already known; considering how new information relates to what is already known; attending to semantic and syntactic constraints; evaluating text for clarity, completeness, and consistency; dealing with failures to understand; and deciding how well information is understood.

Numerous training "programs" for teaching metacognition and strategies are now becoming available (see Mayer, 1984, and Weinstein & Mayer, 1985 for reviews). Their number may be sufficient to beguile instructors who might want to employ them in the design of teaching methods. From the view point of the researcher the development of successful training programs for teaching strategies for learning, problem-solving, comprehension and the like is said to be one of the most powerful tools of current cognitive science (see for example, Palinscar & Brown, 1984). This research has run the gamut from metacognitions or what the learner knows about his or her own learning and memory processes to programs for developing strategies for remembering, studying and comprehension.

As a consequence of its relation to other cognitive models, cognitive skills research takes into consideration

1. what the learner knows about his or her own capabilities and limitations;
2. the learner's world knowledge, or more specifically, what the learner knows about the topic being studied;
3. what the learner knows about learning, studying, or remembering;
4. the conditions of instruction (complexity, density of concepts, consideration of learner knowledge such as familiarity with the material, and mode or rate of presentation, and
5. the kind of evaluation used to judge the success of the training program.

The standard achievement test mode of evaluation has been replaced by more discriminating criteria that acknowledge the need to test for differential outcomes of a learning event. Such criteria might be the ability to use the information in problem solving rather than simply repeating or recognizing the information in verbatim form, the ability to use certain processes in solving given problems (e.g., the use of imagery and inference), and the ability to retrieve knowledge after a delay rather than immediately after learning. To be useful the training of strategies should satisfy such criteria as useability, flexibility, durability, and ultimately decontextualization. Most importantly, the strategy should become self-regulated or self-monitored so that it can be used in situations where the strategy is applicable.

Studies on the simplest of learning strategies such as mnemonic aids, were useful for demonstrating that both visual and acoustic cues may be employed in

associative devices and that activation of appropriate schemata can help to facilitate learning. The early investigations had played a significant role in understanding the nature of some basic generative processes (or, perhaps, simply that
generative processes are important) and some of the factors that allow for more
rapid learning: For example, the use of a unitized image provides for chunking as
well as for retrieval cues. Through development of an artificial knowledge structure, the use of a jingle, research on the pegword system as a memory aid,
illustrated the role of prior knowledge on assimilation and retrieval of new
information. The elements of the stable jingle, which remains constant, provides
a scaffolding for new information that has to be remembered. Despite the theoretical contributions of these studies, the pragmatic value of simple basic strategies for learning foreign languages and the like is dubious. They stop short of
meaningful learning and function mainly as *crutches* in the early part of learning.
Most of the readers of this article know how to use these aids with some degree
of facility, but it is doubtful that many of them use the aids even for attempting to
remember grocery lists.

At the other extreme, are devices such as concept mapping (Novak & Gowin,
1984) and spatial mapping strategies (Dansereau, 1985; Holley & Dansereau,
1984) which make serious attempts to facilitate, and hold more promise for
meaningful learning. They appear to be rooted in the fundamental premise that
the objective of learning ought to be comprehension and understanding, a premise that does not seem to be shared in investigations of mnemonic aids.

Effective research approaches to the study of cognitive skills, learning strategies, and study skills involve (a) the generation of research problems from
theories such as those described above, (b) the identification of procedures
consistently employed by teachers in teaching or procedures consistently employed by learners for learning, and (c) mapping a program in instruction for
teaching the procedure based on sound theoretical principles. The identified
procedures then become the subjects of investigation through such questions as:
What effects does the procedure have? What process does it induce? Under what
conditions? With what students? And, with what effects? Similar questions
might be asked about the strategies that teachers typically use.

Just what skills are to be taught? The list is still growing. However, Sternberg
(1983) has provided a classification that seems useful for incorporating typical
(though not necessarily representative) skills. The general classifications are
executive (self-regulation processes that keep track of one's place in understanding, comprehension, and problem solving) and nonexecutive (selection, monitoring, and verifying processes that are specific to a given task). Within the category of executive skills (Sternberg, 1983, p. 9) are: problem identification; process
selection, representation selection; allocation of resources; solution monitoring;
sensitivity to feedback; translation of feedback into an action plan; and implementation of the action plan. The nonexecutive processes include (Sternberg,
1983, p. 10) selective encoding; selective combination; inference; mapping;

application; comparison; and justification. As can be seen a representative training program for cognitive skills (see, for example, one described by Palinscar & Brown, 1984 on p. 61) typically involves one or more of the skills listed under the executive and nonexecutive categories.

SOCIAL INFLUENCES IN MODELING COGNITIVE SKILLS

The current evidence does not show that modeling has a highly significant role in learning. However, it does deserve some attention here because of its intuitive appeal as well as the empirical evidence in support of its role in social-personal behaviors and in the development of attitudes. Certainly social influences do play a motivational role in typical classroom situations and social factors associated with different cultures have an effect on what is learned and how people in those cultures process information (Cole & Means, 1981).

There are many components of modeling theory that correspond to the components of cognitive theory: For example, in modeling, the characteristics of the model *as perceived* by the observer are important in determining who is modeled. Vicarious reinforcement (i.e., memorial representations of the conditions under which the model is reinforced) is assumed to be a motivational determinant of *future* performance of the modeled behavior by the observer. By encoding observations of a model's behavior a great deal of processing trial and error may be eliminated in the initial performance of a skill by the observer.

Although modeling is often taken simply as an observer activity it is also a generative activity. Modeling theory depends heavily on the perceptual abilities of the learner. Without guidance, in what to observe, learners will only model that which seems apparent to them. Neisser (see "A Conversation with Ulric Neisser," *Psychology Today,* May 1982) reports a study in which it was found that students learning to throw darts at a target improve most, by mental practice, if they vicariously take the position of the dart thrower rather than using mental practice vicariously from the position of the spectator. This finding implies that the student should be engaged in role-playing and that he or she might analyze, at first overtly, and with informative feedback, the activities of a skilled model who excels at understanding, at elaborating, at organizing, and so on, from the standpoint of the model and not that of the spectator. As with other skills, learners can profit from learning *how* to model as well as *what* behaviors to model. It seems reasonable to expect, however, that this conclusion may be true only for the novice. Observations of the "body-movements" and depth of explanations given by expert sports announcers, e.g., suggest that they vicariously take on the role of participant/performer as well as spectator.

Much current research on teaching cognitive skills *is* based on employing vicarious or real social contexts (as are some teaching techniques such as the Socratic Dialogue, the recitation method, and peer tutoring) . . . contexts that are necessary components of imitation and modeling. Palinscar and Brown

(1984) use the modeling procedure in their use of reciprocal teaching for teaching comprehension fostering strategies. A reason for describing their study is to indicate that the methodology (in this case gradual relinquishing of responsibility for learning from teacher to student rather than simply individually instructing students how to use a strategy) can make a difference in the kinds of effects the researcher obtains.

They taught students to learn four concrete activities including: summarizing (self-review), questioning, clarifying, and predicting. Each activity is related to a generative process . . . e.g., clarifying requires critical examination of what the text is saying which, in turn, requires the learner to relate new information to what he or she already knows, to determine how it relates to the wholistic point of view in the text, and, thereby, to enable the possibility that the learner will make the necessary inferences about the material being read to enhance comprehension. Consistent with the generative theory of learning all four activities require *the learner* to relate the material to background knowledge, i. e., require the activations of relevant schemata. The main research approach was to embed the learning of these activities in the context of student-teacher dialogue.

The general procedure involved four steps. First, the teacher modeled the skill completely as the material was being read. The learner acted primarily as observer. Then the learner, as a novice or apprentice, takes on some of the modeled tasks, to the extent of his or her ability. With more experience, the novice assumes more complex tasks, ultimately accepting more responsibility for the conduct of the skill while still sharing the support of the teacher. In the final stage of the learning process the teacher's role of critic and interrogator is taken over by the learner . . .hence the term *reciprocal teaching* is applied to the general procedure. The outcomes of this study, were comparable in two experiments, leading to the conclusions that the skills were maintained over reasonable lengths of time, and that there were improvements in comprehension, transfer to different tasks, and in the quality of summaries and questions used by the learner.

It is unlikely that the success of the reciprocal teaching method is dependent solely or even mainly on social interaction variables. Clearly, the procedure also requires generative processes by the learner. Modeling requires active participation in attending, observing, noting details and the like during the early stages. Second, the observer/learner takes on the role of performer requiring attention to metacognitions ("what will I have to do when the responsibility is mine?"). Third, the learner is required to verbalize his/her own procedures thereby focusing attention on executive functions (planning) required to run off a smooth sequence. Fourth, while describing the procedure the learner's knowledge of the procedure is "made public" thereby requiring the learner to acknowledge nonexecutive metacognitions and providing opportunities for the teacher to use informative feedback and correction. Fifth, the model-observer relation provides a supportive social context that may enhance motivation. Which of these variables (or others not identified here) functions to make reciprocal teaching effective is the subject for future studies.

Given its pervasiveness in the teaching process it is clear that study of how modeling is, or can be used in the classroom warrants further examination. Problems that come to mind are: To what extent is modeling employed currently by teachers? how? for what purposes? For what kinds of objectives is modeling appropriate? What are the necessary conditions for modeling to be successful? Does an expert compared to a novice benefit from modeling? What are the consequences (e.g., durability of training) of modeling? Although the procedures of reciprocal teaching and peer-tutoring provide a beginning to such research it is apparent that much more needs to be known about the role of social factors in learning within the classroom (see Zajonc, 1963).

GENERAL OR DOMAIN-SPECIFIC THINKING SKILLS?

There has been a plethora of literature within the past few years on the teaching of *general* skills for thinking and problem solving (see de Bono, 1985, for a description of one such program). The premise underlying these programs is the assumption that general problem solving or thinking skills can be taught best outside the context of typical curricular content. The programs provide practice on problems that are intentionally abstract (e.g., fictitious sciences) and presumably are independent of the use of prior knowledge for their solution. They may employ such processes as visual imagery, creative combinations, and inference. The assumption is that by requiring the learner to proceed through the problem-solving process in a diversity of situations and contexts, without the need to retrieve domain-specific knowledge, he or she will acquire a generalized skill, will perceive that unique combinations of ideas can be obtained, and will be encouraged (motivated) to seek alternative ways of arriving at solutions in a self-confident manner. Presumably these skills will transfer broadly to a variety of problem-solving and decision-making tasks.

Simon (1980, p. 93) makes a case for teaching problem solving (adaptive production systems) to enhance understanding. Five steps are cited:

1. Cognitive skills can be represented as productions rather than propositions. (He shares with most instructors, for example, the observation that many students do not know the difference between rote learning and learning with understanding; they question why, after thoroughly memorizing texts, they are unable to pass examinations that require applications.)

2. There is now available, from studies on problem solving and artificial intelligence, many tested problem-solving procedures that can be incorporated into school programs. (A technique such as means-end analysis, should be learned by actively engaging the learner in the use of a technique.)

3. Problem-solving procedures can be integrated into the subject matter part of the curriculum. (This procedure allows transfer of procedures learned outside the curriculum, but also shows the learner which procedures, from general to

specific, are, or can be, associated with or embedded within the subject-matter and in which ways.)

4. The teaching of problem solving should involve self-instruction. (The generative process leads to the acquisition of general problem-solving skills rather than specific skills.)

5. The perceptual side of the problem-solving skill needs emphasis. (Pattern recognition is an important prerequisite to the conditional requirements for employing a given action-sequence.)

The issue is not whether general problem-solving skills *should* be taught, but, rather, what is the appropriate combination of general problem-solving skills, domain-specific skills, and domain-specific knowledge? An empirically based technology for teaching problem-solving skills has yet to be developed. Despite their current and enduring popularity there has been little evaluation of even the most popular of the programs for teaching general problem solving. The evidence appears to be that both declarative and procedural knowledge develop concurrently, i.e., that skills are best learned in the context of a given domain (see, for example, Glaser, 1984). Strategies, cognitive skills, metacognitions and the like are probably incapable of being applied without the availability (and accessibility) of specific facts, knowledges, principles, and patterns that exist within a domain.

The view that general thinking skills can be developed out of context dates back at least to the early years of formal discipline and to the search for general problem solving procedures by the Gestalists (e.g., Duncker, 1945; Wertheimer, 1945). However, it has long been noted that these early investigators erred, not in the character of their observations but in the assumption that general transfer of such skills was expected across disciplines. On the basis of current evidence (Glaser, 1984; Greeno, 1980) it would appear that the transfer of such thinking skills may occur mainly within a discipline where both procedural and declarative knowledge are integrated as they seem to be in the development of expertise. We may find that general training programs are effective mainly for novices. Such training programs may have little effect on the training of those persons already experts in a field and may actually interfere with their performance if established and effective strategies must be replaced.

THE LEARNING CONTEXT: CLASSROOM MANAGEMENT AND EFFECTIVE TRAINING

Educational psychologists view not only the learner but the context in which learning takes place—the classroom. This component of the instructional process is considered within the contextualist position among the other influences that affect learning (including what the learner knows and does and what the teacher knows and does and what outcomes are anticipated by both teacher and student). Activity structures (e.g., reading circle, seatwork, and recitation) are set within the constraints of the classroom environment. Each structure plays a different role in the teaching/learning situation and employs different rules and norms known by teachers and students engaged in the activity (Berliner, 1983a, 1983b).

Initially, studies of classroom management examined the relation of simple time-on-task with achievement. The assumption that the more time the learner spent on a task the more would be learned, gained some empirical support. However, it soon gave way to the view that it was not the amount of time that was spent on the task but the *quality* of that time that was the important variable.

Quality-time is a complex variable (see, for example, Peterson & Swing, 1982) since it can be influenced by (a) the teacher's philosophies, methods, and materials that guide his or her assignment of tasks, (b) the way the tasks are to be performed, and (c) the learner's perceptions of the tasks, and so on. Further, quality-time is influenced by the schemata the learner brings to bear on the tasks and the activities actually employed to carry out the tasks. Thus, how the learner processes the information (i.e., the quality of processing) is a complex interaction of *what the teacher knows* and *what the teacher does*, on the one hand, and *what the learner knows* and *what the learner does* on the other (Weinstein & Mayer, 1985).

Studies on classroom management have taken many forms beyond sheer observation of time-on-task. Berliner (1983a), for example, has discussed the teacher-as-executive, pointing out that the managerial functions of the teacher are as complex as those of any executive. He has shown that there are wide differences among teachers in terms of the amount of time they spend on a specific objective such as comprehension. Thus, for example, one teacher might spend only 10% of the time spent by another teacher, during the same overall time period, on some facet of reading such as comprehension. In addition, some teachers indicate that they don't spend as much time as another teacher on a given subject matter area, simply because "they don't like that subject-matter."

At the opposite end of the continuum from direct observation of how time is spent in classroom activities is what the teacher is thinking as she or he is conducting the classroom. This work is being extended to what the student thinks as he or she engages in certain activities such as group work (Peterson & Swing, 1982).

Classes vary on such factors as time actually spent for instruction, rates of attentiveness by students, time spent on subject-matter areas, amount of seat-work assigned, amount of discussion, time students spend on thinking about the subject matter being taught (Good, 1983), and expert and novice teachers knowledge about students and their progress (Leinhart, 1983). The status of this research is much like that of the research on metacognitions. It is certainly sensible to conclude, for example, that a teacher who spends 900 min on comprehension will produce different levels of achievement than one who spends 100 min within a given time span. Nevertheless, it is still the task of the educational psychologist to determine just what those differences are and under what conditions (e.g., intellectual level of learners or how comprehension is taught) differences in achievement occur. Similarly, it is necessary to know the extent to which quality-time can be manipulated to increase productivity (and, of course, the kind of productivity) in the classroom. Regardless of how idealistic the teacher's objectives, thinking, methods, or evaluation procedures may be, they will be of little use if they are overridden by the learner's thinking and activities. (For example, the teacher may state and, indeed, adhere to the principle of teaching for understanding. However, if the learner perceives that the way to achieve *good* grades in that teacher's course is by mere verbatim learning then the learner's activities will take precedence over those learning strategies that might be more effective for achieving understanding.)

MOTIVATION: MAINTAINING LEVELS OF AROUSAL

Motivation has been a valued tool of teachers from the early days of concern over discipline in the classroom to similar concerns today. One of the earlier formal statements related to motivation came with the law of effect (Thorndike, 1932) and continues today as the law of reinforcement, perhaps one of the most enduring principles in psychology. However, the more recent view of this law by cognitive psychologists is that it is not the automatic regulation of behavior by association of negative or positive affect with negative or positive reinforcement that is important. Rather, it is the information that feedback provides that is important, a point also recognized by behaviorists at least as early as Thorndike. (The issue of informative feedback can be seen by comparing Thorndike, 1913, 1932.)

An appealing reinterpretation of the law of effect that is compatible with the cognitive view has been proposed by Lindsay and Norman (1977) which they call the law of causal learning, as follows: "For desirable outcomes, the learner attempts to repeat those particular actions that have an apparent causal relation to desired outcomes. For undesirable outcomes, the learner attempts to avoid those particular actions that have an apparent causal relation to the undesirable outcomes" (pp. 501–502).

The term *apparent* in this causal law implies that learners can only infer logical relationships between actions and outcomes. These may or may not reflect the physical conditions that actually exist in the real world. As can be seen this restatement of the law of effect has a clearly cognitive connotation. In it are rooted explanations for superstitious behavior, expectancies, and attributions, all of which are part of current conceptualizations in motivational theory.

This restatement of the law of effect, makes other important assumptions. One is that the the outcome of an event serves as *information* about that event indicating that informative feedback is, at least as important as the affective properties of feedback. The other assumption is the difference between real and apparent causality. Thus, Lindsay and Norman (pp. 501–502) indicate that humans can only infer causal relations between their behavior and the outcomes of that behavior (pp. 501–502). In fact they may do so even when no such relation exists (as in superstition, e.g.). Obviously, this orientation sets the stage for a number of other traditional theories as well as for refining the law of effect. The link with effectance motivations and attribution theories is apparent.

Motivation as a research area seems to go through varying degrees of interest. Despite sporadic swings some traditional theories have emerged which seem to be of current importance and deserve consideration for further research. Studies and theories of intrinsic sources of motivation have been interestingly summarized by Lepper (1985). The following paragraphs are based on that article. The several theories are separated for purposes of analysis although there is overlap among some of them.

One source of motivation derives from the desire *to use valued skills*. These motives are often described as the *effectance* motives. They include the needs for achievement, competence, and mastery (White, 1960). Under these motives *challenge* is a useful teaching device. However, as attractive and simple as this notion appears to be some cautions need to be observed as illustrated by Lepper (1985). He indicates that one able student, working at a problem-solving task on a computer delivery system, was presented increasingly difficult or challenging tasks whenever tasks at a given level of difficulty were successfully mastered. After a period of time the student expressed a great deal of frustration. When asked, ''Why?'' he replied, ''Everytime I seem to be able to do the problems I begin to miss them all over again.'' Within the cognitive framework such observations would dictate that pupils ought to be informed clearly about the nature and purposes of whatever tasks they may be required to perform, whether it is the purpose for going to school, the purposes of reading, or the reasons why increasingly difficult tasks are assigned.

There is an advantage to exploiting the desire to use valued skills. Opportunities to and motivation for remaining at a task are essential to *tuning* later states of learning. Such opportunities, nevertheless, must be well managed. Some students may need more time than others to merely practice what they have learned and to get satisfaction out of such practice. Optimal amounts of time must be identified for given tasks and practice should provide for breadth of application. However, merely using practice as opportunity for keeping the learner busy (e.g., at rote repetition) may defeat the purposes of practice to tune the use of a skill or knowledge Opportunities for practice ought to provide for the use of skills that coincide with valued personal goals and provide challenges without destroying optimal levels of motivation.

Another area of intrinsic motivation is based on providing optimal levels of *surprise*. The reader will note a link with work of Berlyne (1960) on *epistemic curiousity* and that of Suchman's (1966) use of *incongruity* in the inquiry method of teaching in which a teaching unit is initiated with the incorporation of conflicting ideas. The many studies of this motive include investigations of cognitive dissonance, balance models, incongruity models, the use of conflict, and the use of novelty and complexity of patterns in directing attention. These are also constituents of Piaget's (Flavell, 1963) notion of disequilibration as well. Reasonable levels of surprise, and conflict related to surprise, provide pleasant affect. As a consequence attention can be directed to relevant components of the task.

A third tradition in motivation research is broadly based on *perceived control*. The dominant constructs in perceived control or self determination are locus-of-control and personal controllability. These determine *attributions* (Weiner, 1986). Thus, one's attributions about his or her successes or failures include luck (external and not controllable); task difficulty (external and controllable); ability (internal and uncontrollable); and effort (internal and controllable). The primary thrust at using attribution theory in pragmatic situations is to encourage, through intervention, the use of effort attributions.

Each of the three positions is involved in most learning situations. In addition, educational applications of computer delivery systems may provide the means for integrating the various viewpoints and provide for another form of intrinsic motivation—that of *fantasy* involvement, a little investigated but often integral part of software (and certainly of video games). There are unusual opportunities for providing animated sequences, fictional characters, sound effects, unusual barriers, exciting and unusual visual effects, and story plots. These are but a few of the means for embedding fantasy involvement in learning environments that are capable of attracting and holding learners to the learning task.

Because of these potentialities for incorporating motivational characteristics into teaching events, the computer may be an especially useful tool for (a) developing automaticity of responses (as in pattern recognition such as syllable recognition in words) especially where feedback on speed and accuracy are important and where the student must be kept at the task, (b) achieving traditional curricular goals by embedding problems in functional/imaginary contexts to maintain interest (e.g., learning fractions within the story context of activity in a pizza parlor) such that the relation between the context and content is nonarbitrary (meaningful). And (c) the provision of learning environments (as, for example, the Logo learning environment) in which the learner may acquire the rudiments of thinking skills through creating his or her own simulated microworlds. Presumably, the learner can, through problems provided, evaluate the effects of actions that might reflect those taken in the real world. At the least, she or he is certain to develop quite different metacognitions than in traditional methods of teaching. In less directed learning environments, the learner can engage in exploratory activities such as those necessary for innovative design (e.g., in engineering, manufacturing, or creative problem solving).

Although automaticity and thinking skills might be taught in traditional direct ways, the motivational programs are based on sound cognitive principles in which the learner takes an active generative role in processing information.

Doubtlessly, despite the slight inefficiency of such methods there are advantageous intrinsic motivational characteristics that may be lacking in traditional learning settings. Presumably learners may gain insight into their learning processes (metacognitions), they may learn material in broader contexts, and with elaborations (thereby making the material more meaningful). As a result there would be more high quality time-on-task.

Although none of these asumptions can be made without further study and without qualification, and although most have little or fragile support, they do set exciting prospects for educational psychologists in unraveling the web of complexities surrounding human behavior and the process of human learning.

SUMMARY

I have summarized a number of current cognitive theories to which educational psychologists have contributed. The underlying theories represent primarily the philosophies of constructivism (Cofer, 1973) and contextualism (Jenkins, 1974b) as well as an ecological (Neisser, 1976a, 1982) point of view. As this chapter has been organized one can see that the empirical and theoretical contributions of educational psychologists to understanding instructional process also reflects the classes of variables represented in the tetrahedral model for memory proposed by Jenkins (1974b). The classes of variables that affect learning within this model are the learner characteristics, the learner's activities, the teacher's activities and knowledge, and the means of evaluation. An important assumption in the tetrahedral model is that these classes of variables subsume a number of specific variables. Further, these variables do not operate independently. Rather, they operate interactively. It is doubtful, e.g., that a result from the laboratory in which the effects of a single variable or two have been identified can be transplanted directly to the classroom independently of other considerations. Identifying the *right* combination of variables is part of cognitive engineering and is the responsibility not only of the educational psychologist but of the educator and the instructional designer as well. However, given the complexity of the task of designing instruction for students in settings as different as classes with different teachers and schools with widely different social and cultural settings and given students "as constructors of knowledge," with different histories of learning, with different strategies for learning, and with different metacognitions and expectations about learning, the development of a standardized instructional design or system does not seem to be imminent. For many of the issues raised, it may be necessary to systematically examine what variables account for the apparent success of some existing systems, in what ways they are successful, and whether they work as efficiently for teaching understanding, problem solving, and other higher-order thinking skills as they do for routinized skills.

REFERENCES

Anderson, J. R. (1983). *The architecture of cognition.* Cambridge, MA: Harvard University Press.

Anderson, J. R. (1984). Spreading activation. In J. R. Anderson & S. M. Kosslyn (Eds.), *Tutorials in learning and memory* (pp. 61–90). San Francisco, CA: W. H. Freeman.

Anderson, J. R. (1985a). *Cognitive psychology and its implications* (2nd Ed.). San Francisco, CA: W. H. Freeman.

Anderson, J. R. (1985b). Ebbinghaus's century. *Journal of Experimental Psychology: Learning, Memory and Cognition, 11,* 436–438.

Anderson, R. C. (1984). A schema theoretic view of basic processes in reading. In P. D. Pearson (Ed.), *Handbook of reading research* (pp. 255–292). New York: Longmans.

Anderson, R. C. & Ortony, A. (1975). On putting apples into bottles: A problem of polysemy. *Cognitive Psychology, 7,* 167–180.

Ausubel, D. P. (1968). *Educational psychology: A cognitive view.* New York: Holt, Rinehart and Winston.

Ausubel, D. P., Novak, J. D., & Hanesian, H. (1978). *Educational psychology: A cognitive view* (2nd Ed.). New York: Holt, Rinehart & Winston.

Bartlett, F. C. (1932). *Remembering: A study in experimental and social psychology.* London, England: Cambridge University Press.

Berliner, D. C. (1983a). The executive who manages classrooms. In B. J. Fraser (Ed.), *Classroom management.* Bentley, Australia: Western Australian Institute of Technology.

Berliner, D. C. (1983b). The executive functions of teaching. *Instructor.* September.

Berliner, D. C. (1983c). Developing conceptions of classroom environments: Some light on the T in classroom studies of ATI. *Educational Psychologist, 18,* 1–13.

Berlyne, D. E. (1960). *Conflict, arousal, and curiosity.* New York: McGraw-Hill.

Bloom, B., Engelhart, M., Furst, E. Hill, W., & Krathwohl, D. (1956). *Taxonomy of educational objectives. The classification of educational goals. Handbook I: Cognitive domain.* New York: Longmans Green.

Blumenthal, A. (1970). *Language and psychology.* New York: Wiley.

Bower, G. H., Black, J. B., & Turner, T. J. (1979). Scripts in memory for text. *Cognitive Psychology, 3,* 177–220.

Bransford, J. D. (1979). *Human cognition: Learning, understanding and remembering.* Belmont, CA: Wadsworth.

Bransford, J. D., Stein, B. S., Vye, N. J., Franks, J. J., Auble, P. M., Mezynski, J. J., & Perfetto, G. A. (1982). Differences in approaches to learning: An overview. *Journal of Experimental Psychology: General, 111,* 390–398.

Brown, A. L., Bransford, J. D., Ferrara, R. A., & Campoine, J. C. (1983). Learning, remembering, and understanding. In P. H. Mussen (ed.), *Carmichael's manual of child psychology.* Vol. III. *Cognitive Development* (pp. 77–166). (J. H. Flavell & E. M. Markman, volume editors) (4th Ed.). Hillsdale, NJ: Lawrence Erlbaum Associates.

Chase, W. G., & Ericsson, K. A. (1981). Skilled memory. In J. R. Anderson (Ed.), *Cognitive skills and their acquisition* (pp. 141–190). Hillsdale, NJ: Lawrence Erlbaum Associates.

Chase, W. G., & Simon, H. A. (1973). Perception in chess. *Cognitive Psychology, 4,* 55–81.

Chi, M. T. H., Feltovich, P., & Glaser, R. (1981). Categorization and representation of physics problems in experts and novices. *Cognitive Science, 5,* 121–152.

Chipman, S. F., Segal, J. W., & Glaser, R. (Eds). (1985). *Thinking and learning skills. Vol. 2. Research and open questions.* Hillsdale, NJ: Lawrence Erlbaum Associates.

Cofer, C. N. (1957). Reasoning as an associative process: III. The role of verbal responses in problem solving. *Journal of General Psychology, 57,* 55–68.

Cofer, C. N. (1973). Constructive processes in memory. *American Scientist, 61,* 537–543.

Cole, M., & Means, B. (1981). *Comparative studies of how people think.* Cambridge, MA: Harvard University Press.

Collins, A. (1985). Teaching reasoning skills. In S. F. Chipman, J. W. Segal, & R. Glaser (Eds.), *Thinking and learning skills. Vol. 2. Research and open questions* (pp. 579–586) Hillsdale, NJ: Lawrence Erlbaum Associates.

Dansereau, D. F. (1985). Learning strategy research. In S. F. Chipman, J. W. Segal, & R. Glaser (Eds.), *Thinking and learning skills. Vol. 1. Relating instruction to research* (pp. 209–239). Hillsdale, NJ: Lawrence Erlbaum Associates.

de Bono, E. (1985). The CORT thinking program. In J. W. Segal, S. F. Chipman, & R. Glaser (Eds.), *Thinking and learning skills. Vol. 1. Relating instruction to research* (pp. 363–388). Hillsdale, NJ: Lawrence Erlbaum Associates.

Deese, J. (1969). Behavior and fact. *American Psychologist, 24,* 515–523.

de Groot, A. (1966). Perception and memory versus thought: Some old ideas and recent findings. In. B. Kleinmuntz (Ed.), *Problem solving* (pp. 19–50). New York: Wiley.

Dewey, J. (1910). *How we think.* Boston, MA: Heath.

Dee-Lucas, D., & Di Vesta, F. J. (1981). Learner generated organizational aids: Effects on learning from text. *Journal of Educational Psychology, 73,* 304–311.

Di Vesta, F. J. (1974). Cognitive structure, symbolic processes and education. *Teachers College Record, 75,* 357–370.

Di Vesta, F. J., & Peverly, S. T. (1984). The effects of encoding variability, processing activity, and rule-examples sequence on the transfer of conceptual rules. *Journal of Educational Psychology, 76,* 108–119.

Duncker, K. (1945). On problem-solving. *Psychological Monographs, 58* (Whole No. 270).

Ebbinghaus, H. (1913). *Memory.* (H. A. Ruger & C. E. Bussenius, Translators) New York: Teachers College. (Originally published in 1885).

Fitts, P. M. (1964). Perceptual motor learning. In A. W. Melton (Ed.), *Categories of human learning* (pp. 244–285). New York: Academic Press.

Fitts, P. M., & Posner, M. L. (1967). *Human performance.* Belmont, CA: Wadsworth.

Flanagan, J. C. (1954). The critical incident technique. *Psychological Bulletin, 51,* 327–358.

Flavell, J. H. (1963). *The developmental psychology of Jean Piaget.* New York: Van Nostrand.

Franks, J. J., Vye, N. J., Auble, P. M., Mezynski, K. J., Perfetto, G. A., & Bransford, J. D. (1982). Learning from explicit versus implicit texts. *Journal of Experimental Psychology: General, 111,* 414–422.

Frederiksen, N. (1986). Toward a broader conception of human intelligence. In R. J. Sternberg & R. Wagner (Eds.), *Practical intelligence: Nature and origins of competence in the everyday world* (pp. 84–116). New York: Cambridge University Press.

Frederiksen, N., Saunders, D. R., & Wand, B. (1957). The In-Basket Test. *Psychological Monographs, 71,* (9, Whole No. 438).

Gagne, E. D. (1985). *The cognitive psychology of school learning.* Boston, MA: Little Brown.

Gagne, R. M. (1985). *The conditions of learning* (4th Ed.). New York: Holt, Rinehart and Winston.

Glaser, R. (1984). Education and thinking. *American Psychologist, 39,* 93–104.

Good, T. L. (1983). Classroom research; A decade of progress. *Educational Psychologist, 18,* 127–144.

Greeno, J. G. (1980). Trends in the theory of knowledge for problem solving. In D. T. Tuma & F. Reif (Eds.), *Problem solving and education* (pp. 9–24). Hillsdale, NJ: Lawrence Erlbaum Associates.

Helm, J., & Novak, J. D. (Eds.). (1983). *Proceedings of the International Seminar: Misconceptions in science and mathematics.* Ithaca, NY: Cornell University.

Herman, P. A., Anderson, R., Pearson, P. D., & Nagy, W. E. (1985). *Incidental acquisition of work meanings from expositions that systematically vary text features* (Technical Report No. 364). Champaign, IL: University of Illinois, Center for the Study of Reading.

Holley, C. D., & Dansereau, D. F. (1984). *Spatial larning strategies: Techniques, applications, and related issues.* Orlando, FL: Academic Press.

Huey, E. B. (1908). *The psychology and pedagogy of reading.* Cambridge, MA: M I T. Press. (Reprinted 1968).

Jenkins, J. J. (1974a). Remember that old theory of memory? Well, forget it! *American Psychologist, 29,* 785–795.

Jenkins, J. J. (1974b). Four points to remember: A tetrahedral model of memory experiments. In L. S. Cermak & F. I. M. Craik (Eds.), *Levels of processing and human memory* (pp. 429–446). Hillsdale, NJ: Lawrence Erlbaum Associates.

Kant, I. (1781). *Kritick der reimen Vermuunft.* Leipzig; P. Reclam. English ed., *Critique of pure reason.* (Translated by J. M. D. Meiklejohn) London: George Ball, 1877.

Koffka, D. (1935). *Principles of Gestalt psychology.* New York: Harcourt.

LaBerge, P., & Samuels, S. J. (1974). Toward a theory of automatic information processing in reading. *Cognitive Psychology, 6,* 293–323.

Leinhart, G. (1983). Novice and expert knowledge of individual student's achievement. *Educational Psychologist, 18,* 165–179.

Lepper, M. R. (1985). Microcomputers in education: Motivational and social issues. *American Psychologist, 40,* 1–18.

Lesgold, A. M. (1984). Acquiring expertise. In J. R. Anderson & S. M. Kosslyn (Eds.), *Tutorials in learning and memory* (pp. 31–61). San Francisco, CA: W. H. Freeman.

Linden, M. A., & Wittrock, M. C. (1981). The teaching of reading comprehension according to the model of generative learning. *Reading Research Quarterly, 17,* 44–57.

Lindsay, P. H., & Norman, D. A. (1977). *Human information processing.* New York: Academic Press.

Mager, R. (1962). *Preparing instructional objectives.* Palo Alto, CA: Fearon.

Mayer, R. E. (1979a). Can advance organizers influence meaningful learning? *Review of Educational Research, 49,* 371–383.

Mayer, R. E. (1979b). Twenty years of research on advance organizers: Assimilation theory is still the best predictor of results. *Instructional Science, 8,* 133–167.

Mayer, R. E. (1984). Aids to text comprehension. *Educational Psychologist, 19,* 30–42.

McClelland, D. C. (1973). Testing for competence rather than for "intelligence." *American Psychologist, 28,* 1–14.

Neisser, U. (1967). *Cognitive psychology.* New York: Appleton-Century-Crofts.

Neisser, U. (1976a). General, academic, and artificial intelligence. In L. Resnick (Ed.), *The nature of intelligence* (pp. 135–144). Hillsdale, NJ: Lawrence Erlbaum Press.

Neisser, U. (1976b). *Cognition and reality: Principles and implications of cognitive psychology.* San Francisco, CA: W. H. Freeman.

Neisser, U. (1982). *Memory observed: Remembering in natural contexts.* San Francisco, CA: W. H. Freeman.

Newell, A., & Simon, H. A. (1972). *Human problem solving.* Englewood Cliffs, NJ: Prentice-Hall.

Norman, D. A. (1978). Notes toward a theory of complex learning. In A. M. Lesgold, J. W. Pelligrino, S. D. Fokkema, & R. Glaser (Eds.), *Cognitive psychology and instruction* (pp. 39–48). New York: Plenum.

Norman, D. A. (1980). Cognitive engineering and education. In D. T. Tuma & F. Reif (Eds.), *Problems solving and education: Issues in teaching and research* (pp. 81–96). Hillsdale, NJ: Lawrence Erlbaum Associates.

Norman, D. A. (1982). *Learning and memory.* San Francisco, CA: W. H. Freeman.

Osborne, R. J., & Wittrock, M. C.(1983). Learning science: A generative process. *Science Education, 67,* 489–504.

Novak, J. D., & Gowin, D. B. (1984). *Learning how to learn.* Cambridge, England: Cambridge University Press.

Palinscar, A. S., & Brown, A. L. (1984). Reciprocal teaching of comprehension-fostering and monitoring activities. *Cognition and Instruction, 1,* 117–175.

Peper, R. J., & Mayer, R. E. (1986). Generative effects of note-taking during science lectures. *Journal of Educational Psychology, 78,* 34–38.

Peterson, P. L., & Swing, S. R. (1982). Beyond time on task: Students' reports of their thought processes during direct instruction. *The Elementary School Journal, 82,* 481–491.

Piaget, J. (1926). *The language and thought of the child.* Harcourt Brace Jovanovich.

Rosch, E. (1975). Cognitive representations of semantic categories. *Journal of Experimental Psychology: General, 104,* 192–223.

Rosch, E. (1977). Human categorization. In N. Warren (Ed.), *Advances in cross-cultural psychology.* (Vol. 1). London: Academic Press.

Rumelhart, D. E. (1980). The building blocks of cognition. In R. J. Spiro, B. C. Bruce, & W. F. Brewer (Eds.), *Theoretical issues in reading comprehension* (pp. 33–58). Hillsdale, NJ: Lawrence Erlbaum Associates.

Sachs, J. D. S. (1967). Recognition memory for syntactic and semantic aspects of connected discourse. *Perception and Psychophysics, 2,* 437–422.

Scardamalia, M. (1984). Knowledge telling and knowledge transformation in written composition. Paper presented at the meeting of the AERA, New Orleans.

Schank, R., & Abelson, R. (1977). *Scripts, plans, goals, and understanding.* Hillsdale, NJ: Lawrence Erlbaum Associates.

Schneider, W. (1986). Training of automatic component skills. Paper presented at the AERA Convention in San Francisco.

Schneider, W., & Fisk, A. D. (1982). Degree of consistent training: Improvements in search performance and automatic process development. *Perception and Psychophysics, 31,* 160–168.

Segal, J. W., Chipman, S. F., & Glaser, R. (Eds.). (1985). *Thinking and learning skills. Vol. 1. Relating instruction to research.* Hillsdale, NJ: Lawrence Erlbaum Associates.

Selz, O. (1927). Die umgestaltung der grundanschauungen vom intellektuellen geschehen. *Kantstudien, 32,* 273–280. [Translated as: The revision of the fundamental conceptions of intellectual processes. In J. Mandler & G. Mandler (Eds.), *Thinking: From association of Gestalt.* New York: Wiley, 1964, 225–234].

Shiffrin, W., & Schneider, W. (1977). Controlled and automatic human information processing: II. Perceptual learning, automatic attending, and a general theory. *Psychological Review, 84,* 127–190.

Simon, H. A. (1965). *The shape of automation for men and management.* New York: Harper.

Simon, H. A. (1980). Problem solving and education. In D. T. Tuma & F. Reif (Eds.), *Problem solving and education: Issues in teaching and research* (pp. 81–96). Hillsdale, NJ: Lawrence Erlbaum Associates.

Steffensen, M. S., Joag-Dev, C. J., & Anderson, R. C. (1979). A cross-cultural perspective on reading comprehension. *Reading Research Quarterly, 15,* 10–29.

Sternberg, R. J. (1983). Criteria for intellectual skills training. *Educational Researcher, 12,* 6–12.

Sternberg, R. J. (1984). Facets of human intelligence. In J. R. Anderson & S. M. Kosslyn (Eds.), *Tutorials in learning and memory* (pp. 137–166). San Francisco, CA: W. H. Freeman.

Suchman, J. R. (1966). A model for the analysis of inquiry. In H. J. Klausmeier & C. W. Harris (Eds.), *Analyses of concept learning* (pp. 77–187). New York: Academic Press.

Thorndike, E. L. (1913). *Educational Psychology.* Vol. 2. *The psychology of learning.* New York: Teacher's College.

Thorndike, E. L. (1917). Reading as reasoning. *The Journal of Educational Psychology, VIII,* 323–332.

Thorndike, E. L. (1932). *The fundamentals of learning.* New York: Teachers College.

Thorndyke, P. W. (1984). Applications of schema theory in cognitive research. In J. R. Anderson & S. M. Kosslyn (Eds.), *Tutorials in learning and memory* (pp. 167–191). San Francisco, CA: W. H. Freeman.

Thornton, G. C., & Byham, W. C. (1982). *Assessment careers and managerial performance*. New York: Academic Press.

Tulving, E. (1985a). How many memory systems are there? *American Psychologist, 40*, 385–398.

Tulving, E. (1985b). Ebbinghaus's memory: What did he learn and remember? *Journal of Experimental Psychology: Learning, Memory and Cognition, 11*, 485–490.

Voss, J. F., Greene, T. R., Post, T. A., & Penner, B. C. (1984). Problem solving skill in the social sciences. In G. H. Bower (Ed.), *The psychology of learning and motivation* (Vol. 18) New York: Academic Press.

Wagner, R. K., & Sternberg, R. J. (1985). Practical intelligence in real-world pursuits: The role of tacit knowledge. *Journal of Personality and Social Psychology, 49*, 436–458.

Wagner, R. K., & Sternberg, R. J. (1986). Tacit knowledge and intelligence in the everyday world. In R. J. Sternberg & R. K. Wagner (Eds.), *Practical intellignece: Nature and Origins of competence in the everyday world* (pp. 51–83). New York: Cambridge University Press.

Weiner, B. (1986). *An attributional theory of motivation and emotion*. New York: Springer-Verlag.

Weinstein, C., & Mayer, R. E. (1985). The teaching of learning strategies. In M. C. Wittrock (Ed.), *Handbook of research on teaching* (pp. 315–327). *Third Edition*. New York: Macmillan.

Wertheimer, M. (1945). *Productive thinking*. New York: Harper and Row. (Enlarged edition, M. Wertheimer, editor, 1959).

White, R. W. (1960). Competence and psychological stages. In M. R. Jones (Ed.), *Nebraska symposium on motivation* (pp. 97–141). Lincoln: University of Nebraska Press.

Wittrock, M. C. (1974a). Learning as a generative process. *Educational Psychologist, 11*, 87–95.

Wittrock, M. C. (1974b). A generative model of mathematics learning. *Journal for Research in Mathematics Education, 5*, 181–196.

Wittrock, M. C. (1975). Reading as a generative process. *Journal of Educational Psychology, 67*, 484–489.

Wittrock, M. C. (1985a). *Generative processes of compehension*. Division 15 Presidential address, American Psychological Association Convention, Los Angeles, CA (Mimeo).

Wittrock, M. C. (1985b). *A constructive review of research on learning strategies*. Los Angeles, CA: University of California (Mimeo).

Wittrock, M. C. (1985c). Teaching learners generative strategies for enhancing reading comprehension. *Theory into Practice, 24*, 123–126.

Wittrock, M. C., Marks, C. B., & Doctorow, M. J. (1975). Reading as a generative process. *Journal of Educational Psychology, 67*, 484–489.

Zajonc, R. B. (1963). Social facilitation. *Science, 149*, 269–274.

5 Educational Psychology and The Future of Research in Learning, Instruction, and Teaching

M. C. Wittrock
University of California, Los Angeles

Research in educational psychology that has significance and utility both for improving educational practice while simultaneously refining psychological theory will be prominent in the future. A reciprocal relation between psychology and education, and between theory and application, in which each influences and contributes to the other will replace previous notions about how theory leads through research and development to improved practice.

Lasting improvements in practice will continue to come from advances in theory and models that are applied, evaluated, and revised in empirical research conducted in realistic educational settings. However, the contributions of research in educational psychology to the refinement and development of socially significant psychological theory will be increasingly recognized. Educational practice and psychological theory will profit from these close ties. Educational psychology will be the link that unites the two fields in this reciprocal process that merges theory development with improved practice.

Research in educational psychology on learning, instruction, and teaching will share these same characteristics—reciprocal contributions to practice and to socially relevant theory. Recent research and theory on the cognitive processes of learning, instruction, and teaching shows much promise for the development of these simultaneous contributions to psychological theory and to educational practice. These recent advances in the study of cognition represent, I believe, the beginnings of research that will lead to a coherent understanding of knowledge acquisition and to a useful and prescriptive theory of instruction and teaching.

In what follows, I discuss some recent research on cognition in learning, instruction, and teaching that represents these beginnings, that combines theory development with practical innovations, and that revises earlier notions about how people learn in educational settings. Afterward, I will draw a few implications about where this research is leading us.

Contrary to popular opinion, the recent cognitive research does not invalidate earlier findings about the basic concepts of the field, but it does provide different interpretations of how and why they function, and new implications about educational methods. For example, cognitive research indicates that a reinforcer provides cognitive and affective information which a learner either believes or does not believe and acts upon accordingly. The implication of this finding is that learners must understand the reasons for the reinforcement or it will have little or no effect upon their learning. Reinforcement does not function automatically.

A cognitive model of reinforcement further implies that success at learning is not enough to increase the probability of behavior. From recent research on attribution theory, which is part of the study of the cognitive processes of motivation, when the learners attribute the reinforcement to their own actions they persevere at a task (Weiner, 1979).

Reinforcement still works, but not automatically. What the learner thinks about the reinforcement influences its effects. This recently developed finding leads directly to useful and inexpensive changes in the classroom use of feedback to students.

Similarly, delay of reinforcement does not automatically decrease learning. Learning increases, decreases, or remains the same depending upon what the learners think about or do during the delay (Atkinson, 1969). Recently, Peterson and Swing (1982) found that time to learn does not predict learning as well as time spent *attending* to the task predicts learning. Again, a measure of a learner's cognitive process, such as attention, better predicts learning than does a comparable measure that focuses upon the environment but neglects to measure what the learner does with that environment. The finding also offers fundamental implications about changing educational practices based on the assumption that more time spent in learning will, in and of itself, increase achievement in schools.

By viewing learning as a function of what the learners think and feel about their environments, of the learners' schemata and information processing systems, these and related new implications and possibilities for change arise in educational methods. We cannot discuss all of these possible changes in education. Instead, we focus on some of the research in learning and instruction that has educational applications about learning disabilities, mathematics and science, and reading. Please see a review article (Wittrock, 1986) for further discussion of cognitive research on teaching.

LEARNING DISABILITIES AND MENTAL RETARDATION

Recent research on attention leads to new explanations of some learning disabilities and to new intervention programs for their treatment. The research indicates that attention consists of at least one short-term component, called the orienting response, and at least one long-term or tonic component. The short-term component is often an involuntary reaction to stimuli, and the long-term component often is a voluntary reaction to stimuli. In schools, mentally retarded children tend to react normally to the short-term attention tasks, but abnormally slowly to the long-term attention tasks. In other settings, the mentally retarded children do not show much of a deficit in long-term voluntary attention. It seems that their attentional problems in schools primarily involve volition, or self-control, which might respond to appropriate training.

Recent neuropsychological research on attention also offers new insights into related learning disabilities, such as reading disabilities. Conners (1970) found a high correlation ($-.60$) between a measure of attention, an evoked potential at 200 msec latency, and reading achievement among 3rd and 4th graders. Preston, Guthrie, and Childs (1974) found that 4th graders and 9th graders, who were poor readers, showed a deficit in attention as measured by their brain wave responses at 180 msec latency to light flashes, but not to encoding, measured by the same brain wave responses to words. These studies also implicate attention as a cognitive process that might be deficient in learning disabilities, including reading disabilities.

Hyperactivity is a learning disability that involves attention. Attention explains how stimulant drugs reduce hyperactivity among learning disabled children. Because hyperactivity leads to diffuse and unorganized behavior, drugs that enhance attention, or cognitive intervention strategies that stress self-control over attention, help to focus and organize behavior. They should ameliorate the problem.

Although stimulant drugs increase arousal, they also enhance selective attention, as Conners (1976) found when he measured brain wave reactions to stimuli. The stimulant drugs seem to have their primary effect upon attention. The result is that the children's energies become focused upon the learning task. As a result, they show less diffuse and disorganized motor behavior. They are not necessarily becoming less active, as they might appear. Instead, they probably concentrate their activity on the classroom tasks, rather than diffuse it on irrelevant stimuli. The educational implication is that if hyperactivity is a problem of voluntary attention, then cognitive training strategies that stress self-control of attention, in lieu of, or in addition to drugs, might ameliorate it. This finding has important possibilities for improving classroom learning through the teaching of a cognitive strategy of learner self-control.

We turn now to research on some of the cognitive strategy training programs and their educational implications. Whether they emphasize control of attention, impulsivity, or encoding, cognitive training programs try to change behavior by changing people's cognitions—their thoughts and feelings about that behavior. These cognitive strategy training programs try to change learners' thoughts in many ways, such as by giving the learners instructions to repeat to themselves, by directing their attention, or by teaching them to transform a stimulus by thinking about it in a new way. For example, Mischel and Baker (1975) increased delay of gratification among nursery school children by having them think of food—marshmallows—as inedible objects—clouds. Meichenbaum and Goodman (1971) taught hyperactive 2nd graders to use a "stop, look, and listen" strategy before they acted. The strategy increased performance on the Matching Familiar Figures Test. In a separate experiment reported in the same study, they also found improvements on Porteus Maze problems and on some subtests of the WISC due to the self-instruction training of this strategy.

Camp (1980) taught strategies modeled after Meichenbaum's model. Over several months, she taught impulsive elementary school-age boys to ask themselves (1) what problem they faced, (2) how they were to try to solve it, (3) whether they were following their plan, and (4) how well they did. After 30 sessions the students showed gains in IQ, reading, and social behavior. In addition, these gains generalized to the classroom. This simple strategy has promise for teaching impulsive students to organize their problem solving behavior in classes taught in elementary schools.

Douglas, Parry, Martin, and Garson (1976) also developed a self-instructional cognitive training program to teach 7- and 8-year-olds to use self-verbalization to control their impulsive behavior. After 3 months of training, their scores increased on the Matching Familiar Figures Test, on tests of planning, and on some tests of reading comprehension. Although reading was not taught in this program, the training generalized to school-related tasks, including reading comprehension.

Other researchers have tried to train children to direct their attention in specific ways. Egeland (1974) taught impulsive children to scan all of the alternatives in a visual discrimination task, to look at component parts, to compare them with the standard given to them, and then to eliminate alternatives until only the correct one remains. The training increased performance on the Matching Familiar Figures Test.

Self-monitoring procedures, which include self-recording of results by 8- to 11-year-old learning disabled students, increase attention and school performance in arithmetic and in writing, as measured by the number of arithmetic problems attempted and the amount of writing that the students completed (Hallahan, Lloyd, Kosiewicz, Kauffman, & Graves, 1979; Kneedler & Hallahan, 1981). But quality of performance was usually not improved in these programs that stress attention. Something in addition to attention often seems to be needed to improve the quality of academic performance, such as training in specific academic skills and strategies. Lloyd, Saltzman, and Kauffman (1981) taught learning disabled children to multiply and to divide by teaching them to count in multiples of the multiplicand. The training in this specific strategy enhanced performance on multiplication problems that involved the multiplicand that the children have previously learned to count.

Wittrock (1967) taught 119 2nd graders replacement, nonreplacement, and control strategies for sampling the possible answers to problems. The sampling-without-replacement strategy produced the greatest learning, near transfer, and far transfer, about 20% to 50% improvement over the control group.

The strategies taught in these studies provide an explicit set of steps for the students to follow. These steps usually involve carefully analyzing stimuli before responding to them. The successful programs also often involve extensive training over several months.

Even with these considerations and limitations, the results of these programs indicate that at least some learning disabilities can be remediated in part by teaching procedures that emphasize attention and learning strategies. The cognitive training programs usually provide the greatest amount of generalization, compared with the behavioral and drug programs (Keogh & Glover, 1980).

These findings imply that changes in the teaching of children are worth exploring in the classroom. The teaching of cognitive strategies of self-control may improve the achievement of some of the children and may reduce the need to medicate some of them to control their learning disability.

MATHEMATICS AND NATURAL SCIENCE

These two broad fields provide excellent and educationally important contexts for discussing possible changes in teaching that follow from recent research on learning and instruction. Some of the recent work in these fields focuses on identifying the cognitive structures, models, and strategies children use to learn and to remember science and mathematics.

Roger Osborne studies the models that children use to comprehend basic scientific concepts, such as electric circuits. Some of his research work is summarized in two recent papers (Osborne & Wittrock, 1983, 1985). He finds that elementary school children in the United States, Great Britain, and New Zealand share the same basic models of how electric current flows in a simple circuit involving a battery and a light bulb. For example (Osborne, 1981), some students think that the current flows only in one half of the circuit and in one direction from the battery to the light bulb, where it gets consumed. Other students think that the current flows in two directions, one from each side of the battery. The collision of the two currents at the light bulb causes it to glow. Other children view the current flow in the DC circuit as the physicists view it, in one direction constant in amplitude throughout the circuit.

He also finds that children given evidence that their model is wrong, such as an ammeter showing them that the current flows equally and in the same direction on both sides of the light bulb, seldom change their model. Instead, they maintain that this particular circuit they are viewing is an exceptional one, and that DC electrical circuits in the real world (i.e., outside the school, especially at home) behave according to the children's models.

Osborne's insightful research indicates that one cannot teach the subject matter, or measure the students' lack of knowledge and then teach the difference between their understanding and the scientist's model. The teaching problem is complex. It involves more than teaching what the students do not know. One must help the students to generate a new and more useful model, when the student, often tenaciously, Osborne finds, clings to a less useful model and incorporates events within it, or rejects them as idiosyncratic and unreal when they do not fit it.

These findings imply that revisions are needed in our conceptions of the teaching of scientific concepts. The problem is different from its earlier conception.

The challenge for the teacher consists of learning how to teach a new model, on new information, which will shift the child's perspective. Knowledge about science is not acquired in a vacuum, even among young children. Rather, the acquisition of knowledge about science is more like the generation of a revision in the student's thinking or organization.

Other findings indicate that Osborne's research identifies a serious problem in some current science teaching, which neglects to help children generate and revise their models of basic scientific concepts. For example, Bell (1981) showed that the proportion of children who thought a worm and a spider were animals actually decreased from age 5 to age 11. This finding may explain why children without an accurate biological model of "animal" also have difficulty understanding the meaning of "consumer," which is often equated to the concept of animal in biology courses.

Osborne feels that to improve student understanding of the word consumer in a biology class one may have to teach the meaning of the word animal. Instruction aimed at teaching the meaning of consumer as "all animals are consumers" would not be effective because the problem lies in the older child's limited model of an animal as something with fur and four legs. The subtle implication is that direct teaching of definitions of terms will not, in these cases, be as effective as will be a refinement of the child's understanding of background concepts, such as animal, basic to understanding the new concept, in this case, consumer.

From a different perspective, several researchers study the organization of learners' concepts, or their cognitive structure. Shavelson and his colleagues (Shavelson, 1974, 1981; Shavelson & Stanton, 1975) developed procedures for quantifying and graphically representing hierarchically ordered cognitive structures. By comparing cognitive structures of students, before and after instruction, with comparable structures of teachers or of other students, one can see some of the important qualitative effects of teaching. We can also see differences across students and classes and between teachers and their students. These techniques also measure content structure as it exists in textbooks, or even in lectures by teachers. These methods hold considerable promise for measuring relations among subject matter, teachers' conceptual organizations, and students' learning and memory, as they are organized and represented in hierarchical cognitive structures.

Other researchers study the cognitive strategies people use to learn and to remember mathematics and to solve problems. These researchers feel that one way to improve the teaching of mathematics and science is to identify and to teach specific cognitive strategies useful for solving classes of problems in mathematics or in science.

In recent research on addition and subtraction several people have identified some of the cognitive strategies children customarily use to solve problems of different kinds. Carpenter and Moser (1982) organize addition and subtraction problems into categories based on three dimensions: (1) whether the word problem involves action, in which an initial state is changed, (2) whether the problem involves a set-subset relation or two or more disjoint sets, and (3) whether the problem involves making, or noticing that something is being made, smaller or larger.

With these problems young children use several different strategies in addition. Carpenter and Moser called the most elementary strategy *counting all with models,* which means that the children used their fingers (models) to count all numbers in a problem such as 2 plus 3. They count the union of these two sets starting from one and using three distinct counts: one count for the first given number, 2; then a second count for the second given number, 3; and a third count of the total 2 plus 3, usually simultaneously with the second count. In other words, they used a sophisticated double counting strategy using both hands simultaneously.

The second strategy, *counting all without models,* closely resembles the first strategy but omits the use of fingers as models during the first count. The third strategy is like the second strategy except that the children begin counting from the first or smaller number. This strategy is called *counting on from the first or smaller number.* The next strategy, called *counting on from the larger number,* differs from the earlier strategy only in that the children start with the larger, rather than the smaller, of the two numbers. Other strategies involved applying *number facts* directly, that is memory of the answer, or using a *heuristic,* such as 2 plus 2, and stating that 2 plus 3 is just one more than 2 plus 2.

Carpenter and Moser present further discussion of these strategies and strategies of subtraction in relation to the types of problems previously mentioned. For teaching, their research implies that one should determine the strategy used by a child, such as a *counting all with models,* and then teach the child a more appropriate strategy for that class of problem, if such a strategy exists and if it can be learned. Again, the teaching problem, like the one Roger Osborne described, involves more than teaching information the child does not know. The problem also involves the teaching of a new model or strategy. This teaching begins by identifying the child's model or strategy. The teaching involves realizing that, from the child's perspective, the learning of a new strategy involves a revision of a procedure which works quite well.

In addition, the teaching involves associating different strategies to different types of problems, appropriately and discriminatively. A complicated set of problems involves more than learning to revise old strategies. It involves learning to discriminate among types of addition and subtraction problems and then learning to use the best strategy for each of them.

From the perspective offered by this research, addition and subtraction becomes a different, more differentiated area than it was previously. Because of this recent research on arithmetic we have a better concept of the complicated cognitive processes children can and do use to solve problems of addition and subtraction. In addition, we also have a better understanding of why some word problems, such as those which do not specify an action to be performed by the young child, are difficult for children while other word problems, involving identical mathematical relations, but which state the actions to be performed, are easier for them. The reason is that the child's strategy, which often involves action with models, can be applied more easily when the problem states the action to be performed.

Other lines of research on addition and subtraction also contribute to our understanding of children's cognitive processes. Resnick and her colleagues (Resnick & Ford, 1981; Woods, Resnick, & Groen, 1975) identified cognitive strategies used by children in mathematics, including single digit subtraction problems. These strategies, such as *counting down from the larger number* or *counting up from the smaller number,* complement other findings and indicate a developmental progression in early elementary school years from following fixed rules to using heuristics involving judgment.

Brown and Vanlehn (1982) identified the "bugs" or faulty strategies children commonly use in subtraction problems. Their procedures enable them to classify a series of incorrect answers to subtraction problems into a strategy which can be used to diagnose the learner's mistakes and possibly to teach the child to subtract more accurately by changing strategies. These studies suggest a potential contribution for diagnosing children's difficulties in learning arithmetic through measuring their use of strategies of addition and subtraction.

Another line of research in mathematics learning that has potential for contribution to teaching emphasizes the relation between the strategies and rules taught to the learners and the transfer they show later. Mayer and Greeno (1972) showed that teaching which emphasizes learning to use a formula, binomial probability, compared with comparable instruction that emphasized the meanings of the variables in the formula and the use of heuristics, produced better transfer to familiar items but far worse transfer to unfamiliar problems. The instruction that emphasized understanding the general concept apparently activated previous knowledge structures associated with a broad range of experience—hence the broader transfer. Solter and Mayer (1978) report similar findings with preschool children and simple number concepts. This latter line of research carries one step further the earlier research on identifying strategies children and adults use to solve problems in mathematics and science. The study by Mayer and Greeno shows the results that can occur when one tries to teach new strategies. Their study also shows the important relation between the learners' background knowledge, the new strategy, and the transfer that occurs when these two elements interact with each other.

In sum, some of the recent research on mathematics and science learning has several implications for improving teaching in these areas. The research examined here implies that teaching mathematics and science involves understanding the structures, strategies, and background knowledge that students bring to the learning task. Teaching also involves engaging the students' knowledge in the active revision of strategies or in the reorganization of cognitive structures. Methods for facilitating these revisions and reorganizations are emerging also. But these teaching procedures are not yet well developed.

READING COMPREHENSION

Research on reading flourishes today, especially since the recent and revived focus on cognition and its emphasis on comprehension and understanding. Neuropsychologists, cognitive psychologists, educational psychologists, reading specialists, and teachers of reading find themselves interested in working on problems of reading and its facilitation. The recent focus on reading revises research and theory in the area, and it promises to lead to improvements in the teaching of reading.

Instead of trying to review and to discuss this massive field of research in a few pages, I focus here on a few studies that exemplify educational applications with promise for improving teaching.

Recent research on reading indicates the critical importance of the learners' experience and knowledge in determining comprehension (e.g., Marks, Doctorow, & Wittrock, 1974; Pearson, Hansen, & Gordon, 1979; Wittrock, Marks, & Doctorow, 1975). Familiar words, stories, contexts, and themes clearly facilitate retention and reading comprehension. From these and related studies reading comprehension is the process of constructing meaning for text by relating one's experience and knowledge to it (Wittrock, 1981b), and by relating its words, sentences, and paragraphs to one another.

A second set of studies shows that the comprehension strategies learners use to relate their knowledge and experience to the text influence what and how much they will comprehend as they read (Doctorow, Wittrock, & Marks, 1978; Pichert & Anderson, 1977; Wittrock, 1981b). Studies that ask readers (1) to take a perspective on a story, (2) to relate the text to their experience, and (3) to create interactive images between the text and their experience facilitate comprehension.

A third area of research shows that asking learners to construct relations among the parts of the text, for example, by writing summaries, influences memory and comprehension (e.g., Brown, Campione, & Day, 1981; Doctorow, et al., 1978; Wittrock & Kelly, 1984). Whether they are given to the learners or constructed by them, headings, summaries, interactive images, and main ideas increase learning and comprehension.

Recent research (Wittrock, 1981a, 1981b, 1983) also shows a number of ways to facilitate the construction of relations between text and knowledge and among the parts of the text. In addition to headings and summaries, the following verbal and spatial techniques have been used successfully: familiar stories and contents, adjunct questions, rules, objectives, inferences, metaphors, pictures, graphs, paraphrases, and analogies. With these verbal and spatial elaborations and generations the results often indicate an enhancement of reading comprehension, retention, or both.

A fourth area of research indicates that the teaching of comprehension strategies facilitates reading. For example, in a series of three studies conducted over 2½ years, Wittrock & Kelly (1984) taught learning strategies and metacognitive techniques for facilitating comprehension to 215 marginally literate soldiers on active duty at three army bases. These strategies increased reading comprehension about 20% after 10 hours of classroom instruction. When microcomputers were used to teach a metacognitive strategy, the instructional time needed to learn was reduced from 10 to 6 hours. Other studies on the teaching of comprehension strategies have shown similar effects on reading with other populations of learners (cf. Calfee & Drum, 1986).

Because the implications of these studies for the improvement of the teaching of reading require more discussion than I can give them here, I mention only a few of the ideas for the future that come from this recent work.

The first implication is that the concept of reading itself has been refined to emphasize more than saying words aloud in the presence of the text. Reading comprehension takes on new interest in recent conceptions of reading. Cognitive models of reading comprehension will continue to be the focus of much of the research on reading.

Second, comprehension is a process of constructing meaning for text by relating its parts to one another and to one's knowledge and experience.

Third, the relations within and across texts need not be given to a learner directly nor need they be derived by the learner with little or no structure or prompting. That is, as strange as it may seem, whether they are given to the learners or not, they must still be constructed by them. Sometimes direct teaching and sometimes less structured teaching are appropriate, depending on the learners background knowledge and ability spontaneously to generate elaborations as they read. This implication for reading teaching will influence future research on classroom methods.

Fourth, the learners' background knowledge and learning strategies acquire new and central importance in the teaching of reading. Individual differences remain important, but from a new perspective-differences in cognitive processes related to constructing meaning. This finding has implications for the development of new diagnostic tests of the cognitive processes readers use to comprehend text.

Fifth, teaching becomes refined also. At least it is viewed from a different perspective. Teaching comprehension becomes the process of inducing the learners to construct representations for text as they read. From this perspective, teachers need to know the developmental level of their students' generative processes. What is the learner's model of comprehension? Can they construct images from the text or from pictures? Do they understand an analogy? Can they construct one?

Sixth, there are practical and inexpensive teaching procedures to use to facilitate the construction of representations for text. Michele Linden and I (Linden & Wittrock, 1981) reported an experiment conducted in a public school in which we compared generative teaching procedures with conventional instruction and also with a control procedure that did not require children to construct verbal or spatial elaborations as they read. The data indicated a sizable enhancement of reading comprehension, with no increase in time to learn, due to the children's constructions of verbal and imaginal representations for the text. These methods were easy to teach, inexpensive to use, and quickly learned. They suggest some promising and practical techniques that sometimes facilitate reading comprehension.

FOR THE FUTURE

The recent psychological research on cognitive and affective thought processes of teachers and students sampled in this chapter has contributed to a knowledge base and to a theory relevant to improving teaching. This recent research also gives educational psychologists some practical strategies and procedures useful for improving student learning in schools.

The recent research on attribution indicates that motivation to learn in school does not occur automatically from teachers' frequent, discriminate, and contingent use of reinforcers. Instead, motivation to learn occurs when students attribute success in class to something they have thought further about, controlled, and have performed with success. In the future, we need research on the teaching of attributions, or attribution changes. The potential impact of this research on achievement in schools is sizable, as is its potential contribution to motivation theory.

The recent research on attention implies that the use that students' make of the time they have to learn in school, not the amount of time itself, better predicts their learning. Again, it is what teaching causes the learners to think about that produces learning. These findings imply that further research on the teaching of strategies for self-control of attention has much promise for improving achievement in schools, as well as for developing models of attention.

The recent study of comprehension indicates that decoding and the learning of vocabulary are important but not sufficient conditions for understanding text. To comprehend text, the readers generate its meaning, or its meanings, by building two types of relations: (1) among its words, sentences, and paragraphs as well as across related texts, and (2) between their knowledge and their experience, on the one hand, and the concepts in the text, on the other hand. These findings imply that fundamental changes are needed in the teaching of reading comprehension. In particular, the teaching of reading comprehension should emphasize the learners' relevant background knowledge, learning strategies, and metacognitive processes, which are critical in the generating of meanings for text. Research on these issues has potential for contributing to practice and to models of knowledge acquisition.

In the teaching of other subjects, such as physical science, closely related implications also follow. The teaching of models of scientific principles, such as current flow in a DC circuit, indicates that teachers cannot teach only the physicists' model of the principle. Instead, because students have their own, often conflicting, models of these principles, teaching current flow involves getting the student to abandon their models and to adopt a different model. Because the students' own models usually function well in their daily lives, the teaching of a new model calls for sophisticated teaching strategies that will induce the learners to generate a new model that they believe functions in real-world contexts outside school.

These findings mean that cognitive teaching strategies will need to go beyond the teaching of the scientists' model to include the active mental involvement of the students in the process of generating a new model. Teaching involves getting the learners to think about their experience and their knowledge in a different way, one that leads to a better and more useful model than the one they now have. In the future, I think we will see considerable research on the cognitive processes involved in subject matter learning extending beyond mathematics and the physical sciences. This research also has promise for improving practice and for refining models of knowledge acquisition.

Research on learning strategies and metacognitive processes shows some effective ways for teaching these cognitive processes. This research indicates ways for students to generate new meanings from old ideas, for being aware of and for controlling their cognitive and affective thought processes. In research on motivation, attention, memory, and comprehension these strategies and metacognitive processes have been developed and used, as I discussed in this chapter. When they are taught carefully and regularly over at least 3 months, they usually show a facilitating effect upon learning. Sometimes their effects are substantial, showing a 50% to 200% gain in learning without an increase in the time needed to learn. These potentials are important for theory and practice.

In the next decade we should see these recent conceptual advances researched further and applied to classroom teaching. These individual strategies for enhancing motivation, attention, memory, and comprehension need to be organized into coherent teaching strategies that can be regularly used by teachers in schools at all levels. Further research on the synthesis of these and related thinking skills is to be expected.

Future research in cognitive psychology and in educational methods also needs to continue to profit from the cooperation between these two areas that has characterized the cognitive movement in teaching and instruction over the last 20 years. To enable the fields of teaching and learning to continue to grow there should be a close interaction between relevant psychological theory and research on subject matter teaching. The psychological models that have led to the recent studies and innovations in teaching need to grow and to develop in response to the findings of the research on subject matter teaching.

We must keep the psychologists who study educational methods and teaching strategies working closely with the psychologists who study and develop theory about cognitive and affective thought processes. Both groups of psychological researchers can continue to learn from each other. The cognitive psychologists interested in the development of psychological theory can continue to make progress by taking a responsibility for improving teaching and by studying the learning and the knowledge acquisition that occurs in socially significant educational settings. These contexts are excellent for revising and advancing socially useful theory.

The psychologists who study education can continue to make substantial progress by applying research-based, theory-grounded strategies to the teaching problems they face. These researchers will continue to grow in knowledge about teaching if they continue to value the theory and the research which underlies their teaching strategies, and if they take responsibility for contributing to the development of psychological theory and research about human cognition.

Educational psychology is the appropriate field for sustaining these close relations between cognitive psychologists and psychologists who focus on improving teaching and instruction. If both groups of researchers identify themselves as educational psychologists, and both take responsibility for contributing to the development of the principles of psychology and to the improvement of education, psychological theory and research on human cognition will continue to grow, and so will our ability to teach people.

REFERENCES

Atkinson, R. C. (1969). Information delay in human learning. *Journal of Verbal Learning and Verbal Behavior, 8,* 507–511.

Bell, B. F. (1981). When is an animal not an animal? *Journal of Biological Education, 15,* 213–218.

Brown, A. L., Campione, J. C., & Day, J. D. (1981). Learning to learn: On training students to learn from texts. *Educational Researcher, 10*(2), 14–21.

Brown, J. S., & Vanlehn, K. (1982). Towards a generative theory of "bugs." In T. P. Carpenter, J. Moser, & T. Romberg, (Eds.), *Addition and subtraction: A Developmental perspective.* Hillsdale, NJ: Lawrence Erlbaum Associates.

Calfee, R., & Drum, P. (1986). Research on teaching reading. In M. C. Wittrock (Ed.), *Handbook of research on teaching, 3rd Ed.* New York: Macmillan.

Camp, B. W. (1980). Two psychoeducational treatment programs for young aggressive boys. In C. K. Whalen & B. Henker (Eds.), *Hyperactive children: The social ecology of identification and treatment* (pp. 191–219). New York: Academic Press.

Carpenter, T. P., & Moser, J. M. (1982). The development of addition and subtraction problem solving skills. Chapter in T. P. Carpenter, J. M. Moser, & T. Romberg (Eds.), *Addition and subtraction: A developmental perspective.* Hillsdale, NJ: Lawrence Erlbaum Associates.

Conners, C. K. (1970). Cortical visual evoked response in children with learning disorders. *Psychophysiology, 7,* 418–428.

Conners, C. K. (1976). Learning disabilities and stimulant drugs in children: Theoretical implications. In R. M. Knights & D. J. Bakker (Eds.), *The neuropsychology of learning disorders.* Baltimore, MD: University Park Press.

Doctorow, M. J., Wittrock, M. C., & Marks, C. B. (1978). Generative processes in reading comprehension. *Journal of Educational Psychology, 70,* 109–118.

Douglas, V. I., Parry, P., Martin, P., & Garson, C. (1976). Assessment of a cognitive training program for hyperactive children. *Journal of Abnormal Child Psychology, 4,* 389–410.

Egeland, B. (1974). Training impulsive children in the use of more efficient scanning techniques. *Child Development, 45,* 165–171.

Hallahan, D. P., Lloyd, J., Kosiewicz, M. M., Kauffman, J. M., & Graves, A. W. (1979). Self-Monitoring of attention as a treatment for a learning disabled boy's off-task behavior. *Learning Disabilities Quarterly, 2*(1), 24–32.

Keogh, B. K., & Glover, A. T. (1980). The generalizability and durability of cognitive training effects. *Exceptional Education Quarterly, 1,* 75–82.

Kneedler, R. D., & Hallahan, D. P. (1981). Self-monitoring of on-task behavior with learning disabled children: Current studies and directions. *Exceptional Education Quarterly, 2*(3), 73–81.

Linden, M. A., & Wittrock, M. C. (1981). The teaching of reading comprehension according to the model of generative learning. *Reading Research Quarterly, 17,* 44–57.

Lloyd, J., Saltzman, N. J., & Kauffman, J. M. (1981). Predictable generalization in academic learning as a result of preskills and strategy training. *Learning Disability Quarterly, 4*(2), 203–216.

Marks, C. B., Doctorow, M. J., & Wittrock, M. C. (1974). Word frequency and reading comprehension. *Journal of Educational Psychology, 67,* 259–262.

Mayer, R. E., & Greeno, J. G. (1972). Structural differences between learning outcomes produced in different instructional methods. *Journal of Educational Psychology, 63,* 165–173.

Meichenbaum, D., & Goodman, J. (1971). Training impulsive children to talk to themselves. A means of developing self-control. *Journal of Abnormal Psychology, 77,* 115–126.

Mischel, W., & Baker, N. (1975). Cognitive appraisals and transformations in delay behavior. *Journal of Personality and Social Psychology, 31,* 254–261.

Osborne, R. (1981). Children's ideas about electric current. *New Zealand Science Teacher, 29,* 12–19.

Osborne, R. J., & Wittrock, M. C. (1983). Learning science: A generative process. *Science Education, 67*(4), 489–504.

Osborne, R. J., & Wittrock, M. C. (1985). The generative learning model and its implications for science education. *Studies in Science Education, 12,* 59–87.

Pearson, P. D., Hansen, J., & Gordon, C. (1979). *The effect of background knowledge on young children's comprehension of explicit and implicit information* (Technical Report No. 116). University of Illinois, Urbana Center for the Study of Reading.

Peterson, P. L., & Swing, S. R. (1982). Beyond time on task: Students' reports of their thought processes during direct instruction. *Elementary School Journal, 82,* 481–491.

Pichert, J. W., & Anderson, R. C. (1977). Taking different perspectives on a story. *Journal of Educational Psychology, 69,* 309–315.

Preston, M. S., Guthrie, J. T., & Childs, B. (1974). Visual evoked responses in normal and disabled readers. *Psychophysiology, 11,* 452–457.

Resnick, L. B., & Ford, W. W. (1981). *The psychology of mathematics for instruction.* Hillsdale, NJ: Lawrence Erlbaum Associates.

Shavelson, R. J. (1974). Some methods for examining content structure and cognitive structure in instruction. *Educational Psychologist, 11,* 110–122.

Shavelson, R. J. (1981). Teaching Mathematics: Contributions of cognitive research. *Educational Psychologist, 16,* 23–44.

Shavelson, R. J., & Stanton, G. C. (1975). Construct validation: Methodology and application to three measures of cognitive structure. *Journal of Educational Measurement, 12,* 67–85

Solter, A., & Mayer, M. (1978). Broader transfer produced in guided discovery of number concepts with preschool children. *Journal of Educational Psychology, 70,* 363–371.

Weiner, B. (1979). A theory of motivation for some classroom experiences. *Journal of Educational Psychology, 71,* 3–25.

Wittrock, M. C. (1967). Replacement and nonreplacement strategies in children's problem solving. *Journal of Educational Psychology, 58,* 69–74.

Wittrock, M. C. (1981a). Learning and memory. In F. H. Farley & N. J. Gordon (Eds.), *Psychology and education: The state of the union* (pp. 242–264). Berkeley, CA: McCutchan.

Wittrock, M. C. (1981b). Reading comprehension. In F. J. Pirozzolo & M. C. Wittrock (Eds.), *Neuropsychological and cognitive processes in reading.* New York: Academic Press.

Wittrock, M. C. (1983). Generative reading comprehension. *Ginn Occasional Reports.* Lexington, MA: Ginn Publishing Co.

Wittrock, M. C. (1986). Students' thought processes. In M. C. Wittrock (Ed.), *Handbook of research on teaching, 3rd Ed.* New York: Macmillan.

Wittrock, M. C., & Kelly, R. (1984). *Teaching reading comprehension to adults in basic skills courses.* Final Report, University of California, Los Angeles, Graduate School of Education, Three Volumes.

Wittrock, M. C., Marks, C. B., & Doctorow, M. J. (1975). Reading as a generative process. *Journal of Educational Psychology, 67,* 484–489.

Woods, S. S., Resnick, L. B., & Groen, G. J. (1975). An experimental test of five process models for subtraction. *Journal of Educational Psychology, 67,* 17–21.

6 The Future of Technology in Educational Psychology

Richard E. Clark
University of Southern California

Over a decade ago, Robert Glaser and William Cooley (1973), suggested that technology should be used ". . . as a vehicle for making available to schools what psychologists have learned about learning" (p. 855). My general goal here is to explore the potential benefits and barriers we have encountered in implementing the Glaser and Cooley suggestion. One particular benefit is an expanded definition of technology for Educational Psychology. I argue that technology has a key role in the recent shift from Behavioral to Cognitive learning theories and that historically, technology has replaced craft orientations in medicine and engineering and is therefore likely to become a principal focus for education. Barriers to technology have included our own understanding of prescriptive research and, perhaps, resistances to research-based technologies. Examples of instructional technologies that have been developed are briefly presented. The ideas presented spring from an enthusiastic point of view about the future of technology in Educational Psychology, particularly for those who will enter the field in the next few years.

WHAT IS TECHNOLOGY?

In the context of education, the common use of the word "technology" most often implies mechanical devices and media such as teaching machines, television, and computers. However, many Educational Psychologists have adopted a more formal meaning similar to the definition offered by the economist John Kenneth Galbraith (1967): "Technology means the systematic application of scientific and other organized knowledge to practical tasks" (p. 36). Galbraith regards technology as similar to what John Dewey (1900) called a ". . . linking science . . . between theory and practical work" (p. 110). Television and computers are machines which are the products of a technology. However, the formal use of the term would also include as technological products, all practical educational strategies and devices which owe their origin to scientific endeavor. In addition to "courseware" for "teaching media," our technology of education has produced diverse offspring such as improved tests, organizational strategies like modular scheduling and school consolidation, instructional design models, school building designs, and teaching methods like drill and practice and the Keller Plan. Using this expanded approach, much of Educational Psychology is now concerned with technologies that support the design and evaluation of instruction. During this development, research is conducted with the goal of translating and applying descriptive learning principles uncovered by basic research to the solving of practical instructional problems.

It was Jerome Bruner (1964) who described differences between "descriptive" learning theory and a linking "prescriptive" instructional theory. Descriptive research and theory represents what Robert Glaser (1976) claims is ". . . the task of the sciences and other disciplines in the university—to describe how things are and how they work" (p. 5). Prescriptive theories, Bruner proposed, set forth rules for developing effective instructional methods for promoting achievement and motivation. In the early stages of the development of prescriptive design, it was B. F. Skinner who most successfully pursued an instructional technology. While he denied an interest in theory, Skinner nonetheless contributed a comprehensive and vital set of instructional prescriptions which resulted from descriptive research. His work, more than any other, contributed to an interest in instructional "design."

The behaviorist concern with prescription languished somewhat as Educational Psychology made the gradual shift from behavioral to cognitive theories of learning. Now that the cognitive model is established and producing a sizeable body of exciting studies, interest in new design theories is reawakening. This development has been very attractive for those who choose the profession of Educational Psychology for the challenge of solving practical problems that exist in real instructional settings. Yet, to fully grasp why this prescriptive science is important, it is necessary to describe the educational approach with which it coexists and sometimes competes.

WHAT IS THE ALTERNATIVE TO TECHNOLOGY?

Dewey's attraction to science as a way to solve practical educational problems stemmed from his concern about our failure to provide teachers with effective strategies. As a result, he wrote, the teacher must ". . . fall back upon mere routine traditions of school teaching, or to fly to the latest fad [or] panacea peddled out in school journals or teacher's institutes—just as the old physician relied upon his magic formula'' (Dewey, 1900, p. 113). Dewey's concerns sound very much like a number of the current criticisms of teacher strategies and effectiveness. Nevertheless, both Dewey and the critics of teacher preparation may have oversimplified the problem. The historical roots of the type of ad hoc teaching methods typically taught to teachers in consistent with the type of knowledge taught during the development of all professions. A brief description of these two ways to conceptualize knowledge may help clarify the difference.

Rumelhart and Norman (1981) have suggested that in the distant past, all knowledge developed first as a procedure. Procedural knowledge is defined simply as a series of steps which accomplish a goal. Throughout history, the accidental discovery that certain actions solve a problem often lead to the repetition of the actions and their eventual formalization as procedures. These procedures are then taught to successive generations. In this way human beings first learned to make fire, treat illnesses, raise crops, and (apparently) to teach teachers. Procedural knowledge has the important advantage of efficiency. With a procedure ''. . . specific aspects of the problem domain can be taken directly into account. . . It is therefore possible to employ heuristics that might fail in general but work in specific cases'' (p. 338).

It is procedural knowledge which initially made schools (and the profession of teaching) possible. Because arbitrary procedures make up most of the *knowledge base* of teaching, they are the primary reason many scholars describe teaching as a *craft*. It is the use of ad hoc procedures which is the most dominant feature of craft-based professions. However, the disadvantages of procedural knowledge and therefore of crafts are dramatic. Procedures are arbitrary, difficult to learn and once learned, difficult to change. Most important is that procedures do not generalize beyond a narrow context. Recent cognitive theories of learning have suggested that the alternative to procedures is ''declarative'' knowledge. The difference between the two is that procedures tell us *how* to do something and declarative knowledge deals with knowledge ''that'' something happens (factual information) or with knowledge about *why* it happens (rules, principles, concepts). For example, one might know *how* to boil water and not know *why* water boils or vice versa. Mastering the steps necessary to boil water is not necessarily accompanied by mastery of scientific principles such as Charles Law's (and vice versa). Declarative and procedural learning are two different forms of knowledge. Craftspeople tend to work procedurally and they occasionally have declarative rules or explanations for their procedures. Nevertheless, their procedures generally result from ad hoc observations and their declarative explanations have little more than face validity. Science centers on the development of declarative knowledge which is both reliable and which offers predictive (and other kinds of) validity. Prescriptive research borrows many of the inquiry methods of basic science. It results in the construction of a technology which, in turn, permits the development of procedures to solve practical problems. One critical difference between technology and craft is that technologies derive from science-based declarative knowledge.

An exciting current focus in Educational Psychology is the encouragement of prescriptive research which contributes to the development of a technology. The expectation is that in the future, we will make the fruits of science-based technology available for use in the training and therefore in the professional activities of teachers and administrators. The products of instructional technology in the form of teaching methods, curricula, and courses will be suitable for delivery either by the results of communication technology (e.g., computers, television, video disk) or by human teachers. In the meantime, and for the foreseeable future, craft and technology must coexist. Yet, it is important to recognize their coexistence may occasionally be troubled. Critics have claimed that a craft focus and its accompanying ''anti-intellectualism'' among educators has resulted in active resistance to the implementation of research based technologies. Others have noted the split in Schools of Education and the resistance to systematic, discipline-based research has inhibited the growth of Educational Psychology. At the very least, there is common agreement that craft and science spring from very different assumptions.

BARRIERS TO TECHNOLOGY IN EDUCATION

According to Barbara Ward, the difference between craft and technology is as profound and fundamental as the difference between primitive and advanced societies. In discussing the characteristics of the two types of cultures, Ward (1962) gives technology the credit for the efficiencies which permit the development of advanced societies. She claims that ''. . . there is virtually no science in tribal society. There is a good deal of practical experience, skilled work and early technique. It seems possible, for instance, that primitive farming developed as a result of close observation of nature's cycle. . . But the idea of controlling material things by grasping the inner law of their construction is absent'' (p. 47). Of course craft-based, ad hoc knowledge and practice are the only method of choice in the absence of science-based technology. But critics such as Fred Kerlinger (1977) have suggested that educators may have actively resisted research-based principles in the past because ''Educators have little patience with what they conceive to be 'impractical', 'ivory tower' research . . . the net effect of their impatience is a pervading anti-intellectualism that has a devastating effect on research in education'' (p. 6). Robert Heinich goes even further than Kerlinger. He is concerned that teachers will resist instructional technologies because ''The evidence we have suggests that organized teacher activity parallels the craft union movement in industry. The ways in which the labor movement tried to protect its members from the encroachment of technology are very similar to how teacher groups seek to maintain the labor-intensive character of instruction'' (Heinich, 1984; pp. 77–78). Another critic, Katz (1966), describes the historical origin of the craft versus science split on Schools of Education. He argues that early in this century, due to their craft focus, ''. . . educationists rejected the option of adherence to any one of the established disciplines, proclaimed themselves outspokenly eclectic, and failed to develop a distinctive mode of inquiry or a set of criteria for organizing data for their self-proclaimed science. In the process they lost all criteria for limiting the nature of their inquiry and, instead, tried to construct a discipline through an indiscriminate survey of all factors loosely associated with schools [and] . . . became marked by the survey outlook'' (p. 332). The result, according to Katz, is that research in education tended to lose its normative character and to choose the status quo as its point of reference. In addition, education became a fragmented series of specialties with no internal logic and any ''job'' in education for which someone could be trained became a legitimate subject for study and departmentalization. ''Finally, almost paradoxically, in the attempt to create a discipline education divorced itself from the rest of the academic community. Education preserved some of the techniques of quantitative measurement but severed itself from the methodology and frame of reference of all academic disciplines and failed to develop a distinctive approach of its own'' (p. 333).

IMPEDIMENT OR IMPOVERISHMENT?

The views of Kerlinger, Heinich, and Katz on the barriers or impediments to research-based educational technology are controversial. How well they represent the situation today is uncertain. Many critics of the teaching profession have noted that Schools of Education have done a less than sterling job training our nation's teachers. Kerlinger and Heinich present evidence for teacher resistance to adopt demonstrably successful research-based technologies. Yet, it would be less than fair to ignore the fact that there have been very few optimistic reviews of the quality of educational research until recently. This may account for some of the lack of teacher enthusiasm for using research. There may simply have been very little research available which could be applied—even though there were few teachers who were either adequately trained or predisposed toward research. In addition, the way research was reported might have served to discourage adoption. Despite the craft focus of educational practice, teachers generally view themselves as open to instructional methods which are demonstrably more effective than existing practices. Their resistance to instructional technology may therefore have been, in part, a reluctance to embrace a not very useful set of principles about learning from instruction. In fact, the most conservative conclusion about the past 3 decades of educational research would be that one major impediment to its application has been an impoverishment in its quality and quantity. It has only been in the past decade that we have produced significant amounts of prescriptive work.

As a concrete indicator of how recent this growth is, Lee Shulman notes the number of studies reported in the *Handbook of Research on Teaching,* published every 10 years. The first *Handbook,* published in 1964, focused mainly on problems with the methodology of teaching research. Authors complained about the lack of solid research (Gage, 1963). Ten years later, Geraldine Clifford (1973) in the lead chapter on the historical impact of teaching research for the next *Handbood,* protested about "Insufficient or inconclusive educational research . . . " (p. 37). The editor of the volume that year, Robert Travers (1973), complained that ". . . those who participated in the first *Handbook* would never have never guessed that a decade later the authors of the *Second Handbook* would be having even greater difficulty in finding significant research to report . . ." (p. vii).

So, recent developments in technology may be due both to increased quality and generalizability of current educational research and to a reduction in the resistance of craft-focused practitioners. Shulman (1986) has referred to the years since Katz's critique as " . . . the modern era (since 1965) . . . " (p. 27). He asserts that only during the past 10 to 12 years has there been a significant expansion of "process-product" research on teaching and learning. Katz (1986) contends that during the past 10 to 15 years ". . . findings have proliferated. Many have been replicated and extended. Policymakers and practitioners alike take the research seriously and apply its results to their activities" (p. 33). Those entering the field now will arrive at what appears to be a watershed. It seems that we now support a relatively new and more productive agenda for our field. But, what caused this recent change in the quantity and quality of educational research? Why is technology more viable now than even 2 decades ago? Although there are many possible answers to these questions, the change may be due in large part to recent work which has attempted to clarify the nature of prescriptive studies of teaching and learning in order to produce a "design science."

TECHNOLOGY AND DESIGN SCIENCE

It was an economist colleague of Galbraith's, Herbert Simon, who described the characteristics of "design sciences" in his book, *The Sciences of the Artificial* (1981). He urged educators to think of themselves as applying social science in the same way that successful physicians apply physical sciences. Educational Psychology, when conceptualized in Simon's terms as a design science, would (among other tasks) apply learning and motivation theory to instructional design. Yet, Simon noted, most professional schools either focus on ad hoc craft-based knowledge or they tend to focus more on extending their underlying "descriptive'' sciences. So, the better medical schools tend more to teach biological sciences and deemphasize prescriptive application. And, it might be added, our more solid departments of Educational Psychology until recently have tended to teach descriptive learning theory and so were "applied" in name only.

Of course the *applied* label has often been attached to both well-intentioned failures and to unreliable ad hoc educational approaches to problems. Until recently, it seemed that Educational Psychologists working in professional Schools of Education had two choices. They could associate either with the applied teacher educators or they could join their colleagues who were largely engaged in extending descriptive theories of learning. The friction between these two cultures in our professional schools may have delayed the development of acceptable science-based prescriptive methodology. This historical development has tended to cool the ardor of some Educational Psychologist's for practical work. In addition, the development of our understanding of prescriptive research and theory is a very recent and still-evolving phenomenon. Prescriptive research and theory are neither easy nor are the numerous problems of conceptualization and design well understood (Cook & Campbell, 1979; Landa, 1983). As a result there is a great deal of potential in this domain if recent efforts are an indication of future development. Notable advances have been achieved, for example, in testing and measurement, in the teaching of reading, in instructional design and for the delivery of instruction through computers and television.

One of the intermediate stages in prescriptive theory development is an attempt to specify generalizations which have survived repeated experimental tests. One such list appeared recently in an *Educational Psychologist* article by Stephen Foster. Drawing on the past century of learning research, Foster (1986) recommends the following list of declarative "principles" of learning:

- We learn to do by doing a behavior once (Guthrie)
- We learn to do what we do and not something else (Guthrie)
- Without reinforcement there can be no learning (Skinner)
- Overt practice improves learning and retention (Thorndike/Underwood)
- Practice [beyond that necessary for] task acquisition produces overlearning which results in resistance to extinction. (p. 236)

Foster goes on to show how cognitive prescriptive research has modified these earlier principles. In the case of Guthrie's principle listed first above, learning by "doing" is complemented " . . . by instruction in and/or by images of doing and by observing others doing (Bandura/Gagne)" (1986, p. 237). Implicit in his review is the insight that such recent modifications of older and established principles of learning are neither easy nor simple. In addition, there are many problems to be solved concerning the application of these *principles* directly to practical instructional problems. For example, Foster's final principle (overlearning) results in resistance not only to extinction but also to transfer. There is evidence from prescriptive studies (Clark & Voogel, 1985) that when procedures are practiced to the point of automaticity, they are extrememly difficult or impossible to modify for transfer to different performance contexts or problems. This kind of difficulty indicates a strong need to extend our knowledge about (and investment in) prescriptive inquiry. Another area where attempts to apply the result of descriptive studies in practical settings have failed, is in the computer-based instruction (CBI) area. Here a confusion of technologies may have led to expensive mistakes.

There is strong evidence in recent research on using computers to teach, that professional educators have confused *teaching* technology (used to deliver instructional content and methods) with *instructional* technology (the instructional methods and content that serve as the psychologically *active ingredient* of all teaching). Clark (1983) has provided an analogy to illustrate the differences between the two technologies. "The best current evidence" he stated "is that media are mere vehicles that deliver instruction but do not influence student achievement any more than the truck that delivers our groceries causes changes in our nutrition" (p. 445). Technologies that deliver instructional methods can range from computers to teachers. When a teacher or a computer deliver worthless teaching strategy, no learning results. When a psychologically effective instructional method is available however, it generally will be deliverable by computer, teacher, or some other medium. The medium seems to greatly influence the efficiency (e.g., cost and time) of instruction but they do not control the psychological processes involved in learning.

This claim of Clark's seems to contradict the considerable evidence in meta-analytic reviews of descriptive studies that when CBI is compared to teacher delivered instruction, CBI produces learning scores that are superior by about .5 standard deviations on achievement tests (Kulik, Kulik, & Cohen, 1980). This is a highly significant difference both statistically and practically. This finding has been used by educators as a post hoc justification for the purchase of computer hardware for use in our nation's schools. However, later prescriptive studies of the problem (Clark, 1983; Clark & Salomon, 1986) noticed that when the same teacher designed both the CBI and the *live* presentation of the lesson in an experiment, there was no difference in the resulting learning scores. The goal of one class of prescriptive studies is to discover the *active ingredient* of successful treatments from descriptive research. In this case, Clark (1983) reasoned that the active ingredient in computer-based instruction, when it was more successful in past studies, was the inclusion of robust instructional methods. These same instructional methods were *not* included in the traditional, teacher-taught conditions in the experiments. So, the research only compared successful with unsuccessful instructional methods. The same successful methods provided by computers in that research might have been delivered by teachers (or other media) with the same learning consequences, he claimed. When the same teacher or instuctional designer work on both the CBI and the traditional treatments compared in the CBI studies, the chances are greater that the same instructional methods will be employed in all compared treatments. Clark (1985) found this to be the case when he reanalyzed a large sample of the Kulik college CBI studies. When a meta-analysis is performed on only the studies where instructional method was controlled between computer and traditional treatments, the estimated contribution of computer delivered instruction to student achievement fell to nearly zero (Clark, 1985). This finding would then suggest that the purchase of computers for schools will not necessarily enhance the learning of students. The more general analysis employed implies that a science-based technological focus may help solve some of the more crucial problems confronting educators. In order to pursue those solutions however, we need to know much more about prescriptive research methodology.

WHAT KINDS OF PROBLEMS DOES A TECHNOLOGY SOLVE?

One of the first realities one encounters when attempting to apply descriptive learning research findings to solve instructional problems is that no *direct* transfer is usually possible. For example, one of the most repeated empirical findings in learning research is that increased time on task results in more learning. Yet it would be obviously foolish to suggest that students who encounter problems when learning from instruction only or usually need more time. Landa (1983) has suggested that prescriptive questions need to be structured in a different way than descriptive ones. He notes that descriptive hypotheses usually place treatment or instructional method alternatives in the "If . . ." place and some learning outcome in the "Then . . ." place. As an example, consider a descriptive hypothesis: "If we increase student time on the learning task then we may expect corresponding increases in mastery." An oversimplified prescriptive version of the time hypothesis would suggest that "If we wish to increase mastery for those having difficulties with existing conditions, then we must increase their time on task." While generally accurate in some cases, the prescription is neither complete nor useful for all learners. As is often the case, variables such as time are "proxies" for other more "active" variables. The question one must ask is "What are these students thinking and doing during the extra time it takes them to learn this task?". Prescriptive theories must gain insights about these active variables so that they can *predict* or suggest a teaching method for example, which will serve to activate or model some necessary but unavailable cognitive skill. So a prescriptive hypothesis begins with a description of the learning task and the aptitudes of the students to be taught and then recommends the instructional method(s) needed for the required levels of achievement.

Glaser's (1976) description of the "components of a psychology of instruction'' serve as an overview of the concerns that need to be addressed by prescriptive researchers. He encourages a focus on two types of guiding questions, the first is methodological; ''What can be learned about techniques to be used in the application of psychological knowledge to the design of instruction from the strategies of design used in other fields?'' (p. 7) and the second is substantive; ''Given methodologies for deciding among possible alternatives, what are the substantive components that are required as the data to which these methodologies can be applied?'' (p. 8). To approach this latter question, he lists the types of concerns to be addressed by prescriptive theories of instruction. He divides the area into:

1. the analysis of competent performance
2. descriptions of the initial state of the learner
3. analyses of conditions which foster the acquisition of competence
4. assessment of the effects of instructional implementation

Glaser's list makes it clear that instructional technologies must include an adequate model for:

- conceptualizing learning tasks (specification and assessment of competent performance)
- the individual differences of the learner (initial state)
- instructional methods (conditions which foster acquisition)

Other attempts to characterize prescriptive instructional models have centered on the same three variables—task, learner, and method. In fact, some have suggested that these divisions characterize some of the main subdivisions in Educational Psychology.

EXAMPLES OF CURRENT INSTRUCTIONAL TECHNOLOGIES

This section contains a number of examples of instructional technologies that have been developed from prescriptive research. There are many other outstanding examples that might have been chosen for illustration. Reigeluth (1983) presents expanded views of a number of instructional design models that have research foundations. The following examples were chosen to make the point that design technology is producing solid work in a variety of subdivisions in Educational Psychology. They are based on what appears to be an emerging ''design theory'' in instruction. It appears that most prescriptive studies have focused on two fruitful classes of variables which seem to *predict* instructional methods—task and individual difference variables. In their most general form, these theories may ultimately give us prescriptions that are organized like "If we require Px level of performance on learning task type Tx and for students with relevant aptitudes which range from Aa to Az then use instructional methods Yi to Yq." Task x treatment prescriptions have been the main focus of experimental Educational Psychology. Individual differences x treatment (ATI) prescriptions have occupied researchers in Differential and Developmental Educational Psychology. The examples that follow are drawn from experimental, differential, and developmental research in Educational Psychology.

The Learning Task Focus: Technologies Developed from Experimental *Psychology.*

The best known experimentalist and technologist in psychology has been B. F. Skinner. He has provided a rich and familiar body of prescriptive work on instructional method which has influenced all subsequent work in this area. More recent prescriptive contributors who owe a great deal to experimental psychology, including the new cognitive experimental literature, are instructional technologists such as Robert Gagne and David Merrill. One of the major contributions of the new generation of experimentally based design theorists, is their attempt to match instructional methods to systematic and useful conceptualizations of learning tasks. Gagne's 1967 book *The Conditions of Learning* had tremendous impact on Educational Psychologists who were seeking to apply experimental learning principles to teaching. His eight types of learning were the basis for a number of later elaborations (Gagne & Briggs, 1979) on the way learning tasks have been conceptualized. The more recent work of David Merrill (1983) on "component display theory" is a notable example of current applications in this area. Merrill's "performance-content matrix" (see Fig. 6.1) is one

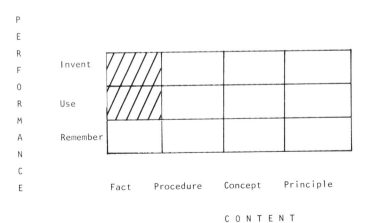

FIG. 6.1. Performance-content matrix following Merrill (1983).

of the more useful conceptualizations of learning tasks now available. Instead of the traditional curriculum characterizations of learning tasks as discipline based, Merrill distinguishes between four types of "content"; facts, procedures, concepts and principles. His definitions for each owe much to experimental studies of memory and concept learning and to later work on the differences between declarative and procedural knowledge. He crosses the four content types with three "performance" types; remember, use, and find (or invent). Merrill has suggested instructional prescriptions for teaching the level of task represented by each cell (excepting find and use fact which he claims are empty cells).

Merrill's technology offers very specific instructional design prescriptions for each cell in the matrix. Generally, these prescriptions advise the use of rule/example sequences and drill/practice/feedback strategies in different mixes for different "cells" in the task matrix. Merrill and other experimentalists generally discourage the consideration of individual difference measures of intelligence in their instructional technology. Their evidence (e.g., Reigeluth, 1983) suggests that only measures of prior knowledge increase the predictive power of their theories. Differential psychologists have disputed the claim (see e.g., Cronbach & Snow, 1977). In fact, it appears that the dispute centers on the fact that the two areas have focused on very different types of learning tasks. The experimentalists have tended to select near transfer memory level and procedural tasks for their learning research. Differential psychologists have typically been more concerned with the farther transfer learning of more abstract concepts and principles.

The Individual Difference Focus: Technologies Developed From Differential Psychology

Richard Snow (e.g., 1977) has explored a variety of prescriptive questions which are concerned with individual differences in learning from instruction. He proposes that the new instructional theories combine questions and findings from both cognitive experimental psychology and cognitive differential psychology. The former has explored the cognitive consequences of different treatments and the latter has described the psychological processes characterizing aptitude for learning. One important prescriptive result of the combination, he suggests, is that aptitude is increasingly viewed as limited by specific task and/or treatment environment.

In his own research, Snow and his colleagues (Snow & Lohman, 1984) have offered prescriptions based on the aptitude x method (ATI) interaction in instruction. They find considerable evidence, for example, that students with higher general ability (G) learn more when instructional methods place more cognitive "load" on them. Lower G students, on the other hand, profit more from methods which decrease their information processing load. This leads to the recommendation that:

> . . . A set of alternative instructional treatments should . . . vary in 'incompleteness'. For lower G learners, the instructional treatment should be made explicit,

direct and structured in detail so as to provide the procedural knowledge . . . conceptual knowledge . . . guided assembly and control during learning. For higher G learners, instructional treatment should be left relatively in-
complete and unstructured so as to allow idiosyncratic exercise of procedural and
conceptual knowledge; assembly and control functions should be unguided. (pp.
372–373)

Snow (1977) has cautioned that when such general prescriptions are translated
for a specific group of learners, the resulting presentation will be "local" and
probably not generalize to other sites. The exception to this limitation is where
"horizontal generalization" is possible when ". . . other schools or communities are found to match this one on relevant variables." (p. 14). Snow's
concern that prescriptive theories will be limited in generalizability has been
controversial. Yet, it does appear that there may be a number of "levels" within
which one might address prescriptive theories. Reigeluth (1983) for example,
distinguished between instructional design theory (which is more general and is
exemplified by Snow's prescription in the preceding paragraph) and instructional
development theory. The latter must accommodate all relevant local conditions
or "constraints" which include factors such as specific amounts and types of
aptitudes in the local population of learners, community instructional goals and
resources for reaching those goals.

Local goals and resources may dictate, for example, that instructional design
be based on the selection of students with specific levels of prior knowledge
rather than the assignment of students to different instructional methods which
have been matched to different aptitude levels. Different goals might focus
design on the training of aptitude rather than selection or assignment. In addition,
the production and delivery of concrete instructional programs involve many
diverse decisions concerning the verbalness or visualness of presentations, the
verbal demands which local students are able to handle and the available means
of delivering instruction. Attempts to accommodate local constraints may often
produce an instructional program which will generalize only to locations where
similar constraints exist. This may be why excellent and independent reviews of
large-scale curriculum development projects by Cronbach and Snow (1977) and
Cooley and Lohnes (1976) found a pattern of failure. It is possible therefore that
a general level of prescriptive theory is possible but that a technology designed
for one location may not work in other locations where important constraints are
different. Much work remains to be done to identify the boundary constraints of
different levels of prescriptive theory.

A Second Individual Difference Focus: Technologies
Which Evolved From Developmental Psychology

The third example of current instructional technologies has evolved from
recent work in Developmental Psychology. Prescriptions from Developmental
Psychology have evolved more slowly than some other substantive areas in

Educational Psychology. This may be due to the fact that early developmental theory emphasized the "implicit" and unmodifiable nature of the "stages" in intellectual development. More recent theories emphasize incremental and more flexible adaptation during development and this approach is more amenable to intervention strategies. While there are a number of people working in this area, the work of Robbie Case (Case, 1978; Case & Bereiter, 1984) is widely acknowledged.

Like Snow, Case (1978) teases instructional generalizations out of the developmental literature: ". . . that young children approach intellectual tasks with strategies that are reasonable but oversimplified, and . . . that young children are incapable of dealing with more than a few items of information at one time" (p. 439). He then develops three main prescriptions to represent the generalizations:

1. Precede the design of instruction with a step by step description not only of the strategy to be taught but also of the strategy . . . that children apply to the instruction spontaneously.

2. Design the instruction in such a way that the limitations of children's spontaneous strategies will be apparent and that the necessity of applying the strategy to be taught will therefore be clear, and

3. Both in selecting the strategy to be taught and in designing the sequence of instructional activities to teach it, reduce the working memory requirements of the learning situation to a bare minimum.

In a later article (Case & Bereiter, 1984) he expresses these three prescriptions as a procedure for designing instruction for both children and older adults.

In Case's work, like Gagne, Merrill, and Snow, one finds clear divisions of concern between task types, individual differences and instructional method. Case and Bereiter (1984) note that their first concern has been on instructional method but that " . . .a second line of inquiry has been devoted to probing the range of tasks and populations for which the developmental method of instructional design may be appropriate" (p. 152). Yet they acknowledge that their suggestions about tasks and individual differences have been primarily *clinical* not experimental.

Future Developments in Prescriptive Research

In the next decade, the amount and quality of prescriptive research will increase and expand into new arenas. It is obvious now that some of that expansion should be in three areas: First, the achievement of the goal Lee Cronbach set for us 30 years ago when he suggested the combination of the "two disciplines of scientific psychology"—experimental and correlational. In terms of the present discussion this goal involves an emphasis on the way that task variables interact with individual difference and developmental variables to *predict* instructional methods.

The second development might be an increased emphasis on producing new prescriptive research methodologies which support the advancement of instructional technology and design science. Here we need to focus on questions of construct validity, generalizability of research findings, levels of prescriptive inquiry, new statistical methods for data analysis. Many methodological issues will be directed to helping us understand the "active ingredients" in the treatments taken from descriptive research (e.g., computer-based instruction studies).

Finally, we need to extend our awareness of the larger arena in which Educational Psychology operates—to the field of Education as a whole—and to understand that the success of our practical efforts will depend on how sensitive we are to the way others perceive problems and solutions. Specifically, we need to expect that the virtues of new psychologically based instructional technologies may not be immediately recognized or adopted. This is the way with most of the dramatic changes in the history of ideas. Yet, the student of Educational Psychology can now expect to play a key role in future developments in Education. The field is in the unsettled but exciting state that usually accompanies major shifts in paradigm. That implies that old alliances and rigid practices are undergoing change. In the midst of that change there is great opportunity for new people.

ACKNOWLEDGMENT

The author wishes to acknowledge Robert Heinich at Indiana University. His research in this area influenced the direction of this chapter and his comments on an earlier version of the manuscript helped guide its development.

REFERENCES

Bruner, J. S. (1964). Some theorems on instruction illustrated with reference to mathematics. *The sixty-third yearbook of the national society for the study of education, Part I, 63*, 306–335.

Case, R. (1978). A developmentally based theory and technology of instruction. *Review of Educational Research, 48*(3), 439–463.

Case, R., & Bereiter, C. (1984). From behaviorism to cognitive behaviorism to cognitive development: Steps in the evolution of instructional design. *Instructional Science, 13*, 141–158.

Clark, R. E. (1983). Reconsidering research on learning from media. *Review of Educational Research, 53*(4), 445–459.

Clark, R. E. (1985). Evidence for confounding in computer-based instruction studies: Analyzing the meta-analyses. *Educational Communication and Technology Journal, 33*(4), 249–262.

Clark, R. E., & Salomon, G. (1986). Media in teaching. In M. C. Wittrock, (Ed.), *Handbook of research on teaching. (2nd edition)*. New York: Macmillan.

Clark, R. E., & Voogel, A. (1985). Transfer of training for instructional design. *Educational Communications and Technology Journal, 33*(2), 113–123.

Clifford, G. (1973). A history of the impact of research on teaching. In R. M. W. Travers, (Ed.), *Second handbook of research on teaching*. New York: Rand McNally.

Cook, T. D., & Campbell, D. T. (1979). *Quasi-experimentation*. Boston: Houghton Mifflin.

Cooley, W. W., & Lohnes, P. R. (1976). *Evaluation research in education*. New York: Irvington.

Cronbach, L. J., & Snow, R. E. (1977). *Aptitudes and instructional methods*. New York: Irvington.

Dewey, J. (1900). Psychology and social practice. *The Psychological Review. 7*, 105–124.

Foster, S. F. (1986). Ten principles of learning revised in accordance with cognitive psychology: With implications for teaching. *Educational Psychologist, 21*(3), 235–243.

Gage, N. L. (Ed.). (1963). *The handbook of* research on Teaching. New York: Rand McNally.

Gagne, R. M. (1967). *The conditions of learning*. New York: Holt, Reinhart & Winston.

Gagne, R. M., & Briggs, L. J. (1979). *Principles of Instructional Design* (2nd edition). New York: Holt Reinhart & Winston.

Galbraith, J. K. (1967). *The new industrial state*. Boston: Houghton Mifflin.

Glaser, R. (1976). Components of a psychology of instruction: Toward a science of design. *Review of Educational Research, 46*(1), 1–24.

Glaser, R., & Cooley, W. W. (1973). Instrumentation for teaching and instructional management. In R. M. W. Travers, (Ed.), *Second handbook of research on teaching*. Chicago: Rand McNally.

Heinich, R. (1984). The proper study of instructional technology. *Educational Communication and Technology Journal, 32*(2), 67–87.

Katz, M. B. (1966). From theory to survey in graduate schools of education. *Journal of Higher Education, 23*, 325–334.

Kerlinger, F. N. (1977, September). The influence of research on education practice. *Educational Researcher*, 5–12.

Kulik, C., Kulik, J., & Cohen, P. (1980). Effectiveness of computer-based college teaching: A meta-analysis of findings. *Review of Educational Research, 50*, 525–544.

Landa, L. N. (1983). Descriptive and prescriptive theories of learning and instruction: An analysis of their relationships and interactions. In C. M. Reigeluth (Ed.), *Instructional design theory and models*. Hillsdale, NJ: Lawrence Erlbaum Associates.

Merrill, M. D. (1983). Component display theory, In C. M. Reigeluth, (Ed.), *Instructional design theory and models,* Hillsdale, NJ: Lawrence Erlbaum Associates.

Reigeluth, C. M. (Ed.). (1983). *Instructional design theories and models*. Hillsdale, NJ: Lawrence Erlbaum Associates.

Rumelhart, D. E., & Norman, D. A. (1981). Analogical processes in learning. In J. R. Anderson, (Ed.), *Cognitive skills and their acquisition*. Hillsdale, NJ: Lawrence Erlbaum Associates.

Shulman, L. S. (1986). Paradigms and research programs in the study of teaching: A contemporary perspective. In M. C. Wittrock, (Ed.), *Handbook of research on teaching (3rd edition)*. New York: Macmillan.

Simon, H. (1981). *The Sciences of the artificial,* Second Edition, Cambridge, MA: MIT Press.

Snow, R. E. (1977, November). Individual differences and instructional theory. *Educational Researcher*, 11–15.

Snow, R. E., & Lohman, D. F. (1984). Toward a cognitive theory of learning from instruction. *Journal of Educational Psychology, 76*(3), 347–376.

Travers, R. M. W. (Ed.). (1973). *Second handbook of research on teaching*. Chicago: Rand McNally.

Ward, B. (1962). *The rich nations and the poor nations*. New York: Norton.

III EMERGING ROLES OF EDUCATIONAL PSYCHOLOGISTS

From the research, theory, and technology discussed in the previous section on emerging directions will come new roles and responsibilities for educational psychologists in universities, colleges, elementary and secondary schools, government, industry, and the military services. As educational psychologists develop their understanding of teaching and learning in different domains and subject matters, their prescriptive knowledge will become increasingly relevant and useful to teachers in all of those contexts.

Sigmund Tobias details contributions of educational psychologists to improving instruction in elementary and secondary schools, industries, and medical settings. He discusses future contributions to elementary and secondary school education of recent research on classroom management, instructional systems design, comprehension, metacognition, measurement, evaluation, computer-assisted instruction, and test-anxiety reduction. In medical settings he shows the possibilities for contributing to improved health through education. His suggestions, echoed by authorities in medicine such as John Knowles, emphasize how national health depends upon an enlightened and widespread understanding of the important daily practices that help to maintain wellness. Nutrition, exercise, weight control, reduction of substance abuse, and stress management contribute to health. From this perspective, physicians, nurses, and other personnel in the health sciences are teachers as well as healers. As teachers, they need to learn and to practice the principles of educational psychology that pertain to effective instruction in health.

Jack Bardon, a school psychologist, takes a different perspective on the future roles of educational psychologists. As someone who is not an educational psychologist, but who is knowledgeable about the field, he was invited to prepare a school psychologist's viewpoint on the future of the field. Bardon argues that educational psychology should respect the domains and the prerogatives of other specialties in psychology, including organizational psychology and school psychology. Educational psychology should retain its place as research-oriented branch of psychology and should not become a competitor with other branches of psychology, whose proper roles are to service schools, businesses, and industries. Bardon's chapter provides a different and useful perspective on the future role and contributions of educational psychology. His chapter also raises the question of the domain of educational psychology.

Beau Fly Jones details the extensive opportunities for educational psychologists to contribute to the development of policies and to the improvement of pedagogy in elementary and secondary schools. The need for improved instructional materials, curricula, and assessment techniques is enormous in these educatinal settings. As educational psychology develops a more differentiated understanding of the domain specific or subject matter specific principles of teaching, it will increasingly become useful to elementary and secondary schools. Consequently, the need for preservice and in-service education will increase, along with the desire to improve the technology of instruction, and the strategies of teaching. These possblities for edcuational psychologists to contribute to schools offer challenges that will have great impact upon the field.

7 New Roles for Educational Psychologists

Sigmund Tobias
City College, City University of New York

The purpose of this chapter is to suggest some new roles for educational psychologists. Traditionally, educational psychologists have worked in college and university environments with the usual teaching and research responsibilities of such faculty (Scandura et al; 1981); they have also assumed special instructional functions in teacher education programs at the undergraduate level. The new roles described here fall into two categories: (1) Positions in elementary and secondary schools with consultative and staff development functions, and (2) Consultative/administrative functions in industry and social agencies for which educational psychologists are uniquely qualified. In many cases the latter roles are not presently being filled at all, or they are being discharged by people with less appropriate training than that of educational psychologists.

The impetus for new roles comes from two directions. First, scientific developments in educational psychology have rarely been more fruitful. Important research in such fields as reading comprehension, study skills and learning strategies, and clarification of the cognitive processes of which intelligence and problem solving are composed have enabled educational psychologists, perhaps for the first time, to be helpful in the improvement of educational practice. Despite this progress, there are relatively few academic positions for educational psychologists (Newsome & Stillwell, 1985), leading to the second stimulus for the new roles to be suggested here. If educational psychologists could enlarge the conceptions of their roles from teaching and research to more activist, interventionist perspectives and broaden their choice of worksites from the college and university environments in which they have traditionally functioned (Scandura et al; 1981) many new opportunities would become available to such fully trained psychologist. This chapter proposes to make such suggestions.

SCHOOL BASED ROLES

The major purpose of the new roles for educational psychologists within schools should be the maintenance and enhancement of students' competence (Levy, 1984) in general, and their academic competence in particular. There are important analogies to these roles in the public health area. It may be surprising to note that the innovation with the greatest impact on public health was *not* any medical treatment involving new technology, not wonder drugs, nor surgery; instead, it was the purification of the water supply (McKeown, 1980). Such purification, of course, prevented many illnesses from developing and made treatment unnecessary. Equally relevant is the finding (Backstrand, 1980) that when a new medical treatment facility is opened its resources are generally absorbed within 3 years and the percentage of the population reporting itself as underserved *remains unchanged*. These data demonstrate dramatically the futility of thinking in terms of treatment models in public health and the importance of shifting to a health maintenance, or prevention perspective. A similar perspective is advocated for the new roles to be described here. Their aim is to enhance the competence of students and their health, in order to reduce the need for educational or psychological remediation or special treatment.

There are educational examples of the relative ineffectiveness of treatment, in the form of remediation, which are similar to those in public health. It is well known, for example, that students receiving remedial reading for a year are *unlikely* to increase their reading ability by a full year (Spreen, 1982). Therefore, even students exposed to successful remedial instruction are most likely to fall further and further behind their peers. Obviously, it is wisest to devote major resources to effective initial instruction rather than remediation. An educational equivalent to the purification of the water supply is needed to help students become and remain competent rather than fall behind in their schoolwork. A number of strategies intended to help accomplish such objectives are described below. Although these strategies may not be as powerful as purification of water, perhaps they can be considered to be an educational analog to the effects of fluoridation.

The suggestions described here should not be considered exhaustive or complete in that similar ends can be accomplished by other roles not mentioned here. Instead, they are intended to be illustrative samples of a large domain of strategies that may be used by educational psychologists to maintain and enhance students' competence and well being. Following the descriptions of these strategies, some general characteristics and requirements of the role are discussed so that educational psychologists can be maximally effective in exercising this role in schools.

Improving Instruction

A substantial body of research relating teacher practices to student achievement has accumulated in recent years (Rosenshine & Stevens, 1986; Brophy & Good, 1986). The results of these investigations are fairly new and have generally *not* been disseminated in either teacher education or in-service teacher training programs. This research has identified and replicated a group of teacher practices that consistently lead to increases in student achievement. Some of these findings are counterintuitive and contradict conventional "teacher wisdom." For example, Anderson, Evertson, and Brophy (1979) found that in small group-based early reading instruction calling on students to respond according to some regular pattern led to superior achievement compared to recognizing volunteers, or selecting students at random. The fact that some of these effective practices are not self-evident makes it all the more important for teachers to learn about them, because they are unlikely otherwise to become familiar with them.

One important role for educational psychologists is to inform teachers about effective teaching practices identified by recent research. In most fields there is a, perhaps inevitable, delay between the development of new knowledge and its utilization. Often this gap is reduced when recently trained individuals assume university teaching positions and disseminate new developments to students and colleagues alike. In view of the fact that there are few academic positions available for newly trained educational psychologists (Newsome & Stilwell, 1985), the knowledge gap in education regarding effective teaching practices is likely to persist for a longer period than usual, making it even more important for psychologists to fulfill this function. Since similar roles were described by both Berliner (1983, in press) and Rosenfield (1984) there is little need for repeating them here.

Behavior Modification

A good deal of research has indicated that a number of practices identified with the behavior modification movement are effective in changing students' behavior. Such procedures as token economies, the systematic reinforcement of some behavior, and preventing the inadvertent reinforcement of behaviors not related to school objectives can significantly improve student achievement, discipline, and teachers' management of classes in general (Sulzer-Azaroff & Reese, (1982). The effectiveness of these practices have been verified in many investigations (Barton, 1982; Kazdin, 1977; Lahey & Drabman, 1981) and are the subject of a large, widely available literature.

Behavior modification techniques should certainly be used more frequently by teachers than they are at present. Educational psychologists should try to disseminate behavioral techniques to teachers, administrators, and counselors. Such dissemination should not consist merely of school-based instruction. Instead, the applications of these techniques to particular students or classes should be discussed in consulting relationships between educational psychologists and educators. Educational psychologists could also model these techniques at school meetings, in classes, or at teacher meetings. Finally, it may be useful to help teachers implement these practices by visiting their classrooms, providing non-evaluative feedback after visits, and modifying or extending these practices after jointly evaluating their effectiveness.

Instructional Systems Design

Research has suggested that when instructional materials follow a series of practices identified as instructional systems design (ISD), improvement in the learning of students using those materials can be expected (Merrill, Kowallis, & Wilson, 1981; Montague, Ellis, & Wulfeck, 1981). Such ISD procedures include having clearly specified instructional objectives, sharing these with students, designing instruction to master the objectives, as well as developing formative and summative evaluation instruments to monitor the degree to which the goals have been attained. Other ISD practices also involve specifying criteria for the attainment of competence, and developing formative evaluation instruments which permit students to loop back for additional instructional cycles if objectives have not been attained to some satisfactory criterion. The Instructional Quality Inventory (Wulfeck et al., 1978) provides a checklist permitting evaluation of the quality of instructional materials, and the degree to which ISD procedures have been systematically followed in their development.

Educational psychologists could inform administrators and teachers of these practices and give specific examples of how they can be applied within the particular setting. They could also act as consultants in the development of instructional materials to suggest that ISD procedures are followed. Furthermore, educational psychologists could also assume a role in evaluating materials created, or acquired by schools to determine whether ISD procedures were used in their development.

Improving Comprehension

If students graduate from school and can not adequately understand what they read, their future is likely to be dim. Advancement in society at any level demands being able to comprehend what is read. Improving students' comprehension is, therefore, an important aim at all educational levels. A case can be made for the proposition that reading comprehension is one of the major objectives of education at the primary level. Poor comprehension inevitably leads to a cycle of increasing and deepening failure at upper school levels, since students with poor comprehension will, obviously, do poorly in all academic fields (Beaugrande, 1984; Mason, 1984; Spreen, 1982). Teaching students effective comprehension skills is, then, a critically important school objective. Two areas of research in educational psychology bear directly on the improvement of comprehension, and suggest avenues by which educational school psychologists can have an important impact in improving students' understanding of their reading. These areas are the use of adjunct questions and metacognitive training.

Adjunct Questions.   A substantial amount of research, reviewed by R. C. Anderson and Biddle (1975), and by others (Hamilton, 1985; Rickards, 1979) indicates that asking students questions about what they have read improves the recall and comprehension of material related to the questions. While there are qualifications about this research, such as the placement of questions (Frase, 1968), their abstractness, and the degree to which they are literal or paraphrased repetitions of the text on which they are based (R.C. Anderson, 1972), the generalization that adjunct questions facilitate the learning of content related to the question is remarkably robust (T.H. Anderson, 1980; Andre, 1979; Rickards, 1979; Rothkopf & Bibiscos, 1967).

Educational school psychologists could instruct teachers in the preparation of questions of text passages assigned to students. These questions could be about homework, seatwork, or any other reading assignments students have to master. Preparing such questions for the most important content is one relatively easy way by which recall and comprehension of this subject matter can be facilitated.

Metacognition.   Metacognition is defined as individuals' monitoring of their knowledge gathering activities (Baker & Brown, 1984; Brown, 1980; Flavell, 1979). With respect to reading comprehension, metacognition refers to students' ability to monitor how well they understand what they read. A substantial amount of research has indicated that both poorer readers, as well as younger readers may not have effective metacognitive strategies to monitor their own comprehension (Brown, 1980; Brown, Armbruster, & Baker, in press; Garner & Kraus, 1981–1982; Markman, 1977).

Recent research (Brown, Palincsar, & Armbruster, 1984; Palincsar & Brown, 1984) has indicated that it is possible to teach students metacognitive strategies to improve their comprehension. Furthermore, there is some evidence that such training generalizes to other tasks (Stevens, 1984). Clearly, educational psychologists could do a great deal to help teachers instruct students in appropriate metacognitive strategies and thus improve their reading comprehension.

Evaluation

Virtually all schools employ some standardized achievement tests. Generally, these are most likely to be norm referenced instruments whose major purpose is to compare the achievement of students to some norm group. Norm referenced tests provide important information for educational administrators at the federal, state, and local levels. They are, however, of limited utility for instructional purposes because they generally do not specify the students' present skills, so that teachers can determine which skills still have to be taught. Nevertheless, students are routinely described by teachers in terms of norm referenced test scores, especially scores derived from grade equivalent norms, despite their well-known limitations.

More useful information for teachers is obtained from either criterion referenced (Berk, 1980; Popham, 1981), or diagnostic tests which are designed to determine students' mastery of particular objectives or skills, instead of comparing them to a norm group. Such information is needed to make effective instructional plans for students. Recently, some widely used norm-referenced tests, such as the California Achievement battery (1978) have attempted to serve both purposes. That is, in addition to comparing students to a norm group, test items are clustered into skill areas, and subtest scores for each area provided. Despite this improvement, teachers tend to emphasize students' grade equivalent scores, rather than criterion referenced information. Many undergraduate and graduate educational psychology courses stress the limitations of norm referenced tests, and the various scores derived from them. Nevertheless, visitors to any school will find teachers who can describe students' grade equivalent scores in most areas, but have a much hazier notion regarding the objectives mastered by students and those which require further instruction.

Educational psychologists could work with teachers to demonstrate the usefulness of criterion referenced tests in planning instructional programs for particular students. Rather than merely instructing teachers (such instruction has obviously had little success despite being covered in many educational psychology courses), workshops and individual conferences with teachers could be scheduled to discuss specific students' learning problems. Such occasions provide opportunities for vivid demonstrations of how little specific information is provided by norm referenced test scores, and how useful criterion referenced tests can be in identifying students' strengths and weaknesses. Demonstrations of the advantages and weaknesses of the two types of scores in planning appropriate interventions could also be given. Conducting such activities in schools may be more effective than in college courses, since the problems of specific students can be clarified and, hopefully, teachers' can realize how little useful information for instructional planning is provided by criterion referenced tests.

Computer Assisted Instruction

The increasing reliance on microcomputers in society is well documented. It may be hard to realize that personal computers have only been sold fairly recently. In January 1975 the first advertisement for a microcomputer kit was published. The first computer store opened in July 1975, and by 1976 there were 56 such stores, and nearly 500 by 1977 (Kinne, 1982). The total factory value of microcomputers sold in 1981 was 1.6 million and by 1983 this figure had risen to an incredible 5.4 billion (Tobias, 1985b). This microcomputer boom has generated enormous pressure for the increased utilization of computers for instructional purposes in schools, homes, and industry.

Virtually all schools have at least some computer assisted instruction (CAI). Becker (1983) surveyed a nationally representative sample of American schools and found that 53% had at least one microcomputer, as did 91% of the secondary schools with more than 1200 students and many had a number of machines for CAI. Unfortunately, CAI in schools is hardly imaginative or exciting and often consists of little more than electronic page turning, i.e., using computers for instructional purposes which could as easily have been accomplished without computers. Becker's (1983) survey also found that drill and practice (e.g., drill ing students on arithmetic computation) is the predominant CAI mode in most schools. Computer literacy and computer programming (mainly BASIC and/or LOGO) were found to be the two subjects most frequently taught via CAI in schools, despite the fact that there is considerable doubt (Bork, 1982; Tobias, 1984a) regarding the utility of teaching students BASIC.

There are many innovative CAI applications (Sleeman & Brown, 1982) using the potential of computers to deliver instruction which can not be accomplished in other ways. For example, intelligent tutoring systems (Sleeman & Brown, 1982) have been devised in which students can be taught well-defined subjects by computer, and many programs are available which simulate the application of scientific principles. Unfortunately, there is little use of such sophisticated CAI in schools, nor is there much use of word processing so that students might learn that making revisions to improve their writing can be a relatively painless process.

Research (Shavelson, 1984) has indicated that there are very few teachers with adequate knowledge about CAI to help their colleagues use computers more imaginatively. Furthermore, even teachers who have learned to program for CAI are most likely to develop additional drill and practice materials which, often, do little more than display multiple choice tests on microcomputers (Tobias, 1984b). Thus, there is an important need to implement more innovative CAI in schools, since even the tiny percentage of teachers who are knowledgeable about computers may know little about more innovative CAI applications.

Schools should also introduce computer managed instruction, in which formative evaluation and instructional sequencing is conducted with the help of computers while learning and teaching occur without computer assistance. Furthermore, the importance of integrating student learning on computers into the total curriculum is a frequently overlooked concern in schools. Experience indicates that students' work on computers often is not reported back to the teacher and, therefore, does not become a part of the curriculum (Tobias, 1985b). Clearly, educational psychologists with training in both instructional design and CAI could enlarge the perspectives of educators to more imaginative and varied instruction which can be delivered by computer.

Test Anxiety Reduction and Study Skills Training

Research (Allen, Elias, & Zlotlow, 1980) has indicated that a variety of test anxiety reduction techniques are effective in decreasing the fear of evaluation so prevalent in schools. Hill (1984) estimated that there are likely to be two or three highly test-anxious students in typical grade 1–12 classrooms, and a total of 4 to 5 million such students nationally. Another 5 million students were thought to have a "significant problem" with test anxiety. Hill found that the impact of test anxiety on achievement test scores increased with age, from correlations of -.20 in 4th grade, to -.40 in 6th grade, to a substantial -.60 in 11th grade. Hill also found that some easily implemented procedures may reduce the debilitating effects of test anxiety. Similarly, Sarason (1987) has indicated that relatively simple directions to students can go a long way towards reducing the debilitating effect of test anxiety on performance.

Research findings indicate that reductions in self-reports of anxiety (Allen et al., 1980; Denney, 1980) are not necessarily accompanied by improvements in cognitive performance. A number of researchers have suggested (Culler & Holahan, 1980; Kirkland & Hollandsworth, 1979, 1980) that what appears to be interference by test anxiety during evaluation may actually be caused by inadequate acquisition due to defective study or test taking skills. It has been suggested (Tobias, 1985c) that the effects of both test anxiety and study skills can be conceptualized as complementary in that the cognitive representation of test anxiety absorbs some portion of students' cognitive capacity leaving less available capacity to devote to task demands. Similarly, good study or test taking skills may reduce the cognitive demands of tasks, enabling students with sound study skills to function more effectively, since less cognitive capacity is required for learning. Naveh-Benjamin (1985) found anxiety reduction training to be most effective for test anxious students with good study skills, and skills instruction most effective for those lacking effective study skills. Further research is clearly required to determine whether test anxiety reduction or study skills training programs are most effective, and what mix of these programs are optimal for different students. Nevertheless, a reasonable interpretation of the available evidence is that both approaches are important in improving student performance.

Clearly, this is an important area of impact for educational school psychologists. Study skills training programs (Dansereau, 1984; McKeachie, 1984) have shown that school performance can be improved by teaching students such skills. As indicated above, test anxiety reduction has been shown to decrease student's reported fear of evaluation. It can safely be assumed that the intense activity in this field will lead to more effective intervention strategies in the near future. While the specific type of applications in this area are presently somewhat vague, more effective intervention strategies are likely to become available in the next few years and form another important area for intervention by educational psychologists.

NEW ROLES IN BUSINESS, INDUSTRY, AND GOVERNMENT AGENCIES

New roles for educational psychologists outside of schools can be suggested by reviewing the implications of some demographic data and the expectations of futurists. These roles were suggested by projects conducted in New York State (Tobias, 1977, 1978, 1980, 1981; Statewide Business Education Review Committee, 1979; Statetewide Health Occupations Education Review Committee, 1982) in which curricula in a number of vocational education programs were revised from a futurist perspective. This perspective seemed especially applicable to vocational education, since teaching secondary school students marketable skills is a major aim of such programs. If curricula were altered to include skills needed at the time the revision process was initiated, they might be obsolete by the time the new curriculum was implemented. Therefore, these projects examined futurist scenarios and demographic data to project societal needs at the beginning of the 21st Century. Extrapolations from these data were then made to recommend changes in vocational education programs to meet the emerging needs.

The model of projecting future needs also has applicability to educational psychology. It is appropriate for the profession in general, and for doctoral programs in particular, to be more concerned about the employability of educational psychologists than they have been. As noted above, since the traditional academic jobs for educational psychologists are now, and will continue to be in short supply (Newsome & Stillwell, 1985; Department of Labor, 1982, p. 129) it becomes vital to envision newer roles, so that students can find productive employment upon graduation.

Demographic Trends

Some major demographic trends are pertinent to this discussion. Much has been made of the post World War II baby boom, referring to the huge increase in the birth rate by 1947 (Bureau of Census, 1976, p. 51) compared to 1946. The boom resulted in overcrowding and split sessions in our elementary and secondary schools in the 1950s, and in the expansion of higher education in the early 1960s. The boom was followed by a "baby bust" in which the birth rate declined sharply, resulting in contraction and retrenchment in schools and colleges by the late 1970s and early 1980s.

Children from the baby boom are now begining to enter their forties. In this decade, demands for medical services typically double (Statewide Health Occupations Review Committee, 1982) compared to earlier periods. The increased need for health services will persist as the baby boomers continue to age. These data are examples of a more general trend—the aging United States population.

Approximately 14.8% of Americans (Bureau of the Census, 1984, p. 8) are likely to be 65-years-old, and presumably retired, by the year 2000. An equally important demographic phenomenon has been the increasing presence of women in the labor force. Estimates are that by 1990 73% of the women will be in the American work force (Department of Labor, 1982).

The demographic data described above have some important implications for educational psychology. The greater need for medical services suggests that the education of medical and allied health personnel will continue to be an area of intense activity. Educational psychologists have been employed in medical schools for some time, filling roles in such areas as research design, consultation, program evaluation, and in the development of instructional materials. The data described earlier suggest that this trend can be expected to increase in the next few years.

New Roles in Medical and Allied Health Contexts.   In addition to medical school settings, however, the aging population, and the greater need for medical services also suggest some new roles for educational psychologists. Alternatives to the medical model, which emphasizes sick care (Garfield, 1979), are being formulated. One of these, referred to as the wellness model (Equitable, undated; Goldbeck, 1980; Department of Health Education and Welfare (HEW), 1978), involves monitoring health by obtaining physiological fitness indices and processing these with the aid of computers to formulate plans designed to maintain and enhance people's health. In addition to monitoring health, wellness programs offer educational services including instruction in such areas as weight control, nutrition, the importance of exercise, reduction of substance abuse (e.g., tobacco, alcohol, and drugs), and stress management (Equitable, undated; Luoto, 1983).

The instructional components of wellness programs have much to gain from the development and implementation of educational materials prepared according to ISD recommendations. Clearly, this is an area where educational psychologists with specialization in human learning and instruction have a great deal to offer. Not only can such training be useful in materials development, but important research is needed to understand how instructional interventions can be designed to alter habits which have proven resistant to change.

As already mentioned, health maintenance and prevention programs, rather than treatment, have the most significant impact on public health. The US Surgeon General's report (HEW, 1979) also reflected this fact by emphasizing that improvements in American health will be made mainly through disease prevention and health promotion programs. In order to be effective, such programs must have major instructional components to which educational psychologists can make a major contribution. In addition to presenting research opportunities, the solution of some of these problems can have vitally important positive implications for health. There is a great need for such programs in school health education courses. For example, the incidence of smoking among male teenagers has dropped from 14.7% in 1968 to 10.7% in 1979, while that of female teens has increased in the same time from 8.4% to 12.7% (Luoto, 1983). One objective of the Department of Health and Human Services (1983) is to reduce the smoking rate to less than 6% among young people. Presumably, the elimination of cigarette smoking can be facilitated by smoking reduction among students in elementary and secondary schools. Concerns such as these are likely to be addressed in the schools of the 21st Century, and educational psychologists should be in the forefront of such efforts by assuming research and evaluation roles, as well as in materials and program development functions.

The aging population also offers other opportunities for educational psychologists. Obviously, such graduate programs with specializations in human development might add offerings in life-span developmental psychology (Havighurst, 1981), including the gerontological area. While other specialties serve this population, educational psychologists might make unique contributions in a number of areas. Specifically, research examining optimal instructional approaches for retired people is one obvious possibility. Such instruction offers a special vantage point for the study of intrinsic motivation since retired individuals are unlikely to study subjects merely for extrinsic reasons. Furthermore, the relationship between learning in older individuals, compared to earlier periods in their life would also be of obvious interest. Equally valuable would be studies of mental ability and its relationship to prior learning indices such as grades in elementary, secondary, and postsecondary schooling. Research on the development of effective instruction to deal with problems occurring as a consequence of retirement would also be of interest.

Some other job opportunities for educational psychologists become available as a consequence of the aging American population. Estimates suggest that medical care in the United States is likely to shift from an emphasis on acute intensive treatment to concentrating on long term chronic care (Statewide Health Occupations Education Committee, 1982). In the latter category will be illnesses, such as the family of arthritis conditions and similar disease entities, in which the major aim is to adjust to long-term disability, rather than to cure it.

Chronic diseases offer other types of challenges and opportunities to educational psychologists. The challenges include understanding the implications of such conditions from the perspective of life span developmental psychology (Havighurst, 1981). Educational psychology programs with concentrations in human development could focus attention on concerns in the second half of the average life span. Greater understanding of the psychological changes occurring in that period will clarify the impact that chronic diseases are likely to have on an older population. Educational psychologists specializing in instruction could participate in the preparation of materials enabling afflicted individuals to adjust to such diseases. Such materials could also aim to teach the chronically ill to exercise caution in evaluating the many panaceas offered by the unscrupulous to a population desperately searching for nonexistent cures.

The shift to a concern with chronic diseases also involves important challenges for the education of medical and allied health personnel. Lifelong care for a disabled, older population places heavy emphasis on kind, patient, and humane treatment (Statewide Health Occupations Education Review Committee, 1982). It can be expected that educating personnel to render such care is likely to be a much more difficult task than training them to administer new medications or to operate elaborate new technological equipment. Teaching medical and allied health personnel to deal with these conditions offers an important challenge to educational psychologists which, again, has both research and service implications. Research needs to identify effective methods to teach human relations techniques so that staff and patients might adapt to the need for life-long care, including the types of personal attention which are not easily rendered by one adult to another. The development of such materials will be an impressive accomplishment for both the aging population and those whose job it is to care for them.

New Roles in Day-Care Contexts.   The increasing presence of women in the work force also has important implications for educational psychology. This trend suggests that there will be increased demands to provide day care for the children of the escalating percentage of working mothers. One can anticipate a continuing increase in such facilities at employment sites in large organizations, in addition to day care offered in proximity to the homes of families with young children. These trends suggest that educational psychology programs with specializations in developmental psychology should stress roles to be assumed in day care facilities by their graduates. For example, educational psychologists can assume leadership roles in the development and administration of day-care centers, in addition to undertaking responsibility for the training of day-care workers and for conducting program evaluations. The applied concerns of educational psychology in general, and the potential bridge between the day-care movement and preschool education suggests that educational psychologists are in a unique position to become actively involved in the day care movement in order to offer something that can truly be called early childhood education, as opposed to the child care services often rendered in such settings.

Futurist Scenarios

The expectations of futurists range from wild-eyed predictions inducing skepticism among many, to relatively reasonable projections of future trends. Among the latter are Toffler's (1980) expectations that the advent of powerful broadcasting and data processing capabilities are likely to lead to major changes in our society. Prominent among these is a tendency to decentralization. Toffler reasoned that large metropolitan complexes were required so that employers would have ready access to a labor pool. Technological changes make such proximity much less important, leading to a reduction in centralization of business and industry and greater concern with the quality of life.

The rapid pace of change in society can, in large part, be attributed to the increasing influence of computers. As indicated above, microcomputers have assumed an extremely important role in all areas of society in a very short time. It can be estimated that decentralization and technological change will continue to alter the duties and responsibilities of the work force for the foreseeable future.

The speed with which society is changing suggests that there will be an incredible need for training and retraining so that workers can cope effectively with new duties. This is likely to affect both the private and public sectors of the economy. As new equipment becomes available, operating that equipment, and altering the responsibilities of personnel will demand a major training effort within the next 20 years. These considerations suggest that the opportunities for individuals with ISD expertise will expand dramatically.

It is well known that small consulting companies preparing such training materials are quite a growth industry. It can be expected that the growing demand for such instruction will substantially increase both the number of training departments in larger organizations, as well as the consulting firms preparing such materials. Conversations with both employers and staff indicate that the materials available for retraining are frequently repetitive, boring, and inefficient. Potential employment for educational psychologists, who have course and practical experience with the development of instructional materials, in these areas is substantial.

An estimate of the training budget in the Department of Defense may be instructive in this context. The total expenditure for individuals in school based training in the Defense Department for fiscal year 1985 is $17.9 billion (Assistant Secretary of Defense, 1984). It should be noted that this figure is based on individualized training in school based programs, but does *not* include training in the field. The budget is somewhat inflated by the fact that the salaries of those receiving training are included in this estimate, as they are in all training programs except those in elementary, secondary, undergraduate, and graduate schools. It can be estimated that the salaries of those receiving training may cost 3 billion dollars leaving a total defense training budget of $14.9 billion for the remaining training costs. This figure includes capital costs for facilities and equipment, salaries of individuals supplying the training, and for research and development efforts in these areas. While the size of the defense training budget is unlikely to be equaled by any single industry in the United States, it can be multiplied many times when the costs of providing training for the next 20 years are projected for the entire private sector.

Clearly, training is an area of major expansion for educational psychologists on which graduate programs should capitalize. A number of university programs in instructional design have sprung up largely separate from traditional educational psychology offerings. Local considerations may well have contributed to the separation of the programs in various universities. It is clear that this is unfortunate since good training in instructional design demands a solid background in human learning, as well as in quantitative and evaluative techniques, surely the staples of most educational psychology programs. It would seem important, though, to assure that subspecializations in the development and evaluation of instructional materials be maintained within educational psychology for both the welfare of those programs, and the adequacy of training to be offered to future instructional designers.

The demand for the development of instructional materials is accompanied by interesting research problems. Investigations will be needed to determine the type of variables that make people either resistant to change, or lead them to welcome it, since the advent of new technology will make one thing quite certain: the responsibilities of various individuals will change, often dramatically. Research to determine the types of instructional techniques which are most likely to enable people to change and the degree to which learner characteristics such as anxiety, locus of control, and originality interact with the ability to change may well be of interest.

A subspecialty for the preparation of training and instructional materials using CAI can be envisioned. Many of the comments made about the failure to use CAI more imaginatively in schools apply to CAI in business and industry as well. On the other hand, industrial training needs lend themselves readily to more sophisticated CAI since some knotty concerns about instructional objectives are less of a problem than they are schools. For example, consensus can more easily be achieved on the goals to be attained by computer simulations of expensive new equipment than by simulations of laws in the social or behavioral sciences. Educational psychologists are in an ideal position to fill roles in the areas of design, evaluation, and development of CAI materials in business, industry, the military, and the government in general.

GENERAL DISCUSSION

A number of new roles have been described that can be assumed by educational psychologists in schools and, more generally in the private and public sector of the society. These were derived from the need to improve the effectiveness of schools, as well as from demographic data and futurists' expectations. As indicated previously, these roles should be considered only a small sample of the new positions that could be assumed by educational psychologists. Many additional roles could have been suggested for which there is substantial research support. These include instruction in learning strategies (Pressley & Levin, 1983), and the possibility of training students in some of the psychological processes of which intelligence is composed (Detterman & Sternberg, 1982; Sternberg, in press). Jones (1985) and Baker (1985) suggested new roles for educational psychologists in curriculum development and in publishing. Finally, some of the activities described, especially those dealing with behavior modification (Sulzer-Azaroff & Reese, 1982), are already being discharged by psychologists working in schools and in the private sector.

The enormous research activity in the general area of cognitive approaches to instruction suggests that some of the procedures by which educational psychologists can discharge the roles described above will probably change considerably in the next few years. Such change is likely because continuing research will probably modify the implications of some of the procedures suggested above, alter others, as well as develop new, more powerful, and more effective interventions which may well replace some of those outlined above.

The roles described demand an unusual breadth of knowledge. Obviously, every educational psychologist can not be equally competent in areas as diverse as instructional systems design, test anxiety reduction, CAI, or metacognition. As roles for educational psychologists within schools multiply, they can exchange services in areas of special competence across schools, or districts so that schools may be served in a variety of these fields. In business, industry, and the government institutional size and needs will determine the number of psychologists needed by a particular institution and their specialties. In smaller settings, psychologists may be retained either as consultants, or on a part time basis. On the other hand, whole educational psychology departments can be envisioned in larger institutions.

The roles described are dynamic in the sense that they mediate between the demands for solutions to very real problems on the one hand and a continually changing body of knowledge on the other. The strength of the research support for the various roles described above varies continually as the knowledge base on which they are based changes. In addition to having an advanced level of professional training, educational psychologist will have to actively monitor new research developments in order to keep abreast of changes in their field. They will also have to conduct research to determine the suitability of various techniques for their particular environment, much as suggested by Cronbach (1975).

Relationship to Consultative Models

Many of the functions within schools outlined above can be considered to be an expansion of the consulting responsibilities initially advocated for school psychologists by Bardon (1963). Consultation roles to be assumed by school psychologists in educational settings have received increasing attention (Alpert & Meyers, 1983; Bardon, 1983a, 1983b; Lambert, 1983a, 1983b; Meyers, 1984; Rosenfield, 1984). Meyers (1973) described a multilevel consultative model for schools varying in terms of the directness of service to students. The functions described here would be considered the least direct form of student assistance, and could be accommodated in Meyers' category of direct service to the school.

A basic approach in most consultative models is to establish an equal relationship between the psychologist and client. Where the activities suggested above can be discharged in one-to-one conferences, an equal consultative relationship can be maintained. Some of the procedures imply that the psychologist assume an instructional function which is somewhat different from that recommended by consultative models. However, once the instructional function has been concluded there is no reason why an equal consultative role can not be resumed.

Training

Many of the activities described above demand a blend of knowledge about recent developments in developmental and cognitive instructional psychology. By virtue of their education and experience educational psychologists would seem to be in ideal positions to assume these new roles, though additional training in a number of areas may be necessary to discharge these roles effectively. Many of the roles require training and experience in consultation. As indicated above, school psychologists have taken leading roles in proposing a variety of school consultation models (Alpert & Meyers, 1983; Lambert, 1983a; Meyers, 1973, 1984; Rosenfield, 1984) which may have application in non-school settings as well. Educational psychologists have much to learn from school psychologists regarding effective functioning in consultative roles, as well as in helping administrators implement the suggestions made earlier.

The activities suggested above demand familiarity with the educational psychology literature describing the knowledge base for the various intervention strategies. In order to be effective in these new roles educational psychologist will also need to acquire techniques to implement them optimally. Although knowledge of the material can readily be acquired in various courses, Lambert (1983b) notes that "Skill in the application of psychological principles to educational practice does not happen automatically as a result of coursework, field experiences or internships, nor simply as a process of maturation" (p. 5). Lambert described a training sequence for school psychologists in which the ability to design instructional approaches and other interventions is at the top of a series of experiences. She suggested, that in order for psychology to be applied to the solution of real problems a broad base of theoretical and empirical experiences were necessary.

As experience with the implementation of these strategies accumulates, comparisons of different training programs will identify the optimal ways to prepare educational psychologists for the roles outlined above. Perhaps some combination of written work, supervised field experiences, and modeling techniques may turn out to be the best way to train individuals in the functions described above. The new roles within schools have been called educational school psychology (Tobias, 1984), as they require a combination of the functions traditionally discharged by educational and school psychologists. Conceivably the training for these new functions would consist of some combination of offerings in educational and school psychology. Because school psychology programs are generally closely affiliated with educational psychology departments, both specialties can cooperate for their mutual benefit in developing appropriate training for the procedures described above.

It is hoped that these considerations will be discussed by faculties in various graduate programs, with a view towards beginning the process of curriculum change to prepare for the roles described. While there is resistance to change in all environments, colleagues in academia are especially well known for avoiding change, and for the formidable rationale they can offer to maintain the status quo. It is hoped that some of the developemnts described here will assist some individuals to assume the role of change agents. Such brave people can start to convince their colleagues, on the many layers of committees by which universities protect themselves from change, about the necessity of moving along some of the lines suggested above in the very near future.

ACKNOWLEDGMENT

This chapter represents an integration of ideas described previously in several papers (Tobias, 1984b, 1985a). Preparation of this paper was facilitated by a grant from the Control Data Corporation.

REFERENCES

Allen, G. J., Elias, M. J., & Zlotlow, S. R. (1980). Behavioral interventions for alleviating test anxiety: A methodological overview of current therapeutic practices. In I. G. Sarason (Ed.), *Test anxiety: theory, research, and applications* (pp. 155–185). Hillsdale, NJ: Lawrence Erlbaum Associates.

Alpert, J. L., & Meyers, J. (1983). *Training in consultation.* Springfield, IL: Charles C. Thomas.

Anderson, L. M., Evertson, C. M., & Brophy, J. E. (1979). An experimental study of effective teaching in first grade reading groups. *Elementary School Journal, 79,* 193–222.

Anderson, R. C. (1972). How to construct achievement tests to assess comprehension. *Review of Educational Research, 42,* 145–170.

Anderson, R. C., & Biddle, W. B. (1975). On asking people questions about what they are reading. In G. H. Bower (Ed.), *The psychology of learning and motivation* (Vol. 9, pp. 89–133). New York: Academic Press.

Anderson, T. H. (1980). Study Strategies and adjunct aids. In R. J. Spiro, B. C. Bruce, & W. F. Brewer (Eds.), *Theoretical issues in reading comprehension* (pp. 483–502). Hillsdale, NJ: Lawrence Erlbaum Associates.

Andre, T. (1979). Does answering higher-level questions while reading facilitate productive learning? *Review of Educational Research, 49,* 280–318.

Assistant Secretary of Defense. (1984). *Military manpower training report for FY 1985. Volume IV: Force readiness report.* Washington, DC: Department of Defense.

Backstrand, G. (1980). *Resources, society and future.* Elmsford, NY: Pergamon.

Baker, L., & Brown, A. L. (1984). Metacognitive skills and reading. In P. D. Pearson (Ed.), *Handbook of reading research* (pp. 353–394). New York: Longman.

Baker, R. F. (1985). Preparing graduates for careers in publishing: A publisher's perspective. *Educational Psychologist 20,* 102–106.

Bardon, J. (1963). Mental health education: A framework for psycho-psychological services in the schools. *Journal of School Psychology, 1,* 20–27.

Bardon, J. (1983a). Psychology applied to education: A specialty in search of an identity. *American Psychologist, 38,* 185–196.

Bardon, J. (1983b, August). *Some actual and potential relationships between education and school psychology.* Paper presented at the annual convention of the American Psychological Association, Anaheim, CA.

Barton, E. J. (1982). Classroom sharing: A critical analysis of assessment facilitation, and generalization procedures. In M. Hersen, R. M. Eisler, & P. M. Miller (Eds.), *Progress in Behavior Modification, 13,* 2–50.

Beaugrande, R. de (1984). Learning to read versus reading to learn: A discourse processing approach. In H. Mandl, N. L. Stein, & T. Trabasso (Eds.), *Learning and comprehension of text* (pp. 159–192). Hillsdale, NJ: Lawrence Erlbaum Associates.

Becker, H. J. (1983, October). *School uses of microcomputers* (Issue No. 3). Baltimore, MD: John Hopkins University, Center for Social Organization of Schools.

Berk, R. (Ed.). (1980). *Criterion-referenced testing: State of the art.* Baltimore, MD: John Hopkins University Press.

Berliner, D. C. (1983, September). *The classroom as a meeting site for educational and school psychology.* Paper presented at the annual convention of the American Psychological Association, Anaheim, CA.

Berliner, D. C. (in press). The clinical educational psychologist: Scientist and practitioner. In J. R. Bergan (Ed.), *School psychology in contemporary society.* Columbus, Ohio: Charles E. Merrill.

Bork, A. (1982, July). *The microcomputer revolution. The computer: Extension of the human mind* (pp. 12–29). Conference proceedings. University of Oregon, College of Education.

Brophy, J. E., & Good, T. L. (1986). Teacher behavior and student achievement. In M. C. Wittrock, (Ed.) *Handbook of research on teaching* (3rd ed., pp. 328–375). New York: Macmillan.

Brown, A. L. (1980). Metacognitive development and reading. In R. J. Spiro, B. Bruce, & W. Brewer (Eds.), *Theoretical issues in reading comprehension* (pp. 453–481). Hillsdale, NJ: Lawrence Erlbaum Associates.

Brown, A. L., Armbruster, B. B., & Baker, L. (in press). The role of metacognition in reading and studying. In J. Orasanu (Ed.), *Reading Comprehension: From research to practice.* Hillsdale, NJ: Lawrence Erlbaum Associates.

Bureau of The Census. (1976). *Historical statistics of The United States: Colonial times to 1970* (Bicentennial ed., Part 1, House Document No. 93–78). Washington, DC: U.S. Government Printing Office.

Bureau of The Census. (1984). *Projections of the population of the United States by age, sex, and race: 1983 to 2080.* (Series P-25, No. 952).Washington, DC: U.S. Government Printing Office.

California Achievement Tests, Forms C and D (1978). Monterey, CA: CTB/McGraw-Hill.

Cronbach, L. J. (1975). Beyond the two disciplines of scientific psychology. *American Psychologist, 30,* 116–127.

Culler, R. E., & Holahan, C. (1980). Test taking and academic performance: The effects of study-related behaviors. *Journal of Educational Psychology, 72,* 16–20.

Dansereau, D. F. (1984, April). *Computer-based learning strategy training modules: A progress report.* Paper presented at the annual meeting of the American Educational Research Association, New Orleans, LA.

Denney, D. R. (1980). Self-control approaches to the treatment of test anxiety. In I. G. Sarason (Ed.), *Test anxiety: Theory, research, and applications* (pp. 209–244). Hillsdale, NJ: Lawrence Erlbaum Associates.

Department of Health, Education, and Welfare. (1978). *Disease prevention and health promotion: Federal programs and prospects.* (PHS Publication No. 79–55071 B). Washington, DC: U.S. Government Printing Office.

Department of Health, Education, and Welfare. (1979). *Healthy people: The Surgeon General's report on health promotion and disease prevention.* (PHS Publication No. 79–55071). Washington, DC: U.S. Government Printing Office.

Department of Health and Human Services-Public Health Service. (1983). *Health, United States* (PHS Publication No. 84–1232). Washington, DC: U.S. Government Printing Office.

Department of Labor. (1982). *Occupational outlook handbook* (BLS Bulletin No. 2200). Washington, DC: U.S. Government Printing Office.

Detterman, D. K., & Sternberg, R. J. (1982). *How and how much can intelligence be increased?* Norwood, NJ: Ablex.

Equitable Life Insurance Company. (Undated). *Model for an equitable wellness program.* New York: Author.

Flavell, J. (1979). Metacognition and cognitive monitoring: A new area of cognitive developmental inquiry. *American Psychologist, 34,* 906–911.

Frase, L. T. (1968). Effect of question location, pacing and mode upon retention of prose material. *Journal of Educational Psychology, 59,* 224–249.

Garfield, S. (1979). Health Testing—A new concept of health care delivery. In G. K. Chacko (Ed.), *Health Handbook* (pp. 179–189). New York: North-Holland.

Garner, R., & Kraus, C. (1981–82). Good and poor comprehender differences in knowing and regulating reading behaviors. *Educational Research Quarterly, 6* (4), 5–12.

Goldbeck, W. (Ed.). (1980). *Mental wellness programs for employees.* New York: Springer-Verlag.

Hamilton, R. J. (1985). A framework for the evaluation of the effectiveness of adjunct questions and objectives. *Review of Educational Research, 55,* 47–85.

Havighurst, R. J. (1981). Life-span development and educational psychology. In F. H. Farley & N. J. Gordon (Ed.), *Psychology and education: The state of the union* (pp. 178–200) Berkeley, CA: McCutchan.

Hill, K. (1984, April). *Test anxiety: The interaction of personality and environmental variables in removing a debilitating affect.* Paper presented at the annual meeting of the American Educational Research Association, New Orleans, LA.

Jones, B. F. (1985). Educational Psychologists—Where are You? Reflections of an Educational Psychologist. *Educational Psychologist, 20,* 83–95.

Kazdin, A. E. (1977). *The token economy: A review and evaluation* (pp. 47–110; 197–214; 225–227). New York: Plenum Press.

Kinne, H. C. (1982, July). *The microcomputer revolution. The computer: Extension of the human mind.* Conference Proceedings. Eugene: University of Oregon, College of Education, pp. 86–90.

Kirkland, K., & Hollandsworth, J. (1979). Test anxiety, study skills, and academic performance. *Journal of College Personnel,* 431–435.

Kirkland, K., & Hollandsworth, J. (1980). Effective test taking: Skills-acquisition versus anxiety-reduction techniques. *Journal of Counseling and Clinical Psychology, 48,* 431–439.

Lahey, B. B., & Drabman, R. S. (1981). Behavior modification in the classroom. In W. E. Craighead, A. E. Kazdin, & M. J. Mahoney (Eds.), *Behavior modification.* Boston: Houghton Mifflin.

Lambert, N. M. (1983a). Perspectives on training school-based consultants. In J. L. Alpert & J. Meyers (Eds.), *Training in consultation* (pp. 29–46).Springfield, IL: Charles C.Thomas.

Lambert, N. M. (1983b, August). *The developmental acquisition of the ability to apply educational psychology to school psychology.* Paper presented at the annual convention of the American Pscychological Association, Anaheim, CA.

Levy, H. (1984). The metamorphosis of clinical psychology: Towards a new charter as human services psychology. *American Psychologist, 39,* (5), 46–494.

Luoto, J. (1983). Reducing the health consequences of smoking—A progress report. *Public Health Reports, 98,* 34–39.

Markman, E. M. (1977). Realizing that you don't understand: A preliminary investigation. *Child Development, 48,* 986–992.

Mason, J. M. (1984). Early reading from a developmental perspective. In P. D. Pearson (Ed.), *Handbook of reading research* (pp. 505–543). New York: Longman.

McKeachie, W. J. (1984, August). *Teaching learning strategies.* Invited address presented at the annual convention of the American Psychological Association, Toronto, Canada.

McKeown, T. (1980). *The role of medicine: Dream, mirage or nemesis?* Princeton, NJ: Princeton University Press.

Merrill, M. D., Kowallis, T., & Wilson, B. G. (1981). Instructional design in transition. In F. H. Farley & N. J. Gordon (Eds.), *Psychology and education: The state of the union* (pp. 298–348). Berkeley, CA: McCutchan.

Meyers, J. (1973). A consultation model of school psychological services. *Journal of School Psychology, 11,* 5–15.

Meyers, J. (1984). *New directions for the practice of psychology in schools.* Paper presented at the annual convention of the American Psychological Association, Toronto, Canada.

Montague, W. E., Ellis, J. A., & Wulfeck, W. H. (1981, April). *After years of instructional research do we know more than grandma did about how to teach people?* Paper presented at the annual meeting of the American Educational Research Association, Los Angeles, CA.

Naveh-Benjamin, M. (1985, August). *Test anxiety: Effects of improving study habits and systematic desenisitization.* Paper presented at the annual convention of the American Psychological Association, Los Angeles, CA.

Newsome, T. I., & Stillwell, W. E. (1985). *Employment opportunities on the industrial-academic interface.* Unpublished manuscript, University of Kentucky.

Palincsar, A. S., & Brown, A. L. (1984). Reciprocal teaching of comprehension fostering and comprehension monitoring activities. *Cognition and Instruction, 1,* 117–175.

Popham, W. J. (1981). *Modern educational measurement.* Englewood Cliffs, NJ: Prentice-Hall.

Pressley, M., & Levin, J. (1983). *Cognitive strategy research: Psychological foundations.* New York: Springer.

Rickards, J. P. (1979). Adjunct postquestions in text: A critical review of methods and processes. *Review of Educational Research,49,* 181–196.

Rosenfield, S. (1984, August). *Instructional consultation.* Paper presented at the annual convention of the American Psychological Association, Toronto, Canada.

Rosenshine, B., & Stevens, R. (1986). Teaching functions. In M. C. Wittrock, (Ed.) *Handbook of research on teaching* (3rd ed., pp. 376–391). New York: Macmillan.

Rothkopf, E. Z., & Bibicos, E. E. (1967). Selective facilitative effects of interspersed questions on learning from written material. *Journal of Educational Psychology, 58,* 56–61.

Sarason, I. G. (1987). Test anxiety, cognitive interference, and performance. In R. E. Snow & M. J. Farr (Ed.), *Aptitude, learning, and instruction: Conative and affective process analyses.* (Vol. 3) Hillsdale, NJ: Lawrence Erlbaum Associates.

Scandura, J. M., Frase, L. T., Gagne, R. M., Stolurow, K. A., Stolurow, L. M., & Groen, G. J. (1981). Current status and future directions of educational psychology as a discipline. In F. H. Farley & N. J. Gordon (Eds.), *Psychology and education: The state of the Union* (pp. 367–388). Berkeley, CA: McCutchan.

Shavelson, R. J. (1984). *Patterns of teachers' microcomputer-based mathematics and science instruction.* Paper presented at the annual convention of the American Psychological Association, Toronto, Canada.

Sleeman, D., & Brown, J. S. (1982). *Intelligent tutoring systems.* New York: Academic Press.

Spreen, 0. (1982). Adult outcomes of reading disorders. In R. N. Malatesha & P. G. Aaron (Eds.), *Reading Disorders.* New York: Academic Press.

Statewide Business Education Review Committee. (1979). *Looking towards the future.* New York: City University of New York, Institute for Research and Development in Occupational Education.

Statewide Health Occupations Education Review Committee. (1982). *Looking towards the future in the health occupations.* New York: City University of New York, Institute for Research and Development in Occupational Education.

Sternberg, R. J. (in press). *Understanding and increasing your intelligence.* New York: Harcourt.

Stevens, R. (1984, June). *The effects of strategy training on the identification of the main idea of expository passages.* Unpublished doctoral dissertation, University of Illinois at Urbana.

Sulzer-Azaroff, B., & Reese, E. P. (1982). *Applying behavioral analysis: A program for developing professional competence.* New York: Holt, Rinehart and Winston.

Tobias, S. (1977). *Statewide business education evaluation committee.* New York: City University of New York, Institute for Research and Development in Occupational Education.

Tobias, S. (1978). *Statewide business education evaluation committee.* New York: City University of New York, Institute for Research and Development in Occupational Education.

Tobias, S. (1980). *Examination of the health occupations education curriculum from a futurist perspective: I.* New York: City University of New York, Institute for Research and Development in Occupational Education.

Tobias, S. (1981). *Examination of the health occupations education curriculum fom a futurist perspective: II.* New York: City University of New York, Institute for Research and Development in Occupational Education.

Tobias, S. (1984a). Computers in the classroom. *Contemporary Education Review, 3,* 387–390.

Tobias, S. (1984b, August). *Implications of wellness models for educational and school psychology.* Paper presented at the annual convention of the American Psychological Association, Toronto, Canada.

Tobias, S. (1985a). New directions for educational psychologists. *Educational Psychologist, 20,* 96–101.

Tobias, S. (1985b). Computer assisted instruction. In M. Wang & H. Walberg (Eds.), *Adapting instruction to individual differences.* Berkeley, CA: McCutchan.

Tobias, S. (1985c). Test anxiety: Interference, defective skills, and cognitive capacity. *Educational Psychologist, 20,* 135–142.

Toffler, A. (1980). *The third wave.* New York: Morrow.

Weinstein, C. E., & Mayer, R. E. (1986). The teaching of learning strategies. In M. C. Wittrock (Ed.), *Handbook of research on teaching* (3rd ed, pp. 315–327). New York: Macmillan.

Wulfeck, W. H. II, Ellis, J. A., Richards, R. E., Wood, N. D., & Merill, M. D. (1978, November). *The instructional quality inventory: I Introduction and overview* (NPRDC SR 79–3). San Diego, CA: Navy Personnel Research & Development center.

8 Relations with Other Disciplines

Jack I. Bardon
University of North Carolina at Greensboro

There is optimism about the future of educational psychology. Tobias (1985) believes that "Scientific developments in the field have rarely been more fruitful in terms of theory, research, and applications to educational practice" (p. 96). Jones (1985) thinks that "At no time in American history have there been so many potential job opportunities for educational psychologists" (p. 83). Other leaders in the field also have recently encouraged educational psychologists to expand their horizons; to enlarge the definition of educational psychology; to consider moving from concern for education in schools to education in homes, the workplace, and in business and industry (Rothkopf, 1984; Wittrock, 1985). There is a growing realization that all learning does not and should not take place in schools; that the very conception of education must reach out into the community to take into consideration the effects of television, the media, the family (White & Duker, 1973). As Fantini (1986) noted, "the school is just one component in a series of educative environments in the community. Substantive restructuring requires functional connections between school and nonschool learning environments" (pp. 136–137). Indeed, educational psychology appears to be in the mainstream of exciting new developments leading to an improved and expanded educational enterprise.

There is also pessimism about the future of educational psychology. Membership in the Division of Educational Psychology of the American Psychological Association (APA) is declining and there are fewer students in doctoral programs in educational psychology (Tobias, 1985). The Committee on Employment and Human Resources, APA (1985) reported an overall decline in traditional academic psychologists of 40% as compared with the 1970s with very rapid increase in employment opportunities in organized human service settings

131

and independent practice. Indeed, educational psychology may be "facing a particularly acute paradox" (Tobias, 1985, p. 96).

This chapter is concerned with the inevitable relationships that will take place as educational psychology itself changes. The problems of research and service delivery processes and role delineation and territoriality are likely to intensify and, therefore, deserve explicit attention in a book on the future of educational psychology.

BOUNDARIES, TERRITORIES, IDENTITY, AND DEFINITIONS

A distinction must be made between what individual persons do who are educated as educational psychologists and what others believe is done in the name of "educational psychology." As part of career development many of us become something other than what we started out to be. There are persons from different disciplines, including educational psychology, who are university and college administrators, publishers, industrial consultants, school administrators, and even politicians. There are also persons who are not identified as educational psychologists per se, but who are employed because of their background and competence at whatever it is they are employed to do. Many of these persons are involved in test development, curriculum development, textbook writing and editing, and education and training in professional schools and government service.

The problem of the identity of the field itself is a long standing one that continues unabated. Grinder (1980, chapter 1, this volume), in tracing the growth of educational psychology as reflected in the history of APA's Division of Educational Psychology, pointed out that the discipline has been fought over by different units in the university, seen as an intermediate or "middle-man" field by some and as a theoretical field by others, at times considered as a field of practice and at other times as a body of organized knowledge. It has been cited as a distinct profession in its own right and also as a branch of psychology.

A mixed image of educational psychology continues to plague the discipline. Snow (1981) observed that "Psychology in education has become much bigger than traditional educational psychology, and there seems to be no unifying theme" (p. 1). It has so far failed to find those kinds of distinctive qualities or competencies which have led other disciplines and specialties of disciplines to be more clearly identified as the disciplines or specialties of choice when certain knowledges or skills are wanted. This failure is not necessarily a problem if it does not really matter whether or not there is an educational psychology as distinct from educational research in a broader sense. However. if it does matter—if there is something that educational psychology can do that others cannot do or cannot do as well—then finding those special attributes becomes a high priority for the field. Good productive relations among disciplines and with other specialties in psychology and education are not really possible until there is a clearer notion of the domains of these specialties, their areas of distinctiveness and overlap, and a clearer understanding of their definitions than now exists.

Within the past several years there have been suggestions made about what educational psychology should be; i.e., what problems it should seek to solve and what activities it should engage in to make it a more useful and identifiable discipline. Within an enlarged definition of the field, the scope of its concerns have been said to include continuation of basic research in learning; cognition and instruction; applied research leading to better research design; program evaluation; the development of instructional materials; creating new types of tests and measures of achievement and process-oriented aptitudes; learning strategies; indirect service to others through instruction and training; in-service education; staff development; bilingual education; writing handbooks for parents and staff about special needs of children; preparing effective curricula; and direct service through teaching literacy to children and adults, career and occupational training, training in health care and preventive medicine; and even testing and counseling individual gifted children and offering group guidance activities (Culcross, 1984; Jones, chapter 9, this volume; Rothkropf, 1983, 1984: Tobias, 1985; Weinstein, 1985, and chapter 10, this volume; Wittrock, 1984, 1985).

Because of the well-established tradition of educational psychology as a field of research about education, however defined, there is little likelihood of concern on the part of other disciplines about its involvement in the conduct of research, basic or applied. Relations with others become more sensitive and strained when educational psychologists offer their services as consultants or in indirect or direct service delivery in settings outside of colleges, universities, and funded research and development centers.

Comparison with Other Specialties in Psychology

There is probably less chance of competition or overlap of functions within an expanded educational psychology in work settings in which clinical and counseling psychologists are typically employed. Because of the emphasis in these psychological specialties on psychopathology and adjustment, and because of the rigorous training and education required by these specialties for professional practice, at least at the doctoral level, it is not likely that educational psychology as a field will seriously impinge on the functions already established by these specialties. In the main, clinical psychology and counseling psychologists are employed in universities where they educate and train others to be what they are; to do research on topics related to human pathology and adjustment; and to work in mental health centers, community clinics, and college counseling centers. They are increasingly involved in the private practice of psychotherapy, counseling, and assessment of individuals and groups. Considering what the literature indicates to be the future worksites and activities of educational psychologists, it is probably in medical centers and perhaps in the military, government, and industry that some overlap of functions with counseling and clinical psychologists may take place. To the extent that educational psychology as a field considers career and occupational training and health care and preventive medicine as within its concerns, to that extent will it be considered as moving into areas in which the field of educational psychology has no particular business. However, if within these more constricted areas of research and practice, educational psychology can identify those problems that specifically related to content and process which is educationally or learning based and can offer research and methodology that help clinical and counseling psychologists to do their jobs better, to that extent it can be seen as an ally, an adjunctive specialty, and a noncompetitor.

As education psychology tries to provide knowledge, consultation, and direct services to industry and business, it will come into conflict with the field of industrial/organizational psychology (I/O). Although I/O psychology also is in a state of flux and cannot be considered a unitary specialty, it has more clearly than has educational psychology delineated the functions it performs in industry and business (Howard, 1981). These include some potential areas of overlap with an expanded educational psychology. Employee and executive selection and placement, test validation, training and development, organizational development, career counseling, and quality of worklife are among the areas in which I/O psychology is already established and areas in which educational psychology and its graduates have been encouraged to engage. As educational psychologists move into business and industry, their competencies to engage in these activities are bound to be challenged.

The situation becomes more complicated when a comparison is made between educational and school psychology. The common use of the terms "educational" and "school" as roughly synonymous has added confusion to the general belief that the two fields are identical or at least very similar (Bardon, 1983b). To add further to the confusion, what is called school psychology in the United States and Canada is called educational psychology in other English speaking countries, such as The United Kingdom, Australia, and New Zealand.

Over at least the past 30 years, school psychology has usually been considered a field whose major contribution to schools has been its provision of psychometric testing for the purpose of classifying children for special education. A secondary, but important, contribution has been the offering of clinical psychological services in schools by assisting with the diagnosis, management, and treatment of children suffering from various forms of pathology. Its uniqueness has been its emphasis on how the practice of child clinical psychology is modified by the school setting in which it occurs (Bardon, 1983b). School psychology, closely controlled by state department of education certification and largely determined by the needs of local school districts for immediate service and by state and federal laws and rules and regulations has been service-oriented to a degree unknown in other practitioner areas of psychology (Bardon, 1982).

Not too many years ago, it was possible, without fear of very much contradiction, to distinguish educational psychology from other fields of psychology, including school psychology, in this way:

> Educational psychology . . . is not an applied psychology in the same sense as is school or clinical psychology. Educational psychology studies the characteristics of students and teachers and explores such topics as learning, motivation, reinforcement, transfer, and the conditions that affect them. Typically, the educational psychologist conducts research on the many factors that influence learning with careful control of elements extraneous to the factors or variables being investigated. According to Donald Ross Green (1964), research in educational psychology can usually be conducted far more carefully in laboratory settings than in school settings. The educational psychologist is most frequently concerned with obtaining results that help us understand the processes of teaching and learning. He [sic] seeks data leading to generalizations that can be applied across educational institutions. (Bardon & Bennett, 1974, p. 7)

Increasingly, the descriptions of American school and educational psychology are changing and merging. The characterizations of both fields mentioned above no longer hold to the same extent as they did even 10 years ago. Within the past several years in particular, there has been a strong movement within school psychology to rediscover its educational roots and special purposes (Bardon, 1983a; Meyers, 1985; Myrick, 1986; Pielstick. 1986). It is looking to research in social, developmental, and educational psychology and to applied behavior analysis as the intermediate bodies of knowledge most likely to offer the theory, methodologies, and justification for greater inclusion in curriculum assessment and consultation, in-service education, systems intervention, and evaluation services. At the same time, educational psychology is seeking challenges and opportunities that move it closer to application and service delivery in schools and in education wherever it might be offered. While school psychology is assuming that educational psychology is still what it has been—a research-oriented field that can offer the bases for a revised psychological practice in educational settings or on educational problems—educational psychology seems either to be assuming that school psychology is what it has been in the past or that it does not matter what it is because it is largely ineffective as an educationally-oriented service. Neither field has yet attempted a rapprochement with the other to try to determine boundary lines and ways in which the two can best cooperate toward the improvement of research and practice in and about education.

The Problems to Be Solved

Block (1985) claimed that "Much of what passes for Educational Psychology research is only peripherally related to problems of schooling and education" (p. 4). If there is to be an improved image of educational psychology, if educational psychology is to become an attractive career choice, and if educators and others are deliberately to turn to educational psychology rather than to others for information, ideas, and services, what are the real-life problems its methods and findings can help resolve or ameliorate *that are not now adequately addressed by other specialties in psychology or by other disciplines?* What do other specialties in psychology and other disciplines and fields (school personnel, business and industry, professional schools, etc.) want that they are not now getting from others? The ability of educational psychology to find its special place in relation to other disciplines is dependent on being able to identify these needs and to decide which, if any, and in what ways it can play particular roles in getting these needs met.

There is increasing recognition from outside educational psychology itself that the kinds of research educational psychologists already carry out do matter and that areas often associated or identified with education psychology knowledge may be the bases for understanding and eventually resolving many practical educational problems. Pryzwansky (1981), for example, representing school psychology, pointed out that school services have been hampered by a "lack of unifying concepts and principles that can tie the totality of knowledge together in ways it can be used" (p. 464). Bailey (1984), concerned about interdisciplinary teams in special education, notes that team functioning in education, health, and psychiatric care settings, social work settings, and in rehabilitation psychology suffer from lack of an adequate conceptual model of how group process and group effectiveness operate. Rosenfield (1985), speaking about children with learning problems, cited the importance of psychological research on instruction and cognition for the improvement of instruction. Hayes-Roth and Thorndyke (1985), referring to the use of intelligent computers, acknowledged that "We are rapidly evolving into collections of 'knowledge workers' in which an increasing number of professionals require the assimilation, evaluation, and production of information by skilled specialists" (p. 231), suggesting the need for the kinds of research that inform such specialists. And Meyers (1985), speaking about psychological assessment in schools, said that "Too often *products* are stressed during assessment in a search for IQ scores, percentiles and even grade equivalent scores. Instead, the *process of learning* should be stressed by assessing *how children learn*. Recent work on information processing and metacognition provide an emerging basis for this focus in assessment" (p. 4).

Beyond the need for basic knowledge generated by educational psychology and associated fields, there is a clear call for knowledge that leads more directly to improved practices and services; i.e., for applied research that serves to link research to practice. Some of the concerns raised by educators and education-related practitioners lead to questions that educational psychology may uniquely be prepared to help address. They illustrate the kinds of questions not now satisfactorily resolved that could eventually direct an educational psychology distinct from other psychological specialties and fields.

How do you make research on cognition and instruction palatable to educators so they can use what is known as part of their own efforts? How do you match the tasks assigned to children in classrooms to their instructional levels? How can teachers best develop acceptable learning plans for children? How can teachers be trained to design quality instructional sequences? How can teachers be helped to understand the logic of the tasks they present to children (Rosenfield, 1985)? How do schools manage resources inside the school; e.g., peer tutors, identifying teaching learning styles, using time effectively and efficiently (school time, after-school time, and home time) (Fantini, 1986)? How can the changing roles of school specialists and regular teachers be better managed, considering that different functions, new work stations, more collaboration, and more public activities are now part of the daily life of those who work in schools (Reynolds & Birch, 1982)? Does educational psychology have anything to say about how the processes of learning and teaching occur in settings and situations other than in schools? Can ways be found to make knowledge "hidden in obscure reports and read only by a limited few" (Rothkopf, 1983, p. 4) available to those who can use such knowledge? How do we offer challenges to the "glib nonsense and cant" (Rothkopf, 1984, p. 4) extant in the educational world? What more needs to be known to help those who work directly with teachers, school administrators and many others about such important educational problems as class management, interpersonal communication, basic academic skills, basic life skills, affective/social skills, parental involvement in the education of their children, classroom organization and social structures, systems development and planning, personnel development, individual differences in development and learning, school-community relations, instruction, and multicultural concerns (School Psychology: A Blueprint, 1984)?

As just one example of a relatively small area of school activity in which basic knowledge and translatable applied research knowledge is badly needed, consider the problem of mandated team participation as part of special education throughout the United States. Here are some of the questions raised in the literature about which little is yet known:

What are the structural and process elements of teacher functioning (Pryzwansky, 1981)? How can cooperation among different pupil personnel workers and teachers be increased (DeBoer & Hayes, 1982; Pfeiffer, 1980)? How can parental and regular teachers' involvement in education planning for exceptional children be increased? What diagnostic information is relevant to the team? Can teams be helped to understand and implement the most meaningful educational decisions (Pfeiffer, 1980)? What psychological processes are involved in expediting the referral process, problem solving on teams, monitoring a child's progress, observing in the classroom, networking to share practices? How are these processes applicable to schooling? How well do they work? Under what conditions can they be best used (Division of Exceptional Children, 1985)? What are the core functions of team members and what are the useful differences among them (Gerken & Minney, 1978)?

It may be useful in responding to these questions to recall the continuum from basic knowledge to application or intervention. That continuum might be presented in this way: basic research—research with indirect implications for practice—applied research intended to address particular generalizable problems of education and training—applied research intended to address particular problems within a particular system or setting—self-referent research intended to study how a particular professional group functions—evaluation of the outcomes of practice—the evaluation of the outcomes of a particular intervention—and the actual carrying out of that intervention. At each step on this continuum others are already there doing their research or engaging in their interventions. Where educational psychology research and practice are most applicable; where educational psychology can best work with others who also do research and engage in educational practices is a matter that deserves more attention.

HOW CAN RELATIONSHIPS WITH OTHERS BE IMPROVED?

Relations with other disciplines, researchers, developers, and educators can be furthered best under certain conditions, some of which have already been mentioned or may be inferred from previous comments.

Educational psychology as a discipline should try to avoid relations with other disciplines and psychological specialties which suggest a zero-sum arrangement in which, if one discipline or specialty wins, others lose. It must avoid defining its expanded role in ways which, directly or inadvertently, move into areas already occupied by others.

It should deliberately seek to define and publicize itself within boundaries that indicate how it can be helpful to others. Wittrock (1985) in an essay on enlarging the conception of educational psychology understood this need.

> If it [educational psychology] enlarges its role, many people who apply psychology to the improvement of instruction will join in the study of educational psychology and will begin to share its primary responsibility to further education. In addition, some educators and educational researchers, who are not trained as psychologists, will see the value of educational psychology and will work with educational psychologists in the study and improvement of teaching and instruction. Other people, who are trained as psychologists, will study psychological models in educational settings with a new responsibility to improve education. (p. 1)

Educational psychology should explicate more clearly how it conceives of the entire educational enterprise and make its views known to other disciplines, its own students, and the public at large. While realizing the range and diversity of views within any field, it is still possible to divide issues related to teaching and learning into categories or components which permit others to understand how and where the field intends to place emphasis. For example—and only as one example—it is possible to conceive of the educational spectrum as having at least three major emphases: education, schools, and schooling (Bardon, 1983a).

Education is the broadest of these terms, describing a process of teaching and learning and its results, formal and informal, which is part of the lives of everyone from birth to death. It involves learning that takes place in the family, the church, the media, the workplace, at play, and also, but certainly not exclusively, in schools. Schools in our culture are special places. They are organized, formal, social, instructional, and cultural institutions that share both commonalities in curriculum and methods of instruction and also are affected by federal, state, and local laws and are influenced by the communities and regions in which they are located. They subsume curriculum and instruction but also are highly social, political, and individualized depending on how they are governed, who attends them, how they are funded, and how they interact with the members of the communities in which they exist. Schooling too often is considered to be what actually takes place in school buildings. This conception is much too narrow to be useful. Schooling may better be understood to be a more encompassing term that can be used to describe and understand how persons interact with any setting in which learning is to take place. It is more constructively and heuristically viewed as the interaction between a person who needs to learn something in contact with a person or materials by which such learning takes place in a setting with particular properties (Bardon, 1986).

These three terms, again only as one example, may help to suggest what educational psychology does that makes it unique. It is conceivable that a broad conception of educational psychology might include research related to teaching and learning from birth to death in all the ways and places that education takes play. Research on basic psychological processes and how they are influenced by development and social/cultural factors would fit here.

Educational psychology certainly is concerned with schools, but to limit its scope to curriculum and classroom instruction is to negate the very nature of schools as educational institutions. By enlarging its mission to understand schools as such, it encompasses areas now seeking to identify themselves as something other than they have been. There are areas of social and developmental psychology increasingly concerned with application, and the dividing line between these fields and educational psychology could be better understood by a broader conception of what educational psychology includes. There are roles in schools—individual schools—that are already performed by others; e.g., school psychologists, guidance counselors, curriculum specialists, and special educators who would not welcome still another specialist among them but would welcome the knowledge about schools and the technical and consultation assistance of applied researchers who can help them do their jobs better through interpretation of research and by conduct of research applicable to solving problems in their school buildings. Recognizing these distinctions and boundaries could help to define the field and avoid professional tensions.

A broad conception of what schooling is all about brings technology, methodology, and theories in educational psychology to bear on an interactive process of teacher-learner-environment interaction in all the ways such a triadic arrangement can take place. It does not confine the field to schools alone but allows it to become a discipline central to understanding a major component of human existence, not, to my knowledge, so far considered as within the purview of the research efforts of any particular field or discipline and, in general, sadly neglected. Schooling is also increasingly a major concern of school psychology as well. The two fields, should, together, consider the points of division between those who furnish the knowledge and much of the methodology by which schooling is understood and the application of such knowledge toward the solution of particular problems of schooling, wherever they occur, including evaluation of these applications.

Albee and Loeffler (1971) pointed out years ago, and Kimble (1984) more recently confirmed, that science and practice are not easily reconciled. The value systems of those attracted to research and those attracted to practice are not likely to be the same. As Albee and Loeffler (1971) indicated,

> It is usually difficult and frequently impossible to make the same person into both a scientist and a professional. Science abhors secrecy but professionals must keep their knowledge secret. Differences exist in personality characteristics in individuals attracted to science or to the profession. Training requirements are clearly different. Readiness to participate in social and political action also differentiates the groups. (p. 465)

Yet, in an expanded educational psychology, especially its applied aspects, science and practice must mesh or knowledgeable educational psychologists will be hampered in their attempts to bring their science to bear on the solution of educational problems.

Perhaps a distinction can be made between basic science and applied science, with those attracted to application already in tune with the values of the practitioner. But, even then, basic scientists these days serve as consultants too, and become involved in making their needs and findings known to naive others. How then can educational psychology help its students to "make career choices in the real world of schools and agencies that serve schools" (Jones, 1985, p. 91) and other work settings as well? How can educational psychologists be educated and trained to understand about the settings in which they may be employed, to deal with the people who are there, to deal with people in general, to consult, to handle resistance to change in operating programs?

Such considerations, already part of the education and training of most practitioner psychologists (Peterson, 1976) and very much part of the concerns of educators or psychologists who work in applied settings (Oakland, 1986) should be considered as integral parts of the education and training of any scientist who plans to work with others about the findings of that science. In the intermediate specialty that is educational psychology, it is even more a pressing need if the discipline is to establish good relations with those it serves and those who use its findings and methods.

Educational psychology should try to find better ways to model what it teaches and asks others to do. Weinstein (1985, chapter 10, this volume) pointed out that one way college instructors can help their students to be independent, responsible, and effective learners is to teach learning strategy skills along with content-based curriculum. To do so, the college instructors themselves must demonstrate how it is done. The education of educational psychologists should include those skills, competencies, strategies, and methods that permit students to demonstrate that they mean what they say. Those who preach must practice if they are to be creditable to those they serve and those who work with them. It may no longer be enough to have elegant theory and research methods and even applicable research findings if the delivery system by which theory, methods, and findings is flawed.

As educational psychology strives to become a broader, enriched, and more important discipline in psychology and in education it will have to be concerned not only with what it finds out but with how it presents its findings and how it relates content and method to the work done by others. As has happened in all other disciplines in which research and practice are combined, attention will have to be paid to the packaging (the psychologists) as well as to the contents of the package (the body of knowledge and methods to be called "educational psychology").

REFERENCES

Albee, G. W., & Loeffler, E. (1971). Role conflicts in psychology and their implications for a reevaluation of training models. *The Canadian Psychologist, 12,* 465–481.

Bailey, D. B., Jr. (1984). A triaxial model of the interdisciplinary team and group process. *Exceptional Children, 51,* 17–25.

Bardon, J. I. (1982). The psychology of school psychology. In C. R. Reynolds & T. B. Gutkin (Eds.). *The handbook of school psychology* (pp. 3–14). New York: Wiley.

Bardon, J. I. (1983a). Psychology applied to education: A specialty in search of an identity. *American Psychologist, 38,* 185–196.

Bardon, J. I. (1983b). *Some actual and potential relationships between educational and school psychology.* Paper presented at the meetings of the American Psychological Association, Anaheim, CA.

Bardon, J. I. (1986). Psychology and schooling: The interrelationships among persons, processes, and products. In S. E. Elliott & J. C. Witt (Eds.), *The delivery of psychological services in schools: Concepts, processes and issues* (pp. 53–79). Hillsdale, NJ: Lawrence Erlbaum Associates.

Bardon, J. I., & Bennett, V. C. (1974). *School psychology.* Englewood Cliffs, NJ: Prentice-Hall.

Block, K. K. (1985, June). What is wrong with educational psychology? *NEP, Newsletter for Educational Psychologists,* pp. 4–6.

Committee on Employment and Human Resources, American Psychological Association (1985, December). *The changing face of American Psychology,* washington, D.C.: author.

Culcross, R. R. (1984, June). Career opportunities for educational psychologists: Consulting with a public school's gifted program. *NEP, Newsletter for Educational Psychologists*, p. 4.

DeBoer, G. E., & Hayes, R. L. (1982). The human services educator: A collaborative model for counselors and teachers. *The Personnel and Guidance Journal, 61*, 77–80.

Division for Exceptional Children, North Carolina Department of Public Instruction (1985, April). Teacher support teams. *DEC Report*, p. 1.

Fantini, M. D. (1986). *Regaining excellence in education.* Columbus, OH: Merrill.

Gerken, K. C., & Minney, J. (1978). Erase the lines of demarcation: The counselor, the psychologist, and the assessment process. *Psychology in the Schools, 15*, 397–400.

Green, D. R. (1964). *Educational psychology.* Englewood Cliffs, NJ: Prentice-Hall.

Grinder, R. E. (1980, November). The growth of educational psychology as reflected in the history of Division 15. *Newsletter for Educational Psychologists*, Division 15, American Psychological Association, pp. 5–9.

Hayes-Roth, B., & Thorndyke, P. W. (1985). Paradigms for intelligent systems. *Educational Psychologist, 20*, 231–241.

Howard, A. (1981, August). *Industrial/organizational psychology: How is it like and how is it different from other practice areas?* Paper presented at the meeting of the American Psychological Association, Los Angeles, CA.

Jones, B. F. (1985). Educational psychologist—Where are you? Reflections of an educational psychologist. *Educational Psychologist, 20*, 83–95.

Kimble, G. A. (1984). Psychology's two cultures. *American Psychologist, 39*, 833–839.

Meyers, J. (1985, August). *Diagnosis diagnosed: Twenty years after.* Presidential address, Division of School Psychology, presented at the meetings of the American Psychological Association, Los Angeles, CA.

Myrick, C. C. (1986, June–July). President's message: OK, let's plan . . . but for what? *Communiqué*, National Association of School Psychologists, pp. 1–2.

Oakland, T. D. (1986). Professionalism within school psychology. *Professional School Psychology, 1*, 9–27.

Peterson, D. R. (1976). Is psychology a profession? *American Psychologist, 31*, 572–581.

Pfeiffer, S. I. (1980). The school-based interprofessional team: Recurring problems and some possible solutions. *Journal of School Psychology, 18*, 390–394.

Pielstick, P. N. L. (1986, February). Priorities in school psychology. *Communiqué*, National Association of School Psychologists, p. 2.

Pryzwansky, W. B. (1981). Mandated team participation: Implications for psychologists working in the schools. *Psychology in the Schools, 18*, 460–466.

Reynolds, M. C., & Birch, J. W. (1982). *Teaching exceptional children in all American Schools.* Arlington, VA: Council for Exceptional Children.

Rosenfield, S. (1985, August). *Classroom intervention techniques for children with learning problems.* Paper presented at the meeting of the American Psychological Association, Los Angeles, CA.

Rothkopf, E. Z. (1983, November). Scientific psychology and education: Agenda for tomorrow. *NEP, Newsletter for Educational Psychologist*, p. 1.

Rothkopf, E. Z. (1984, June). President's message: Go west! *NEP Newsletter for Educational Psychologists*, p. 1.

School psychology: A blueprint for training and practice (1984). Minneapolis, MN: National School Psychology Inservice Training Network.

Snow, R. E. (1981, November). On the future of educational psychology. *Newsletter for Educational Psychologists*, Division 15, American Psychological Association, p. 1.

Tobias, S. (1985). New directions for educational psychologists. *Educational Psychologist, 20*, 96–101.

White, M. A., & Duker, J. (1973). *Education: A conceptual and empirical approach.* New York: Holt, Rinehard & Winston.

Weinstein, C. E. (1985). Learning strategies: The flip-side of teaching strategies. *Innovation Abstracts, VII* (19), 2pp.

Wittrock, M. C. (1984, November). New opportunities for educational psychologists. *NEP, Newsletter for Educational Psychologists,* pp. 1 & 2.

Wittrock, M. C. (1985, June). Enlarging the conception of educational psychology. *NEP, Newsletter for Educational Psychologists,* pp. 1–2.

9 Educational Psychologists Where Are You? Toward Closing the Gap Between Research and Practice

Beau Fly Jones
North Central Regional
Educational Laboratory

At no time in American history have there been so many potential job opportunities for educational psychologists. Schools need a variety of services to plan for and implement change toward greater effectiveness. Policy makers are increasingly involved in the reform movement. Teacher education is in the midst of massive political, demographic, and pedagogical changes. There are widespread concerns about how to train administrators to become instructional leaders, given that this is a relatively new role and considering the estimated turnover of principals. Also widespread are concerns about the meaning and uses of the new technology. In spite of this upsurge of activities requiring the research skills and special perspective of educational psychology, many of the decisions about education, both inside and outside schools, seem to be made by persons other than educational psychologists and/or in contexts in which there is little input from educational psychologists.

The main purpose of this paper is to excite prospective educational psychologists to consider a broad range of job opportunities in schools and school-related organizations, most of which apparently do not currently employ educational psychologists as full-time employees, and many of which do not now seek the advice of educational psychologists. Thus, it is not my goal here to provide a systematic analysis of job hierarchies or definitions of job requirements; nor do I supply statistics about career ladders, salaries, and the like. To the contrary, this paper raises questions within the field of educational psychology about its posture toward applied research and educational reform. I was asked to write this chapter from personal experience as well as from research, and I have some strong beliefs about what tasks are important to reform in schools and school-related organizations. Moreover, I am as interested in channeling educational psychologists into those jobs that relate to those tasks as I am concerned about informing educational psychologists about job opportunities.

This paper is divided into three parts. Part 1 discusses what I think are some key tasks in the educational reform movement and how I perceive the interaction among educational researchers, policy makers, and practitioners. Part 2 describes specific occupations that address these key tasks. Part 3 provides some comments regarding the joys and limitations of working in the field full time.

KEY TASKS IN EDUCATIONAL REFORM

A Nation at Risk (National Commission on Excellence in Education, 1983) has provided unprecedented attention to issues of reform for education. Many good things have already emerged as a direct result of the challenge presented by this document and the spate of reports responding to it. The need for increased requirements in math and science and other subject areas and the recent movement toward restructuring teacher education (e.g., Report of the Holmes Group, 1986) are among the most useful and effective outcomes. Nevertheless, some critical substantive issues have been underaddressed or addressed ineffectively, in my opinion. Of these, quality of instruction and issues of equity are outstanding.

Instruction

Instructional Materials, Curriculum, and Assessment.   The recent hue and cry about textbooks and other instructional materials is a case in point. Educational psychologists such as Osborn (1984) show that a staggering amount of instruction in reading is based on commercial textbooks that frequently do not reflect models of learning and instruction (see also Osborn, Jones, & Stein, 1985). Examinations of basal readers (Durkin, 1981), math texts (Nicely, 1985) and other content texts (Anderson & Armbruster, 1984) indicate that, all too often, prose texts are "inconsiderate"—lacking in cohesion, unity, and appropriate organizational patterns—and are therefore difficult to understand. Additionally, instruction focuses on factual recall rather than thinking and application, and the instruction in teacher manuals frequently provides only "mentioning" and drill and practice, rather than sustained instruction on content and procedures.

Policy makers' response to this problem has been mixed. On the one hand, many national and state legislators apparently interpreted this problem as part of a greater one involving "watering down" or "dumbing down" the curriculum. Consequently, their initial response was to launch a rather large-scale campaign to make textbooks more "rigorous" (meaning more difficult) in an attempt to raise the standards. While raising standards may be necessary and effective, doing so without an equivalent attention to instruction may increase the number of failures considerably (Jones, 1986). There is some evidence of this effect already among both students and prospective teachers, especially among minorities (Gifford, 1985: Hodgkinson, 1985; Resnick, 1985).

On the other hand, legislators in several states utilized the focus on textbooks and educational reform to marshal support for substantial changes in curriculum guides and adoption policies that do reflect recent research on textbooks as well as research on instruction. The state of California, for example, has taken the lead in rejecting reading materials that do not have literary quality and key elements of effective instruction, math texts that do not focus on problem solving, and science texts that do not discuss Darwin's theories (see California State Board of Education, 1984, 1985a, 1985b).

Additionally, some nonadoption states have implemented "the new definition of reading" implied in schema theory in curriculum guides (e.g., Wisconsin Department of Public Instruction, 1986) or in new statewide tests such as in Michigan (Wixson & Peters, 1984; see below also). There are also states such as Connecticut which have implemented various research-based plans for teaching and assessing thinking skills, (e.g., S. Leinwand, personal communication, 1986). These states are leading the country in efforts to close the gap between research and practice.

Having been involved in some of the conferences and networking that were a part of this movement, I believe there is a strong positive relationship between the involvement of educational psychologists and cognitive psychologists and the quality of legislation. That is, I do not think that these differing responses (between the states whose policies reflect recent research and those which do not) arose simply from differences in reading materials among legislators and their aides. To the contrary, some of these conferences were sponsored by particular states in part to receive the input of researchers, and there was a concerted effort among certain researchers to lobby for textbook adoptions, curriculum guides, and tests to reflect recent research. Thus, the very states that have legislation addressing recent research are states in which this partnership among policy makers and researchers is strongest.

In sum, quality of instruction appears to be at the heart of reform in state initiatives involving textbook selection, curriculum development, and assessment in a number of states where interaction with educational researchers has been prominent. However, this number is relatively very small and may not extend to all areas of a given state department. And the general lack of large-scale response among schools for changes in textbook selection and assessment across the nation is noteworthy. Hence, there is still a need to align curriculum, instructional materials, and testing in many states as well as a widespread need to stimulate interest in these issues and policy/researcher partnerships among states and schools that are currently disinterested and/or inactive. Further, spokespersons for the textbook industry have said repeatedly that textbooks will not change until there is a demand from states and schools. Thus, the giant task of relating these changes in demand to the textbook industry remains.

Classroom Teaching.   There is no question that the traditional classroom leaves much to be desired in terms of quality of instruction. Durkin's (1978–1979) landmark study documenting the extensive focus on assessing comprehension rather than comprehension instruction has been replicated and extended repeatedly. Additionally, this theme of the limitations of teaching in the traditional classroom recurs in recent descriptions of mathematics instruction (e.g., Silver, 1985) as well as recent studies on misconceptions in science (e.g., Anderson & Smith, 1987).

The response to this problem among researchers has been exciting and interesting. In fact, Pearson (1985) has termed this reply the comprehension revolution, referring largely to changes in our conception of good and poor readers and to the development of numerous effective instructional strategies in reading. However, there have been significant changes and/or significant shifts in other areas as well, such as research on the nature of intelligence (e.g., Sternberg, 1984), expert teaching and teacher thinking (e.g., Berliner, 1986; Clark & Peterson, 1985; Wittrock, 1985), thinking (e.g., Nickerson, Perkins, & Smith, 1986; Resnick, 1985), metacognition (e.g., Pressley, Borkowski, & Schneider, 1987), writing (e.g., Scardamalia & Bereiter, 1985), technology of text (Jonassen. 1985), problem solving (Schoenfeld, 1985; Silver, 1985), and instruction (e.g., Bransford, Sherwood, Vye, & Riesser, in press; Collins, Brown & Newman, in press; Lesgold, 1986).

This information revolution has been gaining momentum, to be sure, but its progress seems slow and highly variable. Judging intuitively from the research literature and educational news media reports, progress seems to be highly related to specific programs and policies in particular schools and states, though these appear to be disproportionately distributed in the elementary grades generally, as compared to high school grades. Moreover, while I cannot speak from anything but my personal experience with regard to researcher/school collaborations, it seems that the schools with the most research-based perspectives are schools in which key personnel have considerable input regarding recent research in educational psychology and cognitive psychology. This sounds self-evident on the surface, but it reflects what I perceive to be a major change in the interactions among researchers and practitioners. That is, as few as 5 years ago, I saw relatively little evidence of participation among educational psychologists or cognitive psychologists in professional journals, at conventions, and even in schools. Now this is no longer the case for many reasons. Professional journals such as *Educational Leadership* and *Reading Teacher* are increasingly providing a forum for cognitive psychologists to communicate with schools. School personnel are increasingly concerned about the need to teach thinking. And many researchers now see the need to impact on schools as part of their research agenda. Consequently, schools seem much more heavily involved in hiring educational psychologists as consultants to train teachers and work with curriculum specialists. At the same time, this note of encouragement should not suggest that all is well in research and practice. To the contrary, such partnerships are only the beginning; the road to school reform is very rocky and uphill all the way.

Preservice and Inservice Education.   Another factor that influences the quality of education in the classroom is quality of instruction in the various preservice and inservice programs that educate teachers, administrators, and curriculum developers in schools, publishing houses, and computer companies. There are several dimensions to this problem.

First is the question of teacher qualifications. State legislators, the unions, accreditation institutions, schools, and researchers are questioning the requirements for teachers in preservice institutions and for continuing development (e.g.. Carnegie Forum on Education and the Economy, 1986: see also almost any recent issue of *Education Week*). Of particular concern to everyone is the lack of knowledge and experience not only in specific content areas, especially science and math, but also the lack of instructional strategies that reflect recent research on cognition and instruction. As long as there are teacher education institutions that do not require graduating teachers to take college-level math courses (Southern Regional Education Board, 1985), this examination and revision seem worthwhile. However, while this overhaul is necessary, it is not sufficient.

Second, there is the problem of developing models of preservice and inservice that are well designed and well implemented. Joyce and Showers (1980), for example, have documented the paucity of effective staff development models, and there has been a widespread response to develop better models at all levels of education. Some of the new programs involving mentors, master teachers, and training centers such as the Schenley Center in the Pittsburgh Public Schools are cause for good feelings. The efforts of the Holmes group, the American Association of Colleges of Teacher Education, and other groups will undoubtedly alter teacher education in preservice institutions significantly.

In spite of these gains, it concerns me that Howey, Matthes, and Zimpher (1985) conducted a comprehensive review of the literature on professional development and found virtually no discussion of the impact of cognitive psychology or instructional strategies for teachers that reflects what we know about cognition and instruction, a comment that is not intended to reflect on their review but rather on the state of the art of professional development literature. This lack of reference to the need to use principles of cognitive psychology to train teachers is also evident in recent state and local legislation mandating inservice programs for teachers and supervisory personnel. This lack of reference in preservice and professional development literature to what Jones (1986) has termed cognitive instruction contrasts sharply with recent reports of inservice programs that focus on teaching teachers in schools how to apply recent research in reading, writing, metacognition, problem solving, and creative and critical thinking in their classrooms. (See, for example, special issues of *Educational Leadership* on teaching thinking, 1985, and on basic skills instruction, 1986.) At the same time, it is surprising how few of these training programs provide for teachers the sustained, interactive procedural instruction and dialogue that are recommended for teachers to provide for their students.

In addition, the lack of reference to cognitive psychology and educational psychology in preservice institutions is not surprising when one considers the content and quality of textbooks for teachers. Although there has been a flourishing of textbooks that focus on recent research on metacognition and reading comprehension (e.g., McNeil, 1983; Pearson & Johnson, 1978), there is little evidence that these books have replaced traditional textbooks or penetrated either inservice or preservice markets en masse. Nor is there much evidence that the new wave of teacher textbooks provides comprehension instruction for teachers, according to Durkin (1985). Finally, there do not seem to be parallel texts that translate research on critical thinking, problem solving, or content area research, other than those published by professional organizations such as the National Council of Teachers of Mathematics.

Instructional Technology.   Instructional technology has witnessed equally divergent uses of educational psychology within the reform movement as those found in preservice and inservice education. There is, for example, a marked discrepancy between what is available in research laboratories and what is available to schools. That is, there are numerous well-designed and well-documented programs that focus on problem-solving skills and computer programming as well as some good programs that teach reading and writing (e.g., Collins & Brown, in press) and content area subjects (e.g., Yerushalmy & Houde, 1986). Additionally, researchers have recently developed exciting, intelligent tutoring programs (Mandl & Lesgold, in press; Sleeman & Brown, 1982) and programs that allow users to access various levels of text (Tobias, 1984), as well as programs to create student networks, libraries, and data banks (Lesgold & Reif, 1983). These programs could not only improve instruction but also address issues of equity for low and high achieving students (see discussion below).

In contrast, the picture of technology use in schools is often distressing. Much of what is available still seems to be largely drill and practice, which is often poor quality. Thus, what is being developed in laboratory settings does not seem to be communicated and distributed effectively in schools. And often, even when good software is available, it may literally be sitting on the shelf because the teachers do not know how to use it, because it takes longer than the 14 minutes allotted for computer instruction, or because the school staff does not identify it as good software. Or, many students may be deprived of computer experiences because the equipment and software are too costly.

Of course, there are numerous and outstanding exceptions to this dismal picture of technology and schooling. Minnesota, for example, has an exemplary curriculum guide specifying learner outcomes in which students must learn to use technological tools such as data bases and word processing as a means of attaining higher order objectives (Minnesota Department of Public Education, 1985). The Wisconsin Instructional Television (1985) has developed a unique program, called *Story Lords,* to teach reading at primary levels; the program features interactive videos for students and includes 13 inservice video tapes for practitioners, using language and instructional strategies that reflect recent research in reading and metacognition.

Additionally, the Cincinnati Public Schools is involved in a collaboration with a renegade computer software company called WASATCH that develops high-quality, research-based interactive software in diverse subject areas. Cincinnati is the lead school system in a consortium of school systems that support WASATCH by serving as consultants in planning, field testing the materials, and critiquing revisions. Participants argue that this collaboration began because there were so few good products on the commercial market.

While these examples are noteworthy, they are few in number, at least from my perspective, and there is a serious need for the involvement of educational psychologists and other educational researchers such as content experts to work with schools, policy makers, and publishers to provide research-based instructional technology for students. I believe that these new tools have the capability to alter the role of teachers and achievement levels of many students as well as to address serious problems of classroom management and teacher accountability that have plagued schools for years, as suggested by Lesgold and Reif (1983). However, these changes will be a long time in coming, with the current gap between research and practice.

In sum, the movement toward excellence in education must address these complex and interrelated problems of instruction on a larger scale than is currently the case. That is, we must do a better job of developing curriculum, instruction, and assessment that promote thinking and cognitive development. This means that we must do a much more effective job of communicating our research to schools, states, institutions of teacher education, and publishers. I believe that a closer partnership among educational psychologists and other researchers with practitioners and policy makers could accelerate the rate of change considerably.

Equity

One of the most persistent problems in American education is the issue of equity in our schools. Specifically, how do we educate low achieving students so that they benefit maximally from the program of instruction?

Quality of Instruction.   Part of the answer to this question relates to quality of instruction. So many schools provide programs that teach thinking to gifted and talented students but relegate low achieving students to instruction in basic skills and lower level courses (Resnick & Resnick, 1985). This differential access to educational opportunities may have disastrous effects in the long run, because it conflicts with values for equity and because it will probably increase the gap between high and low achieving students (Jones, 1986). Such policies must be questioned when there is so much evidence from training studies demonstrating that low achieving students benefit markedly from direct instruction using higher order thinking/learning strategies (e.g., Brown & Palincsar, in press). This is not to suggest that such instruction is easy to implement: clearly, it is not. Teaching low achieving students to think effectively is difficult (Brown, Campione, & Day, 1981; Derry & Murphy, 1986), and dealing with federal policies is likely to provide serious constraints (Allington, 1986). Yet it can be done on a large scale in schools (e.g., Dorr-Bremme, Keesling, & King, 1984; Educational Testing Service, 1985; Jones & Spady, 1985).

Also important, there are few inservice models that address the needs of urban and rural schools. Consider, for example, the problem of training the 30,000 teachers in the Chicago Public Schools. One could spend a great deal of money training as many as 500 or even 5000. Yet, there would still be over 25,000 who would not benefit from the training. Or consider rural schools. Providing training in schools, substitute teachers, and training centers constitutes a large-scale problem when the school is a one-room schoolhouse, when the district has only 300 students, or when the region covers 10,000 acres.

What is needed are research-based models that address the problem of communicating both with very large numbers of educators in small areas and with small numbers of educators in very large areas. Certainly principles of distance learning and the best of instructional technology could go a long way toward solving these problems, as could much better preservice programs, university/school collaborations, and better models of instruction for training teachers in schools.

Classroom Factors.   Another part of the answer regarding issues of equity lies in classroom organization and the match between each student's level of achievement and the instructional materials used. Continuous progress models seek to individualize instruction so that each student is taught what he or she is ready to learn in a sequence of hierarchically organized objectives. This idea sounds so reasonable in theory. Nevertheless, numerous school systems have abandoned such efforts in favor of whole group instruction (Jones & Spady, 1985). Ostensibly, not enough teachers have the interest in or the management skills needed for providing instruction to all the students in the classroom or even several different small groups. Pull-out programs also have management problems and the stigma of being a low achieving student associated with them.

Whole group instruction has a different set of problems. Traditionally, if classes are heterogeneous, the teacher typically aims for the middle level, leaving many bright students bored and slow students frustrated. If classes are homogeneous, all of the dangers associated with tracking are present, unless instruction is carefully monitored to set challenging goals and movement between levels. The net result is that the most able students tend to do well or survive, whereas the least able students increasingly fall behind (Jones & Spady, 1985).

Some solutions to this problem may be found in effective mastery learning models (e.g., Bloom, 1984; Jones & Spady, 1985); cooperative learning (Slavin et al., 1984), effective classroom grouping practices (e.g., Good & Brophy, 1984), and computer-based instruction which has capabilities to engage students interactively, to provide multi-media and effective individualized instruction, to identify and correct systematic errors, to access utilities and text signaling aids, and to manage record keeping (Sleeman & Brown, 1982).

Each of the issues just described needs the insights and skills of educational psychologists in addition to those of practitioners and policy makers. The following section identifies a broad range of occupations in which key decisions are made about instruction in the classroom, instruction in preservice and inservice institutions, and the instructional applications of technology. Some of these occupations already involve educational psychologists on a large scale; others do not. Thus, for each type of occupation, I describe what type of decisions are made about instruction and the status of educational psychologists. Generalizations about the latter are impressionistic, as stated earlier, because there is no research that I know of which identifies educational psychologists in schools and school-related organizations. Thus, this section is based on my experience and some informal surveys. The generalizations here are essentially heuristic to raise questions for future research and for the future of educational psychology. The descriptions of occupations and fields are organized into two main categories: the public sector and the private sector.

OCCUPATIONS/FIELDS

The Public Sector

Federal Educational Agencies. Policy-making positions exist at the national, state, and local levels and represent a wealth of job opportunities. The National Institute of Education (NIE)—now part of the Office of Educational Research and Improvement (OERI)—the U.S. Army Research Institute (ARI), the Office of Naval Research (ONR), and the Office of Education (OE) are outstanding examples. Each of these bodies makes high-level, large-scale, and far-reaching decisions about what educational research is funded throughout the country. Each employs professional researchers, including educational psychologists, to manage divisions and projects at various levels. These agencies are critical because they investigate and support specific research agendas for the nation. They also fund and monitor labs, centers, and other educational organizations as well as specific projects in universities and independent agencies.

What is most interesting to me, however, is that over the years all of these institutions have become increasingly involved in applying research to solve problems of instruction in school and military settings. Years ago, some of these institutions had little interest in supporting applied research; others supported applied research but not in the areas of text design, learning strategies and high order thinking, or quality of instruction. Now there is very strong federal support for all of these areas. Equally important, there seems to be a need to communicate these findings to practitioners. Thus, for instance, NIE/OERI now strongly encourages researchers to write up their results for media that communicate directly to teachers, administrators, school board members, state legislatures, publishers, and others. These changes of focus are highly significant and undoubtedly have played a critical role in alerting practitioners to key issues and in directing educational psychologists and other researchers toward applied research and involvement in schools.

National and State Legislative Groups.   Senators and congresspersons generally have staff in Washington and in their respective states who are responsible for informing them about educational research, the needs of schools, key problems and issues, and the activities of specific educational agencies. Political aides to legislators may have considerable power in selecting the people and issues that come to the attention of our state and national legislators and in formulating policies for appropriations and political platforms.

State policy is formed in similar ways. Governors, state senators, and chief state school officers have access not only to political aides and staff in state departments of education, state boards of education, and intermediate (regional) state agencies, but also to national agencies such as the national Council of Chief State School Officers (CCSSO), the National Association of State Boards of Education (NASBE), and the National School Boards Association (NSBA), to name but a few. Many of these organizations have separate staff for any or all of the following areas: education of the gifted, bilingual education, learning disabilities, special education, elementary education, secondary education, postsecondary education, curriculum and instruction, research, technology, textbook selection, professional development, and often, specific subject areas such as English and math.

Perhaps one of the most significant changes on the horizon that will shape instruction, teacher education, and issues of equity is the increased importance of the role of the state. This is apparent in the number of state mandates for reform, and many of these reforms are massive in the amount of monies involved and in the scope of state initiatives. Illinois, for example, has just passed reform legislation containing 169 parts, backed up with 400 million dollars. Some of this money will go to schools to buy books and services, but *very* large chunks are earmarked to develop statewide training packages and regional service centers to train unprecedented numbers of teachers and administrators.

Additionally, there are interstate support agencies that serve one or more state legislatures. The Educational Commission of the States (ECS), for example, serves all states as a clearinghouse for information about key educational issues. Located in Denver, ECS has 1000 constituents—governors, legislators and their aides, high-level administrators in schools and institutions of higher education, and members of state boards of education. Besides its clearinghouse function, ECS sponsors forums for policy makers, conducts research, produces several publications, offers technical assistance to states developing new programs or legislation, and serves as a liaison among the different levels of government and between policy makers and educators. Although all of these organizations employ educational researchers, informal inquiries at national and state levels suggest that researchers, aides, and other staff in these agencies are seldom, if ever, educational psychologists. One reason for this arises from long standing competition among legislators and institutions of higher education for control over policy and funding. Nevertheless, the need for instructional applications of technology, professional development, and programs related to instruction is increasing. Educational psychologists might apply for jobs in these areas even if educational psychology is not specified. As more and more states take on education as a key issue, state involvement in education will increase and become more powerful. It is hoped that more educational psychologists will play political roles in the area of education.

In fact, of all the occupations or fields described here, consulting to state legislative groups has perhaps been most influenced by researchers in the area of instruction and text analysis. Besides the examples discussed above, Winograd and Osborn (in press) have documented how the textbook adoption process works in Kentucky, and Winograd is actually a member of the adoption committee. Wixson and Peters (1984) have worked extensively with the Michigan State Department of Education on a collaborative effort with the Michigan Reading Association to redefine reading as an interaction between the reader, the text, and the context. Courtland, Farr, Harris, Tarr, and Treece (1983) have worked extensively with the Indiana State Department of Education to build in criteria for instructional materials that provide instruction in higher order thinking skills. In fact, Indiana has even hired Tarr to work with the department on a full-time basis. Additionally, California's new guidelines for reading are based in part on guidelines being developed by The Center for the Study of Reading (see description in Osborn et al., 1985). Clearly, researchers can make a major impact on practice if they work with states to change textbook selection practices and assessment measures.

Laboratories and Centers. For over 2 decades, the National Institute of Education has funded a network of laboratories and centers. Centers are fewer in number than laboratories and have no regional basis. They were created largely to conduct basic research on specific themes such as reading or teaching. Generally, center personnel do not teach specific courses; or to be more precise, centers do not require their staff to teach. In fact, most centers are located in universities and have staff that teach as part of their responsibilities at the university. Thus, although students may take courses at a given center, centers typically do not give degrees. Currently, there are 14 centers.[1]

Laboratories are quite different. Their primary function is to serve schools on a regional basis as change agents.[2] Toward this end, laboratories (a) translate research conducted in universities and centers for use in schools; (b) disseminate information about research-based educational programs, products, services, and agencies; (c) provide a variety of direct services to schools through consulting, giving workshops and conferences, networking, and conducting collaborative research and development. Some labs also work closely with state departments of education and educational institutions for teachers and administrators.

Generally, lab staff is diverse. Some have school backgrounds; others have worked for national, state, or local legislative agencies or professional organizations. Many lab people have doctorates, but many of these are in the area of curriculum and instruction, or administration. In 1985, I conducted an informal telephone survey of staff for all the laboratories. Considering professional staff only, less than 20 lab employees across the country have doctorates. Although labs often employ educational psychologists as consultants, a surprising number of laboratory staff seems to be relatively unaware of recent research on reading, reading in the content areas, learning strategies, comprehension instruction, the limitations of existing texts, and other research emerging from cognitive psychology.

Laboratories and centers are funded in 5-year cycles with opportunities for

---

[1]The Center for Bilingual Research and Second Language Education in Los Angeles; Center for Education and Employment in New York; Center for Effective Elementary and Middle Schools in Baltimore, Maryland; Center for Effective Secondary Schools in Madison, Wisconsin; Center for Improving Postsecondary Learning and Teaching in Ann Arbor, Michigan; Center for Postsecondary Governance and Finance in College Park, Maryland; Center for State and Local Policy Development and Leadership in New Brunswick, New Jersey; Center for Student Testing Evaluation and Standards: Assessing and Improving Quality in Los Angeles; Center on Teacher Education in East Lansing, Michigan; Center for the Study of Learning in Pittsburgh, Pennsylvania; Center for the Study of Reading in Champaign, Illinois; Center for the Study of Writing in Berkeley, California; Educational Technology Center in Cambridge, Massachusetts; Institute for Research on Teaching in East Lansing, Michigan. Office of Educational Research and Improvement. (1986). *Directory of Institutional Projects*. Washington DC: U.S. Department of Education.

[2]Appalachia Educational Laboratory in Charleston, West Virginia; Far West Laboratory for Educational Research and Development in San Francisco; Mid-continent Regional Educational Laboratory in Aurora, Colorado; Northwest Regional Educational Laboratory in Portland, Oregon: North Central Regional Educational Laboratory in Elmhurst, Illinois; Research for Better Schools in Philadelphia, Pennsylvania; Regional Laboratory for Educational Improvement of the Northeast and Islands in Andover, Massachusetts; Southeastern Educational Improvement Laboratory in Research Triangle Park, North Carolina; and Southwest Educational Development Laboratory in Austin, Texas. Office of Educational Research and Improvement. (1986, July). *Directory of Institutional Projects*. Washington, DC: U.S. Department of Education.

refunding. In 1985, however, there was an open competition that restructured the locations and missions of almost all of the existing laboratories and centers. The new centers focus heavily on themes related to teaching, writing, and policy. The new laboratories serve different regions and are more oriented to working directly with state legislators than in the past. This feature gives laboratories a far greater capability to make an impact on schools than in the past. Thus, future laboratories will have more opportunities to influence state policy and to use the resources of the state. Laboratories could, for example, play a key role in the textbook movement. Laboratories may also utilize the power of the telecommunications systems and other technologies that many states have or plan to install on a statewide basis. If educational psychology seeks to make an impact on schools, involvement in laboratories would be timely and rich with opportunities.

Higher Education.   Obviously, most educational psychologists are likely to choose traditional research positions in universities and colleges because these positions are most consistent with the knowledge, skills, and values that are inculcated in most programs for educational psychology. What is not so clear is the relationship of educational psychology to institutions of teacher education. My experience is that institutions devoted solely to teacher education tend to have far fewer educational psychologists and are not generally oriented toward research. At the same time, an increasing number of teacher institutions are strengthening their requirements for entrants and for their own staff. Moreover, I see some evidence of a trend toward teaching teachers to use research in the classroom, (e.g., Tierney, Tucker, Gallagher, Pearson, & Crismore, 1985).

Schools.   Schools have numerous departments that would provide jobs for educational psychologists in the following areas: curriculum and instruction, staff development, elementary and secondary education, bilingual education, special education, technology, research and evaluation, content area departments, vocational and adult education, and programs for the gifted and talented. Additionally, individual schools often have instructional coordinators, specialists in reading, math, or writing, counselors, and resource teachers.

For 7 years, I was employed by the Chicago Public Schools. During this time, I worked with hundreds of individual schools and school systems in Chicago and throughout the nation. Incredibly, I know only a handful of persons who hold degrees in educational psychology and have been employed full time in a school! (And I hired one of them to work with me.) Generally, those who are responsible for central office jobs in the departments listed earlier are teachers who came up through the ranks. Many of them do not hold doctorates at all, and those who do typically have doctorates in administration, research and evaluation, or curriculum and instruction.

In retrospect, these conditions may be explained by the gap between higher education and schools. Until recently, much of the research conducted in universities and centers was not relevant to school issues and problems. Additionally, the disparity between the backgrounds of researchers and teachers often generated mutual distrust between school staff and hired consultants from higher education. However, these conditions are changing. Increasingly, higher education offers courses and research in areas that are relevant to schools. More and more, schools are engaging in successful school/university collaborations as well as hiring more educational researchers as part-time consultants. In addition, teacher education institutions as well as unions and teacher centers are increasingly emphasizing the importance of teachers becoming knowledgeable about the content of school-relevant research and its uses in the classroom.

The foregoing should not be interpreted to mean that schools should ever have a preponderance of educational psychologists. Nevertheless, it is hoped that the current widespread imbalance will be somewhat shifted. It is also hoped that educational institutions for teachers and administrators will focus more heavily on educational psychology so that teachers are more cognizant of research in learning and instruction and of ways to use research to improve instruction in the classroom.

Professional Organizations.   Agencies that serve schools are organized in various ways. The Association for Supervision and Curriculum Development (ASCD), American Association of School Administrators (AASA), and Phi Delta Kappan (PDK) are the most influential organizations for central office administrators and curriculum developers. Additionally, the National Association of Elementary School Principals (NAESP) and the National Association of Secondary School Principals (NASSP) serve the nation's principals. For teachers, there are two unions: the National Educational Association (NEA) and the American Federation of Teachers (AFT), as well as numerous professional groups for content area specialization such as the National Council for Teachers of English (NCTE), the National Council for the Social Studies (NCSS), the National Science Teachers Association (NSTA), and the International Reading Association (IRA). Finally, there are organizations for minority groups such as the National Alliance of Black School Educators (NABSE), urban schools such as the Urban Education Network (UEN), parent groups such as the Parent Teachers Association (PTA), and educational research agencies such as the American Educational Research Association (AERA) and the National Research Conference (NRC).

In spite of their diversity, these organizational agencies have much in common: (a) each has several educational publications in the form of journals, newsletters, magazines, cassettes, monographs, and so on; (b) each holds conferences, workshops, and institutes; (c) each makes policy statements indirectly through its publications and directly through editorial statements, its elected representatives and appointments, and explicit policy statements. Most of the research agencies employ professional researchers, but many subject-related organizations are run by persons who are trained as administrators or as specialists in the specific content areas. Thus, they are not educational psychologists by and large, and here again there may be opportunities for collaboration and employment.

Three trends in professional organizations seem highly significant to the future of educational psychology because they denote major shifts of interests and activities. First, many of these organizations have become deeply concerned about the quality of instruction in schools, in teacher education institutions, and, indeed, in inservice programs offered by professional organizations themselves, and they have made important efforts to do something about these problems. Several organizations such as the AFT, ASCD, and the NEA, for example, have developed policies and programs that support teaching thinking.

Second, many of these organizations have begun to develop packages of instructional materials for teachers and students to use in the classroom, especially in the area of teaching thinking. If this movement is successful, it could change the publishing industry substantially because these materials are research based, and they will be in competition with materials published commercially. NCTE, for example, has a whole line of products for teachers developed by noted researchers in the areas of reading, writing, and higher order thinking.

Third, groups of professional organizations are increasingly forming collaborations to improve instruction. ASCD, for example, now sponsors a coalition on teaching thinking. This group includes most of the subject area organizations as well as several labs. One of the tasks of this group is to develop guidelines for publishers. Another is to develop a research agenda. Perhaps the most fascinating task of this coalition is to provide a conceptual framework for understanding the thinking skills movement and for helping schools to implement teaching thinking. One product of this task force will be a taxonomy of the thinking skills used in the various thinking programs (Marzano et al., in prep.).

Educational psychologists would play a vital role in these trends by applying their knowledge of instruction to the development of instructional materials and teacher education programs.

Public Television.   Numerous programs within the Public Broadcasting System (PBS) require educational researchers. These range from specific courses offered by universities to designing and implementing programs for *Sesame Street*. Further, the educational division of PBS and other groups have recently embraced an intriguing new set of hardware for narrowcasting. In contrast to broadcasting, narrowcasting involves high frequencies that are beamed directly to specific institutions such as hospitals and schools. The hardware for this concept is now in place in certain areas. What is shown on the air when the system becomes fully operative presumably will be limited only by the imagination of those who design the instructional programs. Currently, the division needs instructional materials for this new type of program, a useful and exciting task for educational psychologists.

The Private Sector

Private Consulting. Most researchers do consulting in addition to their regular jobs. However, it seems that there is an increasing number of researchers who have established small agencies to promote a specific training program. Some have joined large research agencies. Others such as Madeline Hunter have become highly successful in providing training for administrators and teachers. At the other end of the spectrum, Bolt, Beranek, and Newman, a private research agency with hundreds of employees, conducts most of its educational research for the federal government, universities, and centers. Its staff includes many cognitive psychologists, who generally are well known in their respective fields.

High-Technology Companies. These companies range from small corporations of one or two individuals, to medium-sized companies such as The Learning Company and WICAT (World International Computer Assisted Teaching), to giant corporations such as Apple and International Business Machines (IBM). These companies employ educational researchers, including educational psychologists, to design and implement various types of high-tech training programs for schools, health care services, business and industry, and so on. This field of electronic learning is fast moving, high paying, and exciting because there are so many options (e.g., computers, video discs, teleconferencing, electronic mail, electronic bulletin boards) and also because there are no rules; it is a pioneer field. Moreover, there are literally thousands of companies such as Lotus and MicroPro (producer of WordStar) that design instructional software products for the massive computer market.

Although some of these companies have outstanding products, the field in general has a desperate need to develop user-friendly tutorial disks and documentation as well as instructional programs for schools that offer more than drill and practice. Again, my impression is that some of the small, research-based companies employ educational psychologists, but most companies do not. The addition of educational psychologists to company rosters could improve the quality of instruction in software programs considerably.

Big Business. Big businesses conduct various types of educational research, especially in the area of training. Many corporations such as Servicemaster have extensive and very effective programs to train new employees on the job. Others such as Bell Laboratories have large-scale research and development centers to test new ideas, to conduct applied research, and to train employees. Frequently, these companies develop training materials involving various media by hiring consultants. In other instances, they contract with a university or private agency to do extensive research and development. Persons with degrees in educational psychology could do any of these jobs.

Publishers. Because of the movement to improve textbooks, publishers are increasingly sensitive to the need to apply recent research in text analysis, learning, and instruction. As indicated earlier, publishers have begun to hire educational psychologists and other researchers to serve as consultants and authors. A few publishers have even hired noted researchers as full-time staff, both to develop inhouse training programs for staff and to develop instructional materials for the classroom.

Private Funding Agencies. Throughout the United States, there are numerous funding agencies of all sizes. These agencies primarily support universities, schools, and individual researchers. In the past, funding agencies shared this role with national agencies. However, as NIE/OERI has increasingly focused on funding laboratories and centers, universities and others in need of funding have become more dependent on private agencies and big business for funding and collaborative projects. Although a few of the larger foundations may employ educational psychologists as consultants, these seem to be few in number and virtually nonexistent in small funding agencies. Given how much power these agencies have and the importance of research in educational psychology, it might be worthwhile for spokespersons from the profession of educational psychology to take an actual count of employment in this area and lobby for an increasing focus on the employment of educational psychologists. The National Council of Foundations has newsletters and other media for internal communication and for inquiry into key issues. Further, both national and private foundations receive position papers, which are not in themselves requests for money but which provide rationales for spending money in certain areas. It may be worthwhile for prominent educational psychologists to write such papers.

PROBLEMS, SOLUTIONS, ASSUMPTIONS, AND REWARDS OF WORKING IN THE FIELD

As researchers get involved in jobs outside universities and centers, they are likely to encounter problems. Two sets of problems and some solutions are discussed in the following section: (a) the lack of preparation in many universities and schools for making career choices in the real world of schools and agencies that serve schools and (b) the inherent conflict of values between conducting applied research and basic research.

Problems and Solutions

The graduate student or veteran educational psychologist who chooses to leave the world of research in a university or center may be faced with a conflict of values about how to get started in a different context. That is, in many research institutions, there is a specific set of assumptions about what is right and proper in choosing a career and in starting out in that career. Typically, the graduate or veteran is expected, where possible, to apply to a university or center and to select the institution in question according to the specific researchers and re-search programs there. Ideally, one aims for an institution that has prestigious researchers and programs in the area of one's specialization. Once accepted, the newcomer is expected to conduct research in that area of specialization, using all the knowledge and skills for which he or she has been trained. Thus, under traditional employment conditions, when an educational psychologist moves into a department of educational psychology or a job that is traditionally held by an educational psychologist, there is a comfortable sense of consistency between what one has been trained to do and what one is expected to do on the job. Further, there is no expectation of rapid change.

But none of this is true when an educational psychologist applies for a real-world job, especially if that job has never been held by an educational psychol-ogist. First, there is the problem that arises in deciding where to apply and what to apply for. Inasmuch as many jobs will not specifically require an educational psychologist, the normal vehicles for searching for jobs, such as interviewing at the American Educational Research Association and getting referrals by one's professors or friends, may not be as relevant. Second, there is the question of nerve. How could one dare apply for a job for which one has not had formal training?

To address these problems, I would like to suggest the following solutions/guidelines/assumptions:

1. Decide what issues are really important to you. I would hope that the issues you choose will be among those defined here because there is such a great need for them.

2. Ignore the fact that the job description may not specify an educational psychologist or the specific areas of research with which you are most familiar. It will be up to you, however, to show how your training does, in fact, apply directly to the job goals (e.g., to develop curriculum and instruction or training for inhouse staff development).

3. Assume you can learn to do the job well and aim for the highest level of capability. You may be surprised at how easily a persuasive argument showing how your ideas and experiences really are well suited for the job may land the job you desire. You should aim for the top in what you produce, as well. This is especially true for curriculum development, for example. You will plan and mold your instructional design very differently if you assume that it may be a national program or product rather than a local one.

4. Assume that even in top-level jobs, you will need to train yourself, both in terms of management skills, if you have staff working for you, and in terms of knowledge. It is highly unlikely that being a graduate student or a professional researcher can prepare you for the exigencies of jobs outside your field, unless

your professors have a history of collaborative and applied research and you are following an established tradition.

5. Assume that what everyone else did before you may not be the best thing to do. This type of zero-based planning is critical because in many instances traditional textbook materials, traditional instructional strategies and training programs, and traditional definitions are part of the problem. Your job is to sort out what in the traditional product or strategy is valid and useful and what must be abandoned for something fresh and imaginative. I believe deeply that the most creative solutions must build on what is traditional and yet represent a creative synthesis of tradition and innovation.

6. Expect some degree of frustration and injustice, no matter where you work, and a great deal of irrationality if you work in a large bureaucracy that is financially poor and/or heavily dependent on government funding. Delays and problems will occur because of poor planning, cuts in funding, and the syndrome of the right hand not knowing what the left is doing. With practice, you will learn to predict and plan for these problems. and not take "no" for an answer.

7. Become expert at effective problem-solving strategies such as changing the situation when there is no viable solution or converting a problem into an asset.

8. Network at the top. Once you have established an identity for yourself and your program, you will need to identify a reference group for whom your product/services are most relevant. Share your research with those at the top of their fields to get their advice and to make them aware of your contribution. In many instances, there will be no journals or other traditional sources to serve as references or to disseminate your research. In such instances, networking is paramount. You may also lobby to have existing journals refer to the type of applied research you do.

Conducting Research. It should be evident from the foregoing examples that the scale and pace of work outside collegiate institutions may be very different from one's experience in such institutions. More important, work outside collegiate institutions may require doing exactly the opposite of what is the norm in universities and colleges. First, in applied research, much of one's work involves integration and synthesis of many different strands of research (e.g., research on graphics, text design, schema theory, mastery learning, instructional design, learning strategies). Welding together a multiplicity of factors in applied research is quite different from the constant focus on analyzing something complex and breaking it down into isolated factors in basic research. Although reviews of the literature provide some training for tasks involving synthesis, a large part of the problem in conducting applied research is affective; one may always feel somewhat uncomfortable in developing a complex program knowing that it will never be possible to separate out the effects of specific variables.

Second, it may be very discomforting to know that large-scale decisions will be made about revising a program and/or implementing one without clear and substantial evidence regarding what parts of a program work or do not work or, in some cases, without good data on the overall effectiveness of a program. This problem is particularly upsetting to hard-nosed empiricists. However, schools and businesses often cannot wait for researchers to take the time that is needed to obtain unequivocal supporting data. Consider, for example, the decision to implement Program X for which there are numerous positive indications of its effectiveness during field testing. Ideally, one would like summative testing before large-scale implementation, yet the decision to implement must be based, at least in part, on available funding and political support. Sometimes the latter may force a decision you think is premature, yet the very existence of your job and the chance to get additional data may depend on that very decision.

A third critical conflict is the inability in most instances to create the conditions necessary for effective evaluation even when the target program has good funding and political support. Random assignment of classrooms to treatment and control conditions is rare. Random assignment of students in classrooms is rarer still. And there will be numerous factors that will be troublesome in the evaluation analysis: (a) interruptions that may seriously affect both short-term and long-term problems (fire drills, the intrusion of "the pencil lady," announcements, health testing and vaccinations, absent teachers and students, strikes, teacher and student transfers, etc.), and (b) behaviors such as teachers who alter the available instructional time, use additional materials, do not follow instructions, compete with each other or you, and so on. These problems and others are fairly well known in the literature; good school researchers anticipate them and try to develop robust designs that will withstand these predictable problems.

A fourth difference between basic research and research in the field concerns assumptions about the conditions for field testing. Good school researchers try to construct instructional programs and field test conditions that will survive under the worst conditions. To explain, most basic researchers assume that it is critical to have the experimenter or trained designee provide the treatment under ideal conditions with maximum control. Although such experiments produce valuable data about isolated variables and learning under ideal conditions, they do not produce valid data about learning how a whole program works with poor or average teachers under less than ideal classroom conditions. This means that the program and the field test design must be robust.

To solve this problem, Katims and Jones (Jones, Amiran, & Katims. 1985) developed a concept called *criterion-referenced field testing*. Using this concept, researchers establish specific criteria for success before field testing. Then they continue to revise and field test any instructional units that do not obtain the desired student outcomes on criterion-referenced tests. This procedure is the opposite of the concept of learning to criterion in basic research. Using this concept, researchers assume that the students' behavior will change in some way with each successive trial. In criterion-referenced field testing, they assume that we have the technology to generate effective instruction; the materials should make a difference. Therefore, they change the materials.

Rewards

Whatever the problems of real-world jobs, there are numerous rewards. Obviously, money is a key issue. Many of these jobs pay well, especially those in the private sector as well as in the upper echelons of many schools and professional organizations. Salaries in some school systems, for example, range from $25,000 to $60,000 for full-time consultants and from $24,000 to $65,000 or even $85,000 for full-time professional staff, excluding the superintendent position. Day-to-day consulting may be very well paid or not, depending on the funding source. Salaries for professional employees (other than executive directors) in some laboratories and government positions have similar ranges. Although these salaries are generally lower than what could be obtained in the private sector, my impression is that they are at least comparable to, if not better than, average academic salaries.

Power is another factor. Researchers in schools, national agencies, businesses, and state legislatures have an opportunity to influence large numbers of students, teachers, and research that researchers in colleges and universities rarely have. In working for the Chicago Public Schools, for example, the staff within the Bureau of Language Arts was able to provide room libraries consisting of trade book and content texts for more than 33,000 students for one summer school program. My current job involves relating to the state departments, deans of colleges of education and teacher training institutions, and schools within seven states. These seven states comprise 20% of the nation's students, and over half of the nation's teachers are trained in this region. Other rewards include the challenge of solving large-scale problems, constant diversity, opportunities for travel, access to the media, and a strong sense of service to those for whom one's services/products are intended.

IMPLICATIONS

Educational psychology has contributed much to the educational reform movement. Substantively, it offers viable, relevant theories and fresh insight regarding comprehension, learning, and instruction. Methodologically, teachers are beginning to use research in the classroom based in part on models of research in educational psychology. And there is an increasing outreach among educational psychologists to conduct research in schools and to serve as consultants to schools and legislative bodies, as well as to business, industry, and the military. Nevertheless, the vast majority of schools and school-related organizations typically do not hire educational psychologists as full-time employees or as consultants. I have argued that the knowledge and research skills of educational psychologists would be well suited to address practical and political issues in schools and school-related organizations, and that hiring educational psychologists as full-time employees has added benefits compared to hiring them as consultants.

This is not to say that persons currently making decisions about instruction are in any way less capable because they are not educational psychologists or that educational psychologists should predominate in schools and school-related organizations. Clearly, schools need administrators who have training in principles of administration as well as teachers who came up through the ranks, and so on. Thus, the argument is not for the exclusion or replacement of existing people and ideas. That would be frivolous and unwarranted. To the contrary, the argument here in its most general form is for synergy of people, synthesis of ideas, more application of research to practice, and implementation of research-based judgments and programs, all oriented to schools and school-related organizations.

How can departments of educational psychology facilitate these changes—should they decide to do so? First, and perhaps most important, these departments must place a high value on applying research to practice. This means rewarding graduate students and professors for developing instructional materials; participating in inservice and preservice programs; and working with professional organizations, schools, and state departments. This also means encouraging educational psychologists to work in schools, state departments, and teacher education institutions full time. A number of universities and centers already have such rewards.

Second, schools of education need to rethink the curriculum and the quality of instruction for educational psychologists in their own institutions. Specifically, it would be helpful to increase opportunities for indepth learning experiences for educational psychologists in the following areas: curriculum development, instructional design, instructional applications of technology, intervention strategies for low achieving students, teacher education, issues about change and implementation, and the politics of education—including a focus on local and state politics as well as discussion about equity in education. Moreover, it would be helpful to increase the focus on concepts and principles from cognitive psychology since these are not covered well in current texts, according to Goetz and Chatman (1985).

Third, to implement the changes above would require providing some new models and guidelines that go beyond the current focus on experimental research. It is important, for example, to provide new standards of excellence for curriculum development and quality of instruction. Currently, the Center for the Study of Reading is developing guidelines for selection and evaluation of textbooks. These should be incorporated into graduate curricula for educational psychologists. Additionally, it would be important to develop standards of excellence in curriculum development that integrate principles of instructional design with instructional applications of technology and principles of instruction from cognitive psychology. Similarly, we need new models of instruction that integrate research on teaching with research in cognitive psychology.

Fourth, there would need to be a focus on new areas of empirical research such as networking and collaboration. Both are relatively new mechanisms for educational change, learning, and instruction. How do they work? Who belongs to them? How important are they for implementing change? What makes a good network or collaboration? Given how widespread they are, it would be important to include them as a legitimate topic of research for educational psychologists.

Both educational psychology and practice may benefit from closer relations and the proposed changes in the instruction of educational psychology. Educational psychology would be enriched if researchers had firsthand experience in making decisions and applying research in a broad range of real world settings. Educators in schools, school-related organizations, and the private sector would be better informed about decisions related to learning, comprehension, and instruction, and they would be influenced by the models of research offered in educational psychology. Educational psychology has never been more relevant to schooling, richer in ideas, or more capable of making a difference in teacher education and student outcomes. It is truly an opportune time to be an educational psychologist for those working inside academe and for those working in the field.

REFERENCES

Allington, R. L. (1986). Policy constraints and effective compensatory reading programs. In J. V. Hoffman (Ed.), *Effective teaching of reading: Research and practice* (pp. 261–290). DE: International Reading Association.

Anderson, C. W., & Smith, L. (1987). Teaching science. In V. Koehler (Ed.), *The educator's handbook: A research perspective* (pp. 84–110). New York: Longman.

Anderson, T. H., & Armbruster, B. B. (1984). Content area textbooks. In R. C. Anderson, J. Osborn, & R. J. Tierney (Eds.), *Learning to read in American schools: Basal readers and content texts* (pp. 105–226). Hillsdale, NJ: Lawrence Erlbaum Associates.

Berliner, D. C. (1986, April). *In pursuit of the expert pedagogue.* Presidential address presented at the annual meeting of the American Educational Research Association, San Francisco.

Bloom, B. S. (1984). The search for methods of whole group instruction as effective as one-to-one tutoring. *Educational Leadership, 41,* 4–18.

Bransford, J., Sherwood, R., Vye, N., & Rieser, J. (in press). Teaching thinking and problem solving. *American Psychologist.*

Brown, A. L., Campione, J. C., & Day, J. D. (1981, April). Learning to learn: On training students to learn from text. *Educational Researcher, 10,* 14–23.

Brown, A. L., & Palincsar, A. S. (in press). Reciprocal teaching of comprehension strategies: A natural history of one program for enhancing learning. In J. Borkowski & J. D. Day (Eds.), *Intelligence and cognition in special children: Comparative studies of giftedness, mental retardation, and learning disabilities.* Norwood, NJ: Ablex.

California State Board of Education. (1984). English/Language Arts. *Model curriculum standards:*

168   JONES

Grades 9–12 (1st ed., pp. E-1–E-88). Sacramento, CA: California State Department of Education.

California State Board of Education. (1985a). *Assessment of the critical thinking skills in history-social science*. Sacramento, CA: California State Department of Education.

California State Board of Education. (1985b). *Standards for reading textbooks*. Sacramento, CA: California State Department of Education.

Carnegie Forum on Education and the Economy. (1986, May). *A Nation prepared: Teachers for the 21st century*. New York: The Carnegie Foundation.

Clark, C. M., & Peterson, P. L. (1985). Teachers' thought processes. In M. C. Wittrock (Ed.). *Handbook of research on teaching*. New York: Macmillan.

Collins, A., & Brown, J. S. (in press). The computer as a tool for learning through reflection. In H. Mandl & A. Lesgold (Eds.), *Learning uses for intelligent tutoring systems*. New York: Springer.

Collins, A., Brown, J. S., & Newman, S. (in press). Cognitive apprenticeship: Teaching students the craft of reading, writing and mathematics. In L. B. Resnick (Ed.), *Cognition and instruction: Issues and Agendas*. Hillsdale, NJ: Lawrence Erlbaum Associates.

Courtland, M. C., Farr, R., Harris, P., Tarr, J. R., & Treece, L. J. (1983). *A case study of the Indiana state reading textbook adoption process*. Unpublished manuscript, Indiana University, School of Education.

Derry, S. J., & Murphy, D. A. (1986). Designing systems that train learning ability: From theory to practice. *Review of Educational Research, 56,* 1–39.

Dorr-Bremme, D., Keesling, W., & King, N. (1984). *Research in effective and ineffective classroom practices in Chapter I schools* (Publication No. 4501). Los Angeles: Research and Evaluation Branch, Los Angeles Unified School District.

Durkin, D. (1978–1979). What classroom observations reveal about reading comprehension instruction. *Reading Research Quarterly, 15,* 481–533.

Durkin, D. (1981). Reading comprehension instruction in five basal reader series. *Reading Research Quarterly, 4,* 515–544.

Durkin, D. (1985, May). *Comprehension instruction: An analysis of reading methodology textbooks*. Paper presented at the sixth Conference on Reading Research, New Orleans.

Educational Testing Service. (1985). *Educational Testing Service: Evaluation of writing to read*. Princeton, NJ: Educational Testing Service.

Gifford, B. R. (1985, March 20). We must interrupt the cycle of minority group failure. *Education Week*, p. 26.

Goetz, E. T., & Chatman, S. P. (1985). Coverage of cognitive psychology in educational psychology textbooks. *Educational Psychologist, 20,* 41–46.

Good, T. L., & Brophy, J. E. (1984). *Looking in classrooms*. Cambridge, MA: Harper & Row.

Hodgkinson, H. L. (1985). *All one system: Demography of schools, kindergarten through graduate school*. Washington, DC: Institute for Educational Leadership.

Howey, K. R., Matthes, W. A., & Zimpher, N. L. (1985). *Issues and problems in professional development* (Tech. Rep). Elmhurst, IL: North Central Regional Educational Laboratory.

Jonassen, D. H. (Ed.). (1985). *The technology of text*. Englewood Cliffs, NJ: Educational Technology Press.

Jones, B. F. (1986). Quality and equality through cognitive instruction. *Educational Leadership, 43,* 4–13.

Jones, B. F., Amiran, M. R., & Katims, M. (1985). Teaching cognitive strategies and text structures within language arts programs. In J. Segal, S. F. Chipman, & R. Glaser (Eds.), *Thinking and learning skills: Relating basic research to instructional practices* (Vol. 1, pp. 259–295). Hillsdale, NJ: Lawrence Erlbaum Associates.

Jones, B. F., & Spady, W. G. (1985). Enhanced mastery learning and quality of instruction as keys to two sigma results in schools. In D. U. Levine (Ed.), *Improving student achievement through mastery learning programs* (pp. 11–43). San Francisco: Jossey-Bass.

Joyce, B., & Showers, B. (1980). Improving inservice training: The messages of research. *Educational Leadership, 37,* 379–385.

Lesgold, A. M. (1986, April). *Producing automatic performance.* Paper presented at the annual meeting of the American Educational Research Association, San Francisco.

Lesgold, A., & Reif, F. (1983). *Computers in education: Realizing the potential. Report of a research conference.* Washington, DC: Office of the Assistant Secretary for Educational Research and Improvement.

Mandl, H., & Lesgold, A. (Eds.). (in press). *Learning issues for intelligent tutoring systems.* New York: Springer.

Marzano, R., Brandt, R., Hughes, C., Jones, B. F., Presseissen, B., Rankin, S., & Suhor, C. (in preparation). *Dimensions of thinking.* Alexandria, VA: Association for Supervision and Curriculum Development.

McNeil, J. (1983). *Teaching reading comprehension.* Glenview, IL: Scott Foresman.

Minnesota Department of Public Education. (1985). *Information technology learner outcomes.* Minneapolis: State of Minnesota Department of Public Education.

National Commission on Excellence in Education. (1983). *A nation at risk. The imperative for educational reform.* Washington, D.C.: Secretary of Education, U.S. Department of Education.

Nicely, R. F., Jr. (1985). Higher order thinking skills in mathematics textbooks. *Educational Leadership, 42,* 26–30.

Nickerson, R. S., Perkins, D., & Smith, E. (1986). *Teaching thinking.* Hillsdale, NJ: Lawrence Erlbaum Associates.

Osborn, J. (1984). The purposes, uses, and contents of workbooks and some guidelines for teachers and publishers. In R. C. Anderson, J. Osborn, & R. Tierney (Eds.), *Learning to read in American schools: Basal readers and content texts* (pp. 45–112). Hillsdale, NJ: Lawrence Erlbaum Associates.

Osborn, J., Jones, B. F., & Stein, M. (1985). The case for improving textbook programs: An issue of quality. *Educational Leadership, 42,* 9–17.

Pearson, P. D. (Ed.). (1985). *Handbook of reading research.* New York: Longman.

Pearson, P. D., & Johnson, D. D. (1978). *Teaching reading comprehension.* New York: Holt, Rinehart & Winston.

Pressley, M., Borkowski, J. G., & Schneider, W. (1987). Good strategy users coordinate metacognition, strategy use and knowledge. In R. Vasta & G. Whitehurst (Eds.), *Annals of Child Development, 4,* 89–129.

Report of the Holmes Group. (1986). *Tomorrow's teachers.* East Lansing, MI: The Holmes Group.

Resnick, D. P., & Resnick, L. B. (1985). Standards, curriculum, and performance: A historical and comparative perspective. *Educational Researcher, 14,* 5–21.

Resnick, L. B. (1985). Cognitive science as educational research: Why we need it now. In National Academy of Education, *Improving education: Perspectives on educational research* (pp. 36–41). Pittsburgh, PA: University of Pittsburgh, Learning Research and Development Center.

Scardamalia, M., & Bereiter, C. (1985). Research on written composition. In M. Wittrock (Ed.), *Handbook of research on teaching* (3rd ed., pp. 59–84). New York: Macmillan.

Schoenfeld, A. H. (1985). *Mathematical problem solving.* New York: Academic Press.

Silver, E. A. (Ed.). (1985). *Teaching and learning mathematical problem solving.* Hillsdale, NJ: Lawrence Erlbaum Associates.

Sleeman, D., & Brown, J. S. (1982). *Intelligent tutoring systems.* New York: Academic Press.

Slavin, R. E., Sharon, S., Kagan, S., Hertz-Lazarowitz, R., Webb, C., & Schmuck, R. (Eds.). (1984). *Learning to cooperate: Cooperating to learn.* New York: Plenum.

Southern Regional Education Board. (1985). *Teacher preparation: The anatomy of a college degree.* Atlanta: Southern Regional Educational Board.

Sternberg, R. J. (1984). *Beyond IQ: A triarchic theory of human intelligence.* New York: Cambridge University Press.

Tierney, R. J., Tucker, D. L., Gallagher, M., Pearson, P. D., & Crismore, A. (1985, January). *The Metcalf project: A teacher-researcher collaboration in developing reading and writing instructional problem-solving* (Reading Education Report No. 56). Urbana, IL: University of Illinois, Center for the Study of Reading.

Tobias, S. (1984), April). *Macro processes, individual differences, and instructional methods.* Paper presented at the annual meeting of the American Educational Research Association, New Orleans.

Winograd, P., & Osborn, J. (in press). How adoption of reading textbooks works in Kentucky: Some problems and solutions. *Reading Research Quarterly.*

Wisconsin Department of Public Instruction. (1986). *A guide to curriculum planning in reading* (D. Cook, Ed.). Madison. WI: Wisconsin Department of Public Instruction.

Wisconsin Instructional Television. (1985). *Story Lords.* Madison, WI: Wisconsin Instructional Television.

Wittrock, M. C. (Ed.). (1985). *Handbook of research on teaching.* New York: Macmillan.

Wixson, K. K., & Peters, C. W. (1984). Reading redefined: A Michigan Reading Association position paper. *The Michigan Reading Journal, 17,* 4–7.

Yerushalmy, M., & Houde, R. A. (1986). Geometric Supposer: Promoting thinking and learning. *Mathematics Teacher, 79,* 418–422.

IV EDUCATION AND TRAINING

Weinstein opens this final Section with a discussion of the educational preparation of education psychologists in the areas of learning, cognition, human development, and so on, pointing out that much of contemporary training is not well attuned to the changing market place for graduates. One market segment poorly considered in graduate curricula is that of the applied educational psychologist, that is, the service-oriented educational psychologists. To better prepare graduates for a changing market, she outlines a number of innovative curricular developments, showing how some of these have worked in an actual graduate training setting.

Muthen's chapter focuses specifically on education and training in statistics and quantitative methods. He overviews many of the recent and evolving developments in theory and method, pointing out that the increasing use, and complexity, of many procedures necessitate increasingly sophisticated training on the part of educational psychology graduates. To illustrate many of the issues of relevant quantitative methods, and the appropriate training in methods needed by educational psychologists, he puts a particular set of procedures, structural equation modelling, under his microscope. He concludes his chapter by proposing a model of graduate education in quantitative methods for students of educational psychology that would strengthen their methodological sophistication and improve the quality of data analyses in educational psychology. He stresses the need for researchers ''who can bridge the gap between the advanced statistical methods and sound applications.''

10 Educating Educational Psychologists

Claire E. Weinstein
University of Texas at Austin

Defining educational psychology is as difficult as defining common sense. Each of us has some idea of what we are talking about but no one has an inclusive definition that everyone agrees upon. In addition, the areas to which each can be applied are both diverse and constantly evolving. This state of affairs creates particular problems for those of us involved in the graduate preparation of future educational psychologists. We have no official set of professional standards to use as guidelines for the development of our curricula and our students come from varied undergraduate backgrounds, although many major in education or psychology. Our graduates often seek academic positions but increasing numbers are looking elsewhere for employment—business, industry, government, professional schools, private consulting firms, and product development groups are just some of the alternative career options being pursued.

Preparing students for such varied settings requires a flexible and adaptive curriculum supplemented by appropriate professional development experiences and opportunities for specializations outside of the traditional teacher/researcher role (Block, 1985). This chapter focuses on the graduate training needed to prepare future educational psychologists. First, a working definition of educational psychology is developed. Then, I discuss the types of jobs currently occupied by educational psychologists as well as other employment possibilities our students might consider in the future. Finally, I discuss ideas for altering and improving graduate training programs so that they can be more responsive to student needs and the evolving roles that educational psychologists are filling and could be filling in modern society. The continued robust growth and development of our profession is predicated upon our continuing commitment and responsiveness to the evolution of our field and the roles we can play in improving education and training, regardless of the contexts in which they occur.

EDUCATIONAL PSYCHOLOGY: A WORKING DEFINITION

Most textbooks in the field trace its origins to E. L. Thorndikes' first edition of *Educational Psychology,* which was published in 1903. Thorndike described educational psychologists as "middlemen" mediating between the science of psychology and the art of teaching. The contexts for this work were to come from educational settings. The methods were to be those of an inductive science. Practices based on speculation or derived from different schools of philosophy were to be discarded and replaced with the infallible products of scientific inquiry. These view were reinforced in the early articles written for the Journal of Educational Psychology, which was founded in 1910 (Grinder, 1981). It was hoped that this new field could help meet societal needs for an informed and skilled citizenry. Thorndike's emphasis on a purely scientific basis for our field has followed us all the way into the 1980s and is creating problems for educational psychologists trying to adapt to the diversity of approaches and job opportunities currently available.

Many graduate curricula and field experiences overemphasize a scientific or research orientation and forget about the middleman role. The problem is that a growing number of educational psychologists are in what Karen Block (1985) called service-oriented positions, that is, they have entered the field for reasons other than wanting to be researchers. They are interested in applying psychological theory and data in educational and training settings and in helping to create new or enhanced applications. They are interested in translating research findings into forms that are usable to other professionals involved in instruction. They are also interested in translating the research findings into forms that are usable to professionals in other areas, such as marketing, decision information systems, manufacturing, and sales. These goals do not conflict with a definition of educational psychology that stresses furthering the field of education through the application of psychology but they do require a reexamination of what we have really meant by the term in more recent times.

The bylaws of Division 15 of the American Psychological Association (the division focusing on educational psychology) define educational psychology as a field designed to "expand psychological knowledge and theory relevant to education." This portion of the definition has received the lion's share of attention in our journals and in our graduate programs. However, the bylaws continue and also state that the goals of educational psychology include "extending the application of psychological knowledge and services to *all* aspects of education." It is this emphasis that must be expanded in our graduate programs. Service-oriented or applied educational psychologists can fill a number of different niches that already exist and will be able to fill new roles that are yet to be defined. But to perform effectively in these roles requires educational experiences that help to develop the knowledge, skills, and attitudes required. While training in scientific psychology, research skills, and scientific reasoning skills is a tremendous contributor to job performance in a variety of settings, it is not sufficient for preparing applied educational psychologists. This becomes clearer when you examine the range of tasks performed by service-oriented psychologists.

SO YOU ARE AN EDUCATIONAL PSYCHOLOGIST—
BUT WHAT DO YOU DO?

Often when I am introduced as an educational psychologist people ask me what I do in the public schools. They are shocked to find out that I am personally most interested in postsecondary educational settings. When my little niece heard the term she asked me just what I educate psychologists about! The confusions of the public (and my family) over the job categories filled by educational psychologists is just a reflection of the diversity of work settings and job responsibilities performed by educational psychologists. Some of us teach. Some of us conduct research. Some of us design instructional materials or develop assessment instruments. Some of us work in schools. Some of us work in mental health settings. Some of us develop educational products to be used in the home. Some of us own or work in consulting companies. Some of us serve as resource consultants in other professional programs in settings such as medical, dental, social work, education and business schools. Some of us work in training settings in the military or government. This incredible diversity makes it difficult to define the "typical" educational psychologist. However, this lack of apparent unity is also a strength of the profession. In this era of dwindling academic positions, our students still have a number of challenging career options with new ones constantly evolving (Block, 1985a; Jones, 1985; Wittrock, 1985a, 1985b). Part of our responsibility as graduate professors is to help our students to prepare for these career options.

Future educational psychologists will use psychological theory and research to further teaching and learning in many settings, a number of which will be outside of traditional school classrooms (Wittrock, 1985a, 1985b). It is our job to enlarge our students' conceptions of educational psychology to include settings in postsecondary education, the home, the military, and the workplace, as well as in the university and the research laboratory. Education takes place in many forms and many places and there is a tremendous need for research and new applications in these areas. We need to help prepare our students to make career choices that may involve alternate educational contexts, particularly in real-world environments. Making these types of choices involves examining some potential value conflicts (Jones, 1985). For example, in real-world research it is not often possible to clearly identify cause–effect relationships. Control is often traded off for ecological validity. Making these career choices is also complicated by the problem of obtaining adequate information about career options and how best to prepare for these positions. Students need to know what programs will help them to prepare for these jobs and even how to obtain leads since the normal routes such as the APA job placement service are not yet adequate for alternative placements.

HOW CAN WE HELP PREPARE FUTURE EDUCATIONAL PSYCHOLOGISTS?

What types of graduate programs are needed to help prepare future educational psychologists who can meet the challenges presented by diverse job placements in both traditional and nontraditional educational contexts? Most existing graduate programs were designed to prepare students for academic careers, particularly in research-oriented departments at major private and public universities. These models may not be the best for preparing students to function effectively in other career tracks (Baker, 1985; Culross, 1984; Jones, 1985; Tobias, 1985; Walker & Yekovich, 1986; Wittrock, 1985b). Additions, modifications, and perhaps deletions, may be needed if our programs are to educate optimally our future educational psychologists.

Traditional programs focus on a large subset of the following topics: learning, statistics, psychometrics, individual differences, personality, evaluation, instructional design, guidance, human development, and consultation skills. The dominant program themes include helping students to understand the theories and data which comprise the field of educational psychology. With the exception of professional programs in school guidance counseling, school psychology, or counseling psychology, little emphasis is given to applied educational psychology, particularly when it is practiced outside of usual school settings. These programs were designed to train researchers who would also teach in a postsecondary educational setting, although little was done to prepare these students for the teaching portion of their future job responsibilities.

What changes have to be made to these traditional models to help make them accommodate to current needs and realities? First, those of us involved in graduate training will need to reevaluate our own values, attitudes, and prejudices. Educational psychologists have their own brand of elitism. Professors, particularly those at a major research university, and researchers, particularly those at the more prestigious labs and centers, are the royalty of our field. This pride, coupled with an ill-defined disdain for applied educational psychology, makes it difficult for many graduate professors to value the time and effort necessary to reevaluate and experiment with our curricula. Professors and researchers, particularly those who act as mentors, must reconsider their own views. Unless we come to value alternative career options, it will be difficult to help our students who wish to pursue them. We must be willing to spend the necessary time to make contacts outside of university settings.

These changes will not be easy. We have already seen a shift on the part of many faculty to more applied research areas that have increasingly direct applications to classroom and other instructional practices. However, we must still examine and redefine the problems and domains that fall within our purvue. Issues in evaluation, design, consultation, and decision making in real-world contexts must receive our attention. Without role-models to emulate and a sense that alternative careers are valued, it will be difficult for students to pursue their goals in our programs. Over time this could have devastating effects both for our field and for the potential impact our graduates could have on society.

Another change that would be helpful is to broaden the emphasis or options available to students in educational psychology to include direct preparation for alternative career choices. An educational psychologist working in an industrial training center may be conducting little or no research and may not even be involved in any classroom instruction. Developments such as individual work stations and computer-aided training are changing the ways many corporations and industries are conducting continuing education and providing opportunities for job enhancement. Platform instruction is being increasingly replaced by these innovative and cost-effective methods in many military and government settings. Educational psychologists on the staffs of medical, dental, and law schools are often involved in optimizing the teaching/learning process or in the design, development, and management of learning assistance centers. The long-standing model of the scientist/teacher is not adequate for these new roles. Students need to have opportunities to acquire the knowledge and skills required to function in these settings. They need to know how to apply the theories, concepts, facts, and data they have learned to the situations in which they will be working.

An example of a method that could be used to help prepare students to work in nontraditional settings is the implementation of a practicum experience, with opportunities for placements in diverse settings with broad work responsibilities. The requirement or option to have one or more practicum placements in potential work settings provides students with the opportunity to explore alternative work environments, develop the abilities and skills needed to compete successfully for similar positions, develop a professional presence, evaluate their desire to pursue the same, or similar, types of employment, and refine their understanding of professional interpersonal relationships, values, and ethics. A practicum placement can provide students with the opportunity to explore professional options they might not otherwise consider. It can also help students to select electives in their own or in other departments that might contribute significantly to their future performance.

The Department of Educational Psychology at the University of Texas at Austin has implemented a practicum program for their doctoral students majoring in the area called Learning, Cognition, and Instruction. Like most programs in this area, graduates usually found employment in higher education, particularly at research-oriented universities. As the number of jobs in these settings has dwindled, other career options have been selected, or worse, forced upon students. To better prepare our students for these alternative placements and to help them become aware of and select possible options, a number of steps were taken, including the development of a two-semester practicum sequence for second-year students. The course has two major components: a placement on a research, development, or applied project, and a series of professional development workshops.

The placement portion requires a 10-hour commitment to the project. Potential projects are selected and placements are negotiated by the practicum coordinator, a member of the faculty in the area of Learning, Cognition, and Instruction. Over time a large number of settings and field supervisors have been identified and approved. These include faculty research projects (both within the Department of Educational Psychology and within other related departments such as Psychology, Curriculum and Instruction, Special Education, and the Cognitive Science Center); University research programs such as projects originating in the Minority Student Affairs Office or the Office of Institutional Studies; College development projects such as teacher training programs being developed by the Science Education Center or the Reading Program in the Curriculum and Instruction Department; community agencies such as mental health centers, patient education programs in the local hospitals, and county programs for children of migrant workers; publishing and product development centers and companies such as the Southwest Educational Development Laboratory, Learned and Tested (a product development subsidiary of Harcourt, Brace, Jovonovich), and various State Agencies (Austin is the capitol of Texas and many offices of the state government are located here); industrial and business settings such as the Radian Corporation, IBM, and Texas Instruments; and military contexts such as the Air Force Human Resources Laboratory in San Antonio. Texas. In addition, students can suggest placement locations and the coordinator, if she or he judges them to be appropriate, will attempt to negotiate a placement.

Not all sites investigated, nor all locations that request being considered as a potential placement, are approved. Designation as a practicum placement is made only if certain criteria are met. For example, the contact person at the site or the project supervisor must agree, in writing, that the student will have a number of different experiences, receive supervision, have the opportunity to learn and test new skills, and receive feedback. Even after a site is selected, students wishing to go to that placement must still go for an interview and, in consultation with the coordinator and site supervisor, prepare a written statement of their goals for the semester (placements can be for one or two semesters). These goal statements are reviewed at the middle and end of each semester. Student progress is monitored during each semester and, if necessary, placements can be changed. This is not common occurrence but it does happen.

In addition to the 10-hour field work commitment, students also meet as a group and participate in professional development workshops and seminars. These sessions are designed to help teach the tacit knowledge that is so important for a successful and fulfilling career. Topics presented include: how to "do" a

conference, professional networking, writing grant proposals, writing and editing journal articles, management of educational R & D projects, alternative
career options, how to pick a placement, resume writing and interviewing skills,
and professional ethics and responsibilities. Students' experiences in their placements are also discussed with the other members of the practicum class. This
provides both a forum for discussing experiences and/or problems and a means
by which the other students get some idea of what it is like to work in that setting.

The program at the University of Texas at Austin has been outlined in some
detail as a case study of an attempt to develop innovative education and training
for a new future in educational psychology. There are many other innovations at
other universities that could also be described. For example, the modularization
of the curriculum in educational psychology is one way to provide an individualized and varied program. The University of Wisconsin at Madison uses
modules of instruction in educational psychology to provide a wide range of
short-courses, typically one credit each, that cover a wide range of specialized
topics. These topics can be readily changed over time to reflect advances and
developments in the discipline. The modules capitalize on the special strengths
of each faculty member, and allow students to construct a set of courses most
relevant to their goals. The Madison program offers mostly basic courses in these
modules, but a few advanced courses are also provided.

The in-depth discussion of the program at the University of Texas at Austin
was also presented as a case study of one approach to creating a practicum
experience to expose students to challenges and responsibilities of varied work
settings. Curricular innovations in other colleges and universities such as the City
University of New York, Penn State University, TCU, UCLA, the University of
California at Santa Barbara, the University of Michigan, the University of
Wisconsin at Madison, and USC have also included the creation of professional
development sequences that give students an opportunity to learn about and
experience career options. For example, a few programs use the medical model
and provide a rotating series of internship experiences. One program provides a
lab setting and uses simulation techniques to provide these experiences. Other
programs report incorporating this information into area or departmental
colloquia.

New or updated courses are needed that reflect both the changing nature of
educational means and environments as well as the evolving psychological theory and knowledge in our field. For example, courses discussing instructional
practices need to consider alternative settings, such as military bases, industrial
learning centers, home learning, and alternate schools. Restricting ourselves to
discussing educational psychology in traditional elementary and secondary class
settings is no longer sufficient. The relevant age groups discussed in our courses
need to be expanded upwards to reflect the changing demographics in our society
and the evolving models of lifelong learning. Additional courses in cognitive
theory and application need to be developed.

A number of departments, including those mentioned above, have already tried to meet these needs by developing new courses or by expanding or incorporating these topics into existing courses. For example, many programs have included topics in higher education and human resource development. A rapidly growing number of departments are developing courses and whole concentrations in the area of applied cognition. Courses in research design, statistics and psychometrics are including more topics in evaluation and nonlaboratory research.

It is only by capitalizing on the new knowledge available to us and the new career opportunities available to our students that we can continue to be a vital profession that impacts significantly on both the study *and* the practice of education.

REFERENCES

Baker, R. F. (1985). Preparing graduates for careers in publishing: A publisher's perspective. *Educational Psychologist, 20,* 102–106.

Block, K. K. (1985, June). What is wrong with educational psychology? *Newsletter for Educational Psychologists,* p. 4–6.

Culross, R. R. (1984, June). New directions in graduate programs in educational psychology. *Newsletter for Educational Psychologists,* p. 4.

Grinder, R. E. (1981). The ''new'' science of education: Educational psychology in search of a mission. In F. F. Farley & N. J. Gordon (Eds.), *Psychology and education: The state of the union.* Berkeley: McCutchan.

Jones, B. F. (1985). Educational psychologists—Where are you? Reflections of an educational psychologist. *Educational Psychologist, 20,* 83–95.

Tobias, S. (1985). New directions for educational psychologists. *Educational Psychologist, 20,* 96–101.

Walker, C., & Yekovich, R. (1986, July). New directions in graduate programs in educational psychology. *Newsletter for Educational Psychologists,* pp. 1–2.

Wittrock, M. C. (1985a, June). Enlarging the conception of educational psychology. *Newsletter for Educational Psychologists,* pp. 1–2.

Wittrock, M. C. (1985b). Educational psychologists of the future. *Educational Psychologists, 20,* 82.

11 Teaching Students of Educational Psychology New Sophisticated Statistical Techniques

Bengt Muthen
Graduate School of Education
University of California, Los Angeles

BACKGROUND

The methodological training of graduate students in the area of Educational Psychology poses an exceptional challenge. While these students frequently have little background in mathematics and statistics, many of the statistical methods most appropriate for the field are technically complex. This is true both for students whose main interests and specialization lie in a substantive area, and also, perhaps even more so, for those students who specialize in research methods. While the substantive group struggles with basic statistics, the often better quantitative background of the methods group is frequently still a poor match for the sharply increased level of difficulty of the methods they are expected to master. The data analysis related research in the Educational Psychology area poses statistical problems as challenging as they come. Although many methodologically advanced solutions have been proposed in recent years, even the methods students are hard pressed to understand them well enough to make good use of them.

The statistical complexities in Educational Psychology research stem from the fact that data are frequently collected in a nonexperimental setting, often in a hierarchical, multilevel fashion (such as students observed within schools), and almost always involving constructs that are difficult to measure in a valid and reliable way. Prime examples of advanced, statistical answers to these data complexities include maximum-likelihood structural equation modeling (see, Joreskog, 1977) which attempts to simultaneously handle uncontrolled background differences and measurement unreliability, regression analysis with a variance component structure (see, Aitkin & Longford, 1986; Burstein, 1985) to take multilevel measurements into account, and item response theory analysis with a full information, three-parameter logistic approach (see Bock & Aitkin, 1981; Hambleton & Swaminathan, 1984) to properly describe the responses to dichotomously scored achievement items.

When thinking about emerging new research methods that future students of educational psychology will need to learn, the above set of advanced techniques naturally come to mind. However, there are other methods that seem important and go beyond the usually covered areas such as experimental design, multiple regression, measurement theory, and standard multivariate techniques. For instance, there have been several useful developments in regression analysis regarding diagnostic measures such as leverage and influence (see e.g., Atkinson [1985] and Cook & Weisberg [1982]). Many recent developments have been made that extend standard analysis techniques to the frequently encountered situations of categorical and other nonnormal data, such as loglinear modeling (see Bishop, Fienberg, Holland, 1975), extensions of loglinear modeling to ordinal variables (see Agresti, 1984 and references therein to work by Goodman), extensions to factor analysis (see Mislevy, 1986), and more general nonnormal data analyses (see McCullagh & Nelder, 1983). Multidimensional scaling and cluster analysis would seem to be useful emerging data analysis techniques and are described in Schiffman, Reynolds, and Young (1981). Traditional as well as more recent missing data techniques are treated in Little and Rubin (1987). Meta analysis techniques for combining information from several studies are treated in Hedges and Olkin (1985). While many important methods naturally are omitted from the above list, it should give a feel for the great amount of statistical material that is potentially relevant for an educational psychology student's data analysis.

This chapter uses structural equation modeling to discuss the general issues involved in preparing Educational Psychology researchers to properly use advanced statistical methods.

THE METHODS TOPIC

Structural equation modeling is a general term for a set of techniques that cover path analysis, confirmatory factor analysis, and general latent variable models that combine features of path and factor analysis. An attempt is made to describe the methodological issues in as nontechnical a language as possible.

In path analysis a set of linear regression relations are assumed to describe a set of correlated variables. For instance, educational aspiration may be regressed on a set of background variables, while at the same time it may be used as a predictor in another regression, e.g., using educational attainment as the dependent variable. By formulating this system of two regression relations, the researcher may attempt to separate the direct influence of background on attainment from the indirect influence on attainment via aspiration. Statistical tests may be performed to check whether all influence is indirect.

In confirmatory factor analysis, an attempt is made to go beyond the scope of ordinary exploratory factor analysis to not only cluster variables that measure the same constructs, but also test specific hypothesis on the measurement relations between the observed variables and the latent factors. For instance, using a measurement instrument in different populations, it may be of great interest to study whether the measurement relations are the same, and if they are, how the distributions of the common factors differ.

In general structural equation modeling, the above two features are special cases which can be combined in one powerful model that addresses measurement concerns and construct relationships simultaneously. Simple path analysis where all variables are observed can be done by a sequence of ordinary linear multiple regressions and has been in practice for about 20 years. Regular exploratory factor analysis can be performed by standard computer packages and has been in practice even longer. However, the more complex modeling, particularly involving hypothesis testing and latent variables, requires specialized software and did not come in general practice until the popularization of the Joreskog's LISREL program (Joreskog & Sorbom, 1984) about 10 years ago.

THE PROBLEM

Today, general structural equation analyses using LISREL are common in Ed Psych journals such as *Journal of Educational Psychology, Journal of Personality and Social Psychology, American Educational Research Journal, Journal of Educational Measurement, Sociology of Education, Applied Psychological Measurement,* and *Psychological Bulletin.* Grant applications have been turned down if structural equation modeling has not been mentioned among solutions to measurement concerns. Structural equation modeling has become a hot topic among social and behavioral science data analysts, and the fact that it is statistically complex only serves to make it the more alluring. At this point, however, I think we are facing a serious problem which is not confined to the use of structural equation modeling, but is a general one for all new sophisticated methods. There is a multitude of very poor applications of the methodology, including the simpler path analyses. Many research claims are based on flawed or completely erroneous analyses. If this volume of bad applications is not greatly reduced, there is, in my opinion, a strong risk that large portions of research results will not be believable. I think there is a growing credibility problem, which must be stemmed since many important research studies will continue to call for statistical tools of this kind. A few prototypical examples of kinds of poor applications may be of interest. In general, I find that the major problem lies in the transition from substantive, conceptual ideas to statistical analysis—there is a difficulty in moving from conceptual to statistical modeling. The common problem is that measurement issues and statistical assumptions that are incidental to the researchers' conceptual ideas become stumbling blocks that invalidate the statistical analysis.

One frequent misuse involves the omission of important explanatory variables ("x variables") in a certain regression relation, be it in path analysis, structural modeling, or factor analysis (where the factor assumes the role of x). It is common to see studies report regressions on a certain set of x variables of particular interest in the study without imbedding these among other x variables belonging in the equation but not necessarily of prime interest. Perhaps this stems from being trained with experimental research situations, where ANOVA on a randomized sample allows one to exclusively concentrate on the *manipulated* factors. However, with regression in a nonexperimental setting, this use of a minimal set of x's is likely to cause severe bias in the estimated regression slopes, which has been called omitted variable bias.

A frequently occurring problem is associated with the increasing use of "confirmatory" analysis, i.e. using a chi-square test of model fit to assess the appropriateness of a certain theory as specified in terms of a covariance structure. Here, the common mistake is to consider estimates and significance of parameters from models that do not fit the data, i.e., use "predictions" from a model that has little to do with the data at hand. A not uncommon version is to compare a sequence of models built from various competing theories, to discuss differences in estimates, and *choose* the model that has the best chi-square—even when each of the chi-square values indicate a strong rejection of the model at hand. Again, perhaps the misuse stems from being used to ANOVA, where one usually does not worry about the "fit of a model" (indeed ANOVA is perhaps not even thought of as a model) but merely wants to look at the "effects."

More complex misuses arise with latent variable modeling, where the researcher may not fully realize that the questionnaire format used or the particular phenomenon intended to be measured causes complications for the latent variable modeling to be carried out in a standard structural modeling framework. The indicator variables may be nonlinearly related to the latent variable; they may, by the question format, have certain direct dependencies; and measurement errors may be likely to be correlated with the latent variable and have strongly heteroscedastic variances. These examples show that structural equation modeling can be a very complex topic, which to be well mastered takes years of hard study.

Part of the methodological/statistical community is becoming skeptical about these methods. For instance, the Summer 1987 issue of *Journal of Educational Statistics* is devoted to the discussion of the strengths and weaknesses of path analysis, where the seminal article is by the statistician David Freedman who is strongly critical of path analysis usage due to violated statistical assumptions. As a discussant in a recent conference on test validity (see Wainer & Braun, 1987), the statistician Don Rubin voiced his concern over bad structural equation modeling removing the analyst to far from his or her data. Many of us interested in psychometrics are concerned. Cliff (1983) stated:

> Initially, these methods seemed a great boon to social science research, but there is some danger that they may instead become a disaster, a disaster because they seem to encourage one to suspend his normal critical faculties. Somehow the use of one of these computer procedures lends an air of unchallengeable sanctity to conclusions that would otherwise be subjected to the most intense scrutiny. These methods have greatly increased the rigor with which one can analyze his correlational data, and they solve many major statistical problems that have plagued this kind of data. However, they solve a much smaller proportion of the interpretational— inferential in the broader sense—problems that go with such data. These interpretational problems are particularly severe in those increasingly common cases where the investigator wishes to make causal interpretations of his analyses.

Five or 10 years ago, poor published applications of structural equation modeling could be excused as demonstration pieces, promoting the method itself. But the average quality has not risen as much as it should since then. One explanation may be related to the publication pressure, where researchers are not allowed to present analysis failures, but where published models must fit the data well at any cost, and where complex analyses are favored over more mundane ones. Such an atmosphere does not stimulate good applications. Some psychometricians emphasize the improvement of the statistical methods to better fit real data, and development of new computer software which is technically less demanding, giving more time to consider the basic analysis problem.

In my own view, however, the largest part of the problem and the largest part of its solution does not lie in the domain of publishing or in methodology development, but in education. Presently, there is not enough done in the education of the ultimate users of these new statistical techniques for them to learn the methodological part of their research trade well. I do not think there is a real problem with the methodology and I am by no means ready to throw out the baby with the bath water. The methods can surely be improved, and that is important. We methodologists should probably also be much more careful of not overselling our new developments. However, the most important way to change the quality of applications is to put more emphasis on training students of the topic to learn it well.

METHODOLOGICAL TRAINING

Like other areas of advanced statistical methods for the social sciences, structural equation modeling has a group of contributors of theory and methods. Hence, recently many new powerful techniques have been proposed in psychometric journals such as *Psychometrika* and *British Journal of Mathematical Psychology*.

As is also the case with item response theory, for example, the group of theoretical structural modelers is rather small, concentrated in a subgroup of *Psychometric Society,* which itself meets with only about 200 members. The ratio of providers to consumer is presumably very small, and this poses a difficult educational problem. There is a distinct lack of people who can bridge the gap between the theory provided and the intelligent use of these methods in practice.

I believe that this problem has caused a pressure for people who are not well trained themselves to assume the role of *bridgers,* teaching and advising those even less knowledgeable in less than optimal ways. And since these people may not always have conveyed a message of methodological rigor, many purely substantive researchers may have felt that it was all right for them too to dabble on their own with the advanced methods. At least that is the impression I am often left with from reading applied journal articles and listening to talks at professional conferences. In my opinion, these methods—or computer programs, as they are often viewed—should not be taken as "everyman's causal modeling" tools.

It is time to take this problem seriously and to consciously educate students to assume various methodological roles. Not everyone should be using these methods. Most people should not use them without intimate guidance and involvement of a truly knowledgeable person (a *bridger* or a theoretical expert). Not everyone should attempt to become an expert.

For the purposes of discussing methodological training, it may be useful to distinguish between three types of Ed Psych students: those who emphasize substantive interest, those who emphasize methodological interest but do not aspire to contribute to methodology, and those who place a strong emphasis on methodology and have aspirations to in some way enhance the methodology.

The first group of substantive students will ultimately constitute a major portion of "the users" of a given methodology, here structural equation modeling. In my view, these students need only an overview of the potential of the techniques, explained in a largely conceptual way. The major message should be to seek intimate cooperation with an expert if a need for structural modeling arises. These students should not be encouraged to *wing it* on their own and should be discouraged from seeking automated sofware solutions. I believe that a large portion of today's poor state of applications is due to the enticement of such students to be self sufficient. While this is laudable and advisable regarding more straightforward, standard statistical techniques, it is not a healthy attitude regarding a new, sophisticated technique such as structural modeling, a topic which it takes years to master well.

Both the second and third group of students, choosing a methodological emphasis, are very much needed in the Ed Psych area. They can fill the void of people at various levels of bridgers and in various degrees make connections between the theorists and the users. They have the potential know-how to move beyond poor and mediocre applications. With a good and intensive methods training they have the distinct advantage over pure statisticians of having a good understanding of their substantive area. They should be trained in making the transition from conceptual, substantive *modeling* to statistical analysis. On the other hand, they should not be expected to become statisticians.

The methodological curriculum should make a distinction between the second and third group. The goal of the second group may suitably be to have a strong grasp of the methods, being able to understand advanced applications, e.g., in publications, and be able to use the methods in their own substantive research with only minor assistance from more expert colleagues. We might call this group low-level bridgers. With this goal, the students certainly need to be quantitatively adept, but need not take special courses in mathematics and statistics. They need courses in regression analysis, ANOVA, and multivariate statistics. The structural equation modeling topic may be studied in two ten week courses, covering factor analysis, path analysis with observed variables, and general structural equation modeling. Some technical detail is needed. However, the emphasis should lie on sound use of the methods, and that can be taught well without taking a large portion of time for statistical theory. This group may also cover other areas of advanced methods, such as item response theory, and so become general methodologists.

The third group, the most methodologically oriented, constitutes a relatively small group that can be trained as applied statisticians or psychometricians with an Ed Psych specialization. These can serve as high-level bridgers. They need considerable technical training, and to assimilate that, need to have previous or parallel mathematical and statistical training in areas such as calculus, matrix algebra, and mathematical statistical theory on an undergraduate introductory level. This knowledge is best achieved by a Master's degree in applied statistics. A degree of this type is strongly recommended for high level bridgers.

Following applied Ed Psych training in areas of regression analysis, experimental design, and multivariate statistics, the study of structural equation modeling for high-level bridgers necessitates a sequence of three ten week courses covering general factor analysis, path analyis, and advanced structural equation modeling. In addition, independent studies with the students working on their own data, followed up by specialized seminars would be needed. In my view, nothing less prepares the student for penetrating the topic to a degree that makes him or her serve in the role as advanced bridger. This person must be able to read and communicate to users the latest advanced developments as presented in the original sources, and must come beyond the point of initial fascination with the methods and their technical aspects to know both strengths and weaknesses well. This will admittedly leave relatively little room for penetrating studies of other topics and hence the group will be a highly specialized one. However, I believe that this is necessary to do the training well—or else, the aim should be a different one.

The last group will be a small, but very important one. Few Ed Psych students are suited for this training. The present rarity of candidates for mastering advanced methodology is certainly a problem worthy of attention. Suitable candidates, for example, are students with a Master's degree in Statistics or applied Mathematics. There is a challenging recruitment effort involved in conveying that they are needed in the Ed Psych methods arena.

CONCLUSION

Using the case of structural equation modeling, the general problem of teaching advanced statistical methods to students in Educational Psychology has been outlined. Due to a lack of attention to the difficulty level of structural modeling, the training of past students has been inadequate. This is having serious ramifications, in that a large number of poor applications of the method has been appearing in scientific journals. Research conclusions have been based on flawed analyses. The importance of breaking a trend towards such analyses not being taken seriously was pointed out. The future need of researchers who can bridge the gap between the advanced statistical methods and sound applications was stressed. The production of such bridgers can only be accomplished by stronger emphasis on thorough methods training. For high level bridgers this requires a strong degree of methods specialization.

ACKNOWLEDGMENT

This work has benefitted from discussions with Leigh Burstein and Linda K. Muthen.

REFERENCES

Aitkin, M. A., & Longford, N. (1986). Statistical modeling issues in school effectiveness studies. *Journal of the Royal Statistical Society, Series A,* 149, 1–35.

Agresti, A. (1984). *Analysis of ordinal categorical data.* New York: Wiley.

Atkinson, A. C. (1985). *Plots, transformations and regression.* London: Oxford University Press.

Bishop, Y. M., Fienberg, S. E., & Holland, P. W. (1975). *Discrete multivariate analysis: Theory and practice.* Cambridge, MA.: MIT Press.

Bock, R. D., & Aitkin, M. (1981). Marginal maximum likelihood estimation of item parameters: Application of an EM algorithm. *Psychometrika, 46,* 443–459.

Burstein, L. (1985). Units of analysis. *International Encyclopedia of Education.* London, England: Pergamon Press, 5368–5375. Also reprinted in International Encyclopedia of Teaching and Teacher Education (forthcoming).

Cliff, N. (1983). Some cautions concerning the application of causal modeling methods. *Multivariate Behavioral Research, 18,* 115–126.

Cook, R. D., & Weisberg, S. (1982). Residuals and influence in regression. New York: Chapman and Hall.

Hambleton, R. K. & Swaminathan, H. (1984). Item response theory. *Principles and applications.* Boston: Kluwer-Nijhoff.

Hedges, L. V., & Olkin, I. (1985). *Statistical methods for meta-analysis.* New York: Academic Press.

Joreskog, K. G. (1977). Structural equation models in the social sciences: Specification, estimation and testing. In P. R. Krishnaiah (Ed.), *Applications of statistics.* Amsterdam: North-Holland.

Joreskog, K. G., & Sorbom, D. (1984). *LISREL VI Analysis of linear structural relationships by the method of maximum likelihood.* User's guide. Mooresville, IN: Scientific Software Inc.

Little, R. & Rubin, D. (1987). *Statistical analysis with missing data.* New York: Wiley.

McCullagh, P., & Nelder, J. A. (1983). *Generalized linear models.* London: Chapman & Hall.

Mislevy, R. J. (1986). *Recent developments* in the factor analysis of categorical variables. *Journal of Educational Statistics, 11,* 3–31.

Schiffman, S. S., Reynolds, M. L., & Young, F. W. (1981). *Introduction to multidimensional scaling. Theory, methods and Applications.* New York: Academic Press.

Wainer, H. & Braun, H. (1987). *Test validity.* Hillsdale, NJ: Lawrence Erlbaum Associates.

V A BLUEPRINT FOR THE FUTURE

12 Toward a Blueprint for Educational Psychology

M. C. Wittrock
University of California, Los Angeles

Frank Farley
University of Wisconsin, Madison

WHAT IS A BLUEPRINT?

The building of a new structure requires a blueprint. The purpose of a blueprint, or plan, is to guide the builders of the new structure.

A blueprint also guides the process of rebuilding or modernizing a structure, including the structure of a discipline. The time to reconstruct an applied discipline occurs when major progress in theory and research in the field lead to fundamental advances in knowledge, technology, and implications for practice that compel a reorganization of its structure. In this final chapter of *The Future of Educational Psychology*, we begin the process of preparing a blueprint for our field.

Educational psychology has recently produced fundamental advances in knowledge and technology that have far-reaching implications for practice. Because of recent progress, a major examination of the present structure of educational psychology is needed. Our mission here is to begin the process of examining the structure and organization of educational psychology. The goal of the book and of this blueprint is to contribute to the building of a future for educational psychology that will enable it to continue to be a leading field in psychology, productive of useful research, of coherent theory, and of effective implications for practice.

Other fields of psychology have profited from a process of self-examination, which have led to recommendations for sustaining the healthy development of their disciplines. For example, clinical psychology has rebuilt its discipline through ideas and documents growing from its Boulder Conference and its Vail Conference. School psychology, through its Thayer Conference, Spring Hill

Conference, and Olympia Conference, has similarly facilitated the rebuilding of its discipline.

Unlike these fields, educational psychology has little experience at reorganization. The blueprint we offer attempts to begin the process of reorganization and remodeling of educational psychology, with the goal of contributing one small step toward securing its long and productive future as a leading field in psychology and in education.

SETTING THE STAGE: THE CHANGING NATURE OF EDUCATIONAL PSYCHOLOGY

As several of the contributors to this volume have stated, educational psychology has recently made substantial progress in theory, research, and in the development of implications for improving education, teaching methods, assessment, and the technology of instruction. The recent resurgence of interest in cognitive models of learning, knowledge acquisition, and individual differences has led to research on students' and teachers' thought processes involved in increasing achievement in the schools. These studies explore topics in motivation, attention, anxiety, learning strategies, aptitudes, and metacognition from a new perspective. From the research on these and related topics, educational psychologists have advanced their understanding of how learners construct knowledge from teaching and understanding from experience. Educational psychology continues to be in the center of psychological research on these topics.

The field is now moving into the development of a prescriptive science useful for improving the teaching of subjects in schools to children, youth, and adults. The design of teaching procedures, strategies of instruction, models of measurement, and models of assessment of achievement that will be practical and functional in schools is now occurring. These advances promise to lead to improvements in school achievement.

Ironically, the flourish of research and technology has led some educators and psychologists to move from educational psychology to the application of its recently discovered principles in the teaching of subject matters. It is as if the knowledge-base were adequately developed, and it was time to move onto the more pressing applied problems of teaching subjects in schools.

We believe it is critically important for theory and research in educational psychology to continue to develop out of the applied research on teaching, knowledge acquisition. technology, individual differences, and motivation. For this reason it is important for the research in these applied areas to continue to be the central part of the field of educational psychology. The people who do the research in these applied areas need to continue to contribute to research in educational psychology, as they draw ideas and theory from it.

A primary function of a blueprint for educational psychology is to facilitate the research in education that will lead to improved educational practice through the theory-based scientific study of its problems. Educational psychology is the appropriate field to unite psychological theory and research with the scientific study of education. Educational psychology should attract and retain, as active participants, the researchers who use psychological principles to further their research and development in education. In turn, these researchers should contribute to the knowledge-base and theory development of educational psychology. The community needs these types of close interactions to continue to grow and to improve teaching.

To move toward the development of a blueprint, and to respond to the changing nature of the field of educational psychology, we focus on two areas: (1) a definition of educational psychology, and (2) a core curriculum for graduate education in educational psychology.

A DEFINITION OF EDUCATIONAL PSYCHOLOGY

During the year that he was President of the Division of Educational Psychology of APA, the senior editor of this volume published a definition of educational psychology in the Division 15 Newsletter (Wittrock, 1984, 1985). He also appointed a Division 15, APA Committee called "The Future of Educational Psychology" to consider further the problem of defining educational psychology. In 1987, this committee prepared the following definition of Educational Psychology, which has since been approved in the Executive Committee of the Division of Educational Psychology and adopted by the membership of the Division (see p. 196).

EDUCATING THE NEW EDUCATIONAL PSYCHOLOGISTS

The changing job market for educational psychologists, and the changing nature of the research and theory in the discipline, necessitate revisions of the graduate curricula. From the chapters in this volume it is clear that sophistication in cognitive psychology and familiarity with multivariate statistical analysis procedures and causal inference techniques are essential for analyzing much present and future research in educational psychology. A limited core curriculum, combined with a wide range of optional courses directed at certain segments of the marketplace for educational psychologists, would be one effective model for the training of educational psychologists. The optional course portfolio should involve not only courses within an educational psychology department or program,

Definition of Educational Psychology

The science and profession of educational psychology is the branch of psychology that is concerned with the development, evaluation, and application of (a) theories and principles of human learning, teaching, and instruction and (b) theory-derived educational materials, programs, strategies, and techniques that can enhance lifelong educational activities and processes.

Functions	Purposes	Processes
A. Development of theories and principles of learning and instruction • Basic Theories • Applied Theories	To *enhance* educational activities and processes, e.g., • Instruction • Learning • Assessment • Evaluation • Diagnosis • Intervention	• Theory formulation, integration, and modification • Field and laboratory observation, testing and evaluation • Identification of learning and instructional principles • Dissemination of theories and principles
B. Development of theory-derived educational programs, materials, and techniques • From Research • From Practice	To *demonstrate* appropriate application of theory to practice, e.g., • Education (e.g., special population, adults, early childhood as well as traditional school-aged children) • Training (e.g., industry, military, teachers, interns) • Testing (e.g., placement, achievement, grading) • Evaluation (e.g., educational practices, legislation, policies)	• Design of theory-derived educational products • Field and laboratory observation, testing and evaluation • Dissemination of guidelines and products

Note: This definition was prepared in 1987 by the APA Division of Educational Psychology Committee on the "Future of Educational Psychology." The Committee members who prepared the definition are: Barbara McCombs, Chair; Margaret Clifford; William Asher; Frank Farley; Sigmund Tobias; and Merlin Wittrock.

but also courses outside that program. The development of joint courses with a cognate program, such as computer science, brain science, anthropology, sociology, statistics, curriculum and instruction, among others, is encouraged.

The Core Curriculum

It seems to us an inescapable conclusion that the further development of educational psychology as a discipline will require competencies of our new graduates in the following "core areas" and topics, as well as in a significant sampling of the following additional areas and topics. Our list here is not exhaustive but is illustrative of the range of intellectual exposure we recommend.

Although educational psychology is expanding into non-traditional settings, and is undergoing changes in focus and direction, as documented in the foregoing chapters, we feel there are domains of scholarship and skill that are essential for the educational psychologist and that are best represented in the academic subjects of:

Cognition and instruction
Motivation and emotion
Human development
Individual differences
Social psychology
Technology, learning, and instruction
History and systems of psychology
Measurement
Research methods (quantitative and qualitative) and statistical analysis of data (including the powerful new multivariate techniques)
Research practicum

In addition to the above "core" list, proficiency in a range of additional, and sometimes related, areas is encouraged, with a sample of such areas including:

Instructional design
Thinking
The educational psychology of special populations
Evaluation methods
Teacher preparation and education
Artificial intelligence and education
Brain, cognition, and education
The educational psychology of health and wellness
The educational psychology of literacy
Issues in professional training

THE FUTURE OF EDUCATIONAL PSYCHOLOGY

Educational psychology plays a reciprocal role in education and psychology. It contributes to the development of theory, research, and knowledge in both of these fields.

Throughout its existence, educational psychology has played a major role in the development of psychology as a discipline. In the areas of learning, measurement, testing, individual differences, counseling, development, and evaluation, educational psychology has consistently contributed major advances to the theory, research, and knowledge of psychology since its beginning as an empirical science.

Educational psychology also contributes to the development of theory and knowledge in the growing field of educational research. Since its infancy, much of the empirical scientific research in education, including educational research methods, owes much to the educational psychologists who applied psychological theory and methods to the study of teaching, instruction, measurement, evaluation, and test development. From their pioneering work came important contributions in educational research to learning theory, test theory, measurement theory, and to the theory and practice of teaching and testing.

Within the last twenty five years, the theories and methods of educational psychology have grown and have progressed considerably. The advent of cognitive psychology, which educational psychology pioneered along with other divisions of psychology, introduced new theories and methods appropriate for studying knowledge acquisition, attention, motivation, achievement, measurement. evaluation, and testing. These theories and methods provided new and useful perspectives toward problems in these areas, such as how student and teacher thought processes and affective reactions mediate achievement in educational contexts.

This recent advent of cognitive psychology also heralded interest in education and training that occurs in industry, government, professions, and other educational settings outside the usual school contexts. These changes in the conception of educational settings have expanded the legitimate areas of interest and study of educational psychology. Its reciprocal role within education and psychology fostered progress in the development of cognitive approaches to research in both of these fields.

In this volume we have attempted to show how its recent advances in theory and research methods and its new found areas of interest and application can be synthesized to advance research in educational psychology, while still retaining the dual role and reciprocal nature of the field. In this blueprint for a future we have emphasized three main points. First, educational psychology has seen much progress recently in its theory, research, technology, and in its applications to education. Second, as a result of this progress, a revised definition of the field is needed to synthesize these advances and to provide direction and coherence to the future. Third, a core curriculum for graduate study in educational psychology, emphasizing the added knowledge and skill now needed to function effectively as an educational psychologist, is needed to insure future progress in the field.

Through the discussions of the recent advances in theories and research methods, through the redefinition of the field, through a reconceptualization of the roles of educational psychologists, and through the suggested revisions in graduate curricula we have tried to present a framework that will give coherence and direction to the future of educational psychology. We hope that the framework will help to sustain and facilitate the reciprocal contributions of the field to the study of education and the science of psychology.

REFERENCES

Wittrock, M. C. (1984). The president's message: New opportunities for educational psychologists. *Newsletter for Educational Psychologists, 8*(1), 1–2.

Wittrock, M. C. (1985). The president's message: Enlarging the conception of educational psychology. *Newsletter for Educational Psychologists, 8*(2), 1–2.

Author Index

Page numbers in *italics* refer to reference pages.

A

Abelson, R., 45, *72*
Agresti, A., 182, *188*
Aitkin, M. A., 181, 182, *188*
Albee, G. W., 140, *141*
Allen, G. J., 116, *125*
Allington, R. L., 152, *167*
Alpert, J. L., 123, 124, *125*
Amiran, M. R., 164, *168*
Anderson, C. W., 148, *167*
Anderson, J. R., 46, 48, 50, 52, 69
Anderson, L. M., 111, *125*
Anderosn, R. C., 45, 46, 49, 50, *69, 70,* 83, *89,* 113, *125*
Anderson, T. H., 113, *125, 126,* 146, *167*
Andre, T., 113, *125*
Armbruster, B. B., 113, *126,* 146, *167*
Ash, M. J., 20, *29*
Atkinson, A. C., 182, *188*
Atkinson, R. C., 76, *87*
Auble, P. M., 56, *69, 70*
Ausubel, D. P., 15, *16,* 39, 44, 46, 54, *69*

B

Backstrand, G., 110, *125*
Bailey, D. B., Jr., 135, *141*

Baker, L., 113, *125, 126*
Baker, N., 77, *88*
Baker, R. F., 122, *125,* 176, *180*
Bardon, J. I., 123, *125, 126,* 134, 135, 139, *141*
Bartlett, F. C., 44, 54, *69*
Barton, E. J., 111, *126*
Beaugrande, R., de, 112, *126*
Becker, H. J., 115, *126*
Bell, B. F., 80, *87*
Bennett, V. C., 135, *141*
Bereiter, C., 104, *105,* 148, *169*
Berliner, C. D., 56, 64, *69,* 111, *126,* 148, *167*
Berk, R., 114, *126*
Berlyne, D. E., 66, *69*
Bevan, W., 12, *17*
Bibicos, E. E., 113, *128*
Biddle, W. B., 113, *125*
Birch, J. W., 137, *142*
Bishop, Y. M., 182, *188*
Black, J. B., 45, *69*
Block, K. K., 135, *141,* 173, 175, *180*
Bloom, B., 42, *69*
Bloom, B. S., 153, *167*
Blumenthal, A. L., 10, *16,* 39, *69*
Bock, R. D., 182, *188*
Bork, A., 115, *126*
Borkowski, J. G., 148, *169*

Subject Index